54-32

HARVARD EAST ASIAN MONOGRAPHS

20

FEUDAL CONTROL IN TOKUGAWA JAPAN:
THE SANKIN KŌTAI SYSTEM

FEUDAL CONTROL IN TOKUGAWA JAPAN:
THE SANKIN KŌTAI SYSTEM


by

Toshio G. Tsukahira


Published by the

East Asian Research Center

Harvard University


Distributed by

Harvard University Press

Cambridge, Mass.

1970

The East Asian Research Center at Harvard
University administers research projects
designed to further scholarly understanding
of China, Japan, Korea, and Vietnam and
adjacent areas.  These studies have been
assisted by grants from the Ford Foundation.

Library of Congress No. 67-3532

SBN 674-29900-0

To Lilly

# CONTENTS

# FOREWORD

Some doctoral dissertations become standard works on
their subjects and circulate on interlibrary loan like medieval
manuscripts.  If their authors have meanwhile moved from academic
life into a different profession, publication may be delayed and
dissertations still in manuscript may become "rare books" without
ever having been published.

Dr. Tsukahira completed this study of the sankin kōtai
system in 1951 under Professors Serge Elisseeff, John K. Fairbank,
and Edwin O. Reischauer, and, after a brief period of teaching
Modern Japanese History at Harvard, entered government service.
He has now served in the Department of State in Washington and
in the American Embassy in Tokyo, with no time for further
historical research.  Yet his dissertation remains a basic
contribution.  We are therefore very glad to have the opportunity
to make it more widely available in this present form.

East Asian Research Center

April 1966

ix

PREFACE

This study of the <u>sankin kōtai</u> system was originally
written as a Ph.D. dissertation at Harvard University in 1951.
I regret that since that time I have not found it possible to
conduct further research on the subject or to undertake an
extensive revision which would take into account subsequent
studies bearing on the Tokugawa political and economic setting.
I am satisifed, however, that while more detail might be added,
no basic change in the original thesis is called for as a result
of these more recent studies.  Continuing requests for the
dissertation in its unpublished form have indicated that it might
usefully be made more widely available.  I have, therefore, been
encouraged to offer it for publication even without major revision
or updating, in the series of Harvard East Asian Monographs.

I wish to take this opportunity to express my gratitude
to Professor Serge Elisseeff, Professor John K. Fairbank and
former Professor (now Ambassador to Japan) Edwin O. Reischauer
for the inspiration and guidance they gave me as my teachers in
Far Eastern studies and as chairmen of my doctoral committee.
This monograph owes much to their advice and to their valuable
suggestions, but, needless to say, its shortcomings are entirely
my own responsibility.

I am indebted also to the staff of the Harvard-Yenching
Institute, to my former colleagues at Boylston Hall, and, not
the least, to my wife, for their help and encouragement during

xi

the long months this study was in preparation.  Finally, I
wish to express my appreciation to the American Council of
Learned Societies and the Harvard-Yenching Institute, whose
generous assistance permitted me to pursue my graduate work
at Harvard, and to the East Asian Research Center, which has
made it possible for this study to be published.

T.G. Tsukahira

Tokyo, Japan
May 1966

# INTRODUCTION

The sankin kōtai (lit., "alternate attendance") system
was a device of the Tokugawa shogunate, the government of Japan
from 1603 to 1868, designed to insure political control by the
regime over the daimyo, or territorial lords, who exercised
virtually autonomous authority over the more than 260 feudal
states into which four-fifths of the country was divided.
Under this system most of the daimyo were required to travel
biennially from their domains to the capital of the Tokugawa
at Edo (present day Tokyo) and to spend alternate years in
personal attendance at the shogunal court. Each daimyo
was also required to maintain residences at the capital
where his wife and children were permanently detained.

This sytem for the control of the daimyo was one of
the key elements in the ingenious system of checks and balances
which the Tokugawa devised to maintain themselves in power.
It was essentially a polite form of hostage based on feudal
custom but designed to serve as a negative check on the centri-
fugal forces inherent in the feudally organized society which
the Tokugawa inherited and strove to maintain. By requiring
the periodic attendance of the daimyo at the capital, the
system subjected them to the constant and direct surveillance
of the central authorities. The enforced residence of their
families in Edo acted as a deterrent to any attempt at rebellion, while the costly journeys to and from Edo and the
expense of maintaining two establishments, one in the metropolis and the other in the domain, kept the lords financially,
and hence militarily, weak.

During its long life of over two centuries, the
sankin kōtai system exerted a powerful influence on Tokugawa
society.  In the political sphere, its main effect was to
consolidate power in a single center and to destroy feudal
autonomy in fact, if not in name.  By collecting the daimyo
in Edo it transformed them from independent territorial
rulers into what amounted to a species of bureaucratic agents
of a powerful national government.  The daimyo as a class
became fainéants with respect to their domains, which as
luxury-loving courtiers of the shogun they tended on the
whole to regard primarily as sources of revenue to support
them at the capital.  The resulting loss of power and initiative
in the local areas meant a corresponding concentration of power
in Edo.  The system, therefore, played a major role in creating
the highly centralized regime which was one of the chief legacies
of the Tokugawa to the new Japan of the Meiji Restoration.

The impact of the system on Tokugawa society was
perhaps most profound in the economic and social sphere.  The
regular journeys to and from the capital by daimyo from all
parts of the country accompanied by their large retinues inevitably fostered the development of a nationwide communications
system.  The concentration of the feudal aristocracy in Edo
created a huge demand for goods and services and directly
contributed to the burgeoning of the population of the
capital city, which by the end of the eighteenth century was
one of the most populous in the world.  The growth and prosperity of Osaka as the commercial center of the nation was
also directly related to the operation of the sankin kōtai,
for it was in Osaka that most of the lords converted their
rice revenues into money for their sankin expenses.  The
sankin kōtai system thus had a direct role in stimulating

the development of a commercial economy and was thereby
instrumental in preparing Japan for the modernization of
the nineteenth century.  In a Japan that was deliberately
cut off from trade with the outside world, the sankin kōtai
was virtually the only stimulus to the growth of an internal
commerce that was national in scope and to the development
of industries which depended on more than a purely local
market.  The social consequences of this system designed
to maintain the political status quo were ironically to
promote the wealth and power of the merchant class and
eventually to weaken that of the entire feudal ruling class,
from the ordinary samurai and the daimyo up to the shogunate
itself.

Another important contribution of the operation of
the sankin kōtai system to the modernization of Japan was
to promote the intellectual and cultural unification of the
country.  The sankin kōtai served to bring a large part of
the leadership elements from the whole country together in
one place and to keep a constant stream of leaders and in-
tellectuals moving back and forth between the capital and
all parts of the country.  This was important in giving Japan
the tremendous intellectual unity with which it faced the
West in the nineteenth century.  It also enabled the people
at large to have a stronger sense of national unity than
would have been the case had the system not existed.  By serving
as the vehicle which spread the culture of Edo and Osaka to
the countryside, the system influenced the diffusion of a truly
national culture.

To cover all the ramifications of the sankin kōtai system
as it impinged on Tokugawa political, economic, and cultural
development would require nothing less than a complete social

4

history of Tokugawa Japan. This study attempts only a pre-
liminary survey of the system as it developed and functioned
within the Tokugawa political and economic setting. Particular
attention has been focused on the economic impact of the sankin
kōtai on the finances of the daimyo, for it is the general
thesis of the author that while the sankin kōtai was a useful
instrument of political control over a feudal order, it also
provided the chief stimulus for those very changes which
made it unworkable. It made possible a remarkable centralization
of power which laid the foundation for the emergence of a modern
state in the latter half of the nineteenth century, but its very
effectiveness as a system of feudal control prevented the evolu-
tion of a truly centralized state system under the Tokugawa.
Like the regime which produced it, the sankin kōtai system was
feudal in theory and in form, but was essentially anti-feudal
in its function. Thus, although it was used to support the
status quo, it helped generate forces which eventually under-
mined the economic foundations of the Tokugawa political structure
and promoted the ultimate dissolution of the Tokugawa state.

Chapter I

THE TOKUGAWA REGIME

It is the purpose of this chapter to provide a
general background for an understanding of the nature and
function of the sankin kōtai system as a socio-political
institution. Why was the system necessary? By what sanctions,
traditional or arbitrary, was it enforced? Why did it take
the form that it did? In order to answer these questions,
we must briefly sketch the historical circumstances under
which the Tokugawa achieved their supremacy over their
rivals and established their hegemony over the entire country;
we must examine the theoretical basis and structure of the
Tokugawa political system; and finally, we must note how the
daimyo were treated as vassal-subjects of the Tokugawa house.

1. The Establishment of the Shogunate

The unification of feudal Japan under the control
of the Tokugawa family was the culmination of a process of
conquest and consolidation of power begun after the middle
of the sixteenth century by Oda Nobunaga (1534-1582) and
further continued by Toyotomi Hideyoshi (1536-1598), who
finally succeeded in pacifying the entire country and
establishing his hegemony over the nation. By reducing
the daimyo or local barons to the position of vassals and
subjecting them to his autocratic control, Hideyoshi managed
to centralize political power at his capital in Osaka, the
seat of his military government. Hideyoshi's death in 1598
precipitated a struggle for power among his daimyo vassals,

strongest of whom was Tokugawa Ieyasu (1542-1616). Ieyasu by
adroit diplomacy succeeded in winning the support of several key
lords and in 1600 with the aid of his allies decisively defeated a rival coalition at the battle of Sekigahara.
Less than three years later he set up a shogunate or hereditary
military government at Edo (the present Tokyo) and by a skillful
combination of force and persuasion made all the daimyo submit
to its authority. In 1615 Ieyasu eliminated the last remnants
of Hideyoshi's family when he seized Osaka castle and destroyed
Hideyori (1593-1615), the son of his former chief. With this
event Tokugawa hegemony over Japan was complete.

Ieyasu and his immediate successors, Hidetada (1579-
1632) and Iemitsu (1604-1651), devoted their energies to the
task of consolidating and centralizing Tokugawa power and
systematically devising safeguards against all foreseeable
threats to the security of the Tokugawa house. The chief source
of danger to the new regime was from the daimyo, who, though
temporarily cowed, still retained their territorial possessions
and military resources and hence the potential for successful
revolt, especially if they could act in combination with one
another. It became, therefore, the chief preoccupation of the
early Tokugawa to weaken and divide the daimyo and at the
same time to make their own position as impregnable as possible.[1]

One of Ieyasu's first moves after Sekigahara was to
rearrange the feudal map of Japan to improve his strategic
position. As a result of the battle, about one-third of the
territory of the country had fallen into his hands. Ieyasu
used most of these spoils to reward his independent allies, in
payment for their past services and to insure their continued
support. He also, however, transferred most of the independent
daimyo who had fiefs in the central part of Japan between the

Kantō plain on the east and the Kyoto-Osaka district on the
west to new fiefs in western Japan.[2] These dispositions
placed the strategic heart of the nation almost entirely
under Tokugawa control. It was now held directly by the
Tokugawa family and its branches or entrusted to hereditary
vassals (fudai) of the Tokugawa house, the larger of whom--
with fiefs of over 10,000 koku--became known as fudai daimyo.[3]
The country was thus divided into a great central zone held
or dominated by the Tokugawa and the realms of the non-Tokugawa
or tozama ("outside") lords, who were now concentrated in
northern and western Honshu, Shikoku, and Kyushu. Later,
under Hidetada and Iemitsu, the Tokugawa domain and the
fiefs of the fudai daimyo were increased by further confiscations and arbitrary transfers and extended to the north
and west.[4] These acquisitions were so interpersed among the
holdings of tozama daimyo that any hostile movement against
the Tokugawa stronghold was made extremely difficult.

Beginning immediately after his investiture as shogun
in 1603, Ieyasu quickly expanded his castle at Edo into an
imposing fortress unrivaled in strength and grandeur even by
Hideyoshi's great citadel at Osaka. Surrounding the castle
he had built a formidable system of protective moats, embank-
ments, and walls. This not only strengthened the Tokugawa
defenses but simultaneously served to weaken his potential
enemies, since the work was done with manpower and materials
requisitioned by the shogun from the daimyo.

While securing his military position vis-à-vis the
daimyo in this fashion, Ieyasu also exploited all the means
at his command to extend his political domination over the
"outside" lords. A diplomat and politician, Ieyasu sought
to control his daimyo rivals more by manipulation than by
overt force. His policy was to conciliate wherever possible

and to induce the barons to submit voluntarily to his mastery.
To win the good will of the more powerful of his former peers,
he liberally dispensed honors and rewards and treated them
ceremonially as equals.  The heads of the great daimyo houses
of Maeda, Shimazu, Date, and Mōri, for example, were given
high court rank and the honorary Tokugawa surname of Matsudaira.[5]
They were received with a great show of deference when they
visited the Tokugawa capital.  Practically all of the leading
tozama families were bound to the Tokugawa house by marriage
ties.  The daimyo were encouraged to send hostages to Edo and
to establish residence for themselves and their families at
the Tokugawa capital.

    The daimyo, anxious to gain the favor of the Tokugawa
and fearful of the consequences of non-cooperation, readily
submitted to the will of the shogun.  The shogunate soon was
able to take a more dictatorial attitude and impose its controls
arbitrarily by fiat.  In 1610, all daimyo were ordered to send
hostages to Edo, and a year later the tozama were gathered
together at Kyoto and Edo and forced to sign a written oath
by which they swore loyally to serve the shogunate, to obey
its orders, and to refuse aid and comfort to its enemies.[6]
Finally, in 1615, a year before his death, Ieyasu caused the
first buke shohatto or "Laws for the Military Houses" to be
promulgated.  Some of these so-called laws were maxims and
prescriptions for the proper personal and social behavior
of the military class and their proper conduct as administrators
and rulers, but they also included injunctions against the
construction of castles, the repair of which had to be reported
to Edo, and against the unauthorized contracting of marriages
between lords.    Each daimyo was ordered to report on suspicious
activities within the fief of his neighbor.[7]  To insure the

observance of these laws and other regulations of the shogunate,
an elaborate system of espionage was organized. Under this
system secret political police, supervised by a group of
officials called metsuke ("censors"), were sent into the
domains and the very households of lords suspected of mis-
conduct toward the bakufu.

Ieyasu's policy of daimyo control was continued and
carried forward by his two immediate successors in a most
thoroughgoing manner. Ieyasu had left them with a tremendous
legacy of material wealth and power. After most of Ieyasu's
proud contemporaries, whom he had to treat as equals, had died,
it was possible for the bakufu to subject their successors to
more stringent controls. Under Hidetada and Iemitsu the shogun's right to demand the assistance of the daimyo in expensive
public undertakings was exercised with such frequency that the
finances of even the wealthiest daimyo were seriously strained.[8]
The writ of Edo was gradually extended into the internal administration of the daimyo territories. The extent to which
the bakufu tried to regulate the governance of the daimyo
fiefs is indicated by Iemitsu's buke shohatto of 1635.[9] This
revision of Ieyasu's original statute required, among other
things, that the daimyo report all cases of capital punishment
and banishment inflicted on their vassals, govern their fiefs
with justice and maintain them in a prosperous condition, keep
communication routes and facilities operational, abolish
private customs barriers, respect the established rights
of temples and shrines within their domains, prohibit
Christianity, curb sedition, and finally, pattern their
legislation in all things after the laws of Edo.

These strategic dispositions and legislative measures
against the daimyo were not the only means by which Tokugawa

power was consolidated and secured. The founders of the regime
took careful steps to control and neutralize all other forces
which might jeopardize their monopoly of power. The imperial
court was one such force. The Tokugawa gave formal recognition
to the emperor's position as the ultimate source of authority
and the fountainhead of honor, and the imperial household and
court aristocracy were given relatively generous incomes.[10]
But at the same time, care was taken to deprive the throne
of any administrative function. Even the lands which were
allotted for the support of the imperial household were administered by agents of the bakufu.[11] Kyoto, the imperial
city, was placed under the supervision of a Tokugawa military
governor among whose functions was to keep the court under
constant surveillance and to prevent it from becoming a rallying point for disaffected daimyo. The shogunate also laid
down strict rules for the conduct of the emperor and his court,
subjecting them to even more thorough control than the daimyo
received.[12]

        Another force which the early Tokugawa came to regard
as perilous to their interest, and which they took drastic
action to eradicate, was the influence of foreign traders
and missionaries in Japan. The policy of seclusion which was
adopted after 1637 closed Japan almost completely for two
centuries to all free intercourse with outside nations. This
policy was largely the result of the fear of the political
consequences of such intercourse. The Christian propaganda
of the missionaries and the commercial activities of the
traders were intolerable because they struck at the ideological
and economic foundations of the feudal order which the Tokugawa
sought to preserve. But a more urgent reason for seclusion,
as Sansom points out, was the fear that the moral and material

support of the foreigners might be used by the daimyo **against**
the ruling house.[13]


2.  The Theory of the Shogunate

The  Tokugawa regime was not founded upon any consistent
theory of government, nor was it built up according to any
rational scheme.  It was constituted of expedients which were
found useful for the consolidation and preservation of Tokugawa
power.  The founders of the regime, as we have seen, were past
masters at power politics, but they knew that if their rule
was to survive, mastery gained by might had to be transformed
into right, and obedience imposed by  force had, if possible,
to be transformed into duty.  Thus while they borrowed freely
from the strategic and centralist policies of their predecessors,
Hideyoshi and Nobunaga, they also sought to establish a moral
and legal basis for their exercise of power.  They found this
basis in the institution of the shogunate, which since the
twelfth century, when the first shogunate was founded, had been
the traditional repository of both feudal and public powers
over the entire country.

The legal authority of the shogunate derived from the
fiction that the office of shogun or generalissimo was the
surrogate of the sovereign emperor.  The doctrine that the
sovereign emperor, the ultimate source of all political
authority, should delegate governing powers to his responsible
ministers had existed in Japan since the seventh century,[14]
and had been used since that time to justify de facto rule
of the country by several powerful families.  In 1192, under
Minamoto no Yoritomo (1147-1199), the theory was applied
to establish a new form of government known as the bakufu
or shogunate which set the pattern for almost seven centuries

of military rule. The office of shogun originally implied little
if any governing power. In pre-feudal times, it was only a temporary commission given to commanders of military campaigns against
the Ainu.[15] But after Yoritomo it became hereditary and acquired
civil as well as military functions, and by the first half of the
thirteenth century, the Kamakura shogunate (1192-1333) had become
the real central government of the nation. The civil government
of the emperor and his court at Kyoto continued formally in existence but was gradually shorn of all actual power by the feudal
regime which now took its place.[16] Thus was developed the dual
system of government, with the emperor as sovereign and the shogun
as ruler, which was to last until the end of the Tokugawa period.

Throughout the feudal ages the theory of imperial sovereignty
had reinforced the position of the shogun as the chief suzerain of
the realm and had strengthened his authority as a public ruler.
This was because the prestige, if not the power, of the imperial
throne remained a living force even during the long ascendancy
of military rule. After the collapse of the Kamakura shogunate
in 1333 a new bakufu was established by the Ashikaga family,
and although it failed to maintain unified control over its
vassals, it retained its continuity for fifteen successive generations, from 1336 to 1573. Both Nobunaga and Hideyoshi, as they
reunified Japan under their suzerainty, aspired to the prestige
and authority of the shogunate but were unsuccessful because of
their lineage. Ieyasu was, fortunately, able to claim descent
from the Minamoto line and was thus in a position to assume the
title of shogun, which had been in abeyance since the death of the
last Ashikaga shogun in 1597, and to set up a new bakufu at Edo.
Before becoming shogun Ieyasu had already seized the reality of
power, but the re-establishment of the shogunate gave permanence

and stability to the new regime.

## 3. The Tokugawa Political Structure

The Tokugawa state was composed of a central directing force, the bakufu or shogunate, at the apex of the hierarchical pyramid, and a number of local authorities who shared with it the actual government of the land and the people. The bakufu, as we have seen, claimed legal and traditional authority over the entire country under the fiction that the sovereign emperor had delegated ruling powers to the shogun, who was also, by virtue of his Minamoto lineage, the supreme suzerain of the entire military ruling class. In his dual capacity as chief of state and supreme suzerain, the shogun exercised general public authority over national defense and foreign affairs and legislated for the entire country. He controlled the minting of money, standardized weights and measures, and regulated trade, but his administrative monopoly was not complete. His power to collect taxes, maintain local order, dispense justice, and to manage the civil service was confined to his own domains. In four-fifths of the realm these powers were held by local rulers, whom he controlled feudally, i.e. indirectly, as his vassals.

In theory, all land belonged to the emperor and was held in trust by the shogun. The latter, as dispenser of the land, parceled it out among his vassals, who were divided into three general classes according to the size of the fief they were granted. In the first class were the daimyo, who possessed fiefs 10,000 koku and over in assessed productivity and who received investiture directly from the shogun. (Vassals of the daimyo often had sub-fiefs of over 10,000 koku, but these had no independent status in the feudal hierarchy under the shogun.)

14

The second class was made up of the hatamoto, or "banner-men,"
who had fiefs of less than 10,000 koku and who enjoyed the
privilege of audience before the shogun; while in the third
class were gokenin, or "house-men," who were granted fiefs
of less than 100 koku and denied audience privileges. In
1722 there were 264 daimyo, 5,205 hatamoto, and 17,399 gokenin.[17/]
These three categories were mutually independent, each owing
allegiance directly to the shogun and the bakufu. While the
daimyo were more or less autonomous territorial rulers, the
great majority of the hatamoto and gokenin enjoyed few if any
independent governing powers over the land and people. Only
a limited number of the hatamoto actually resided in their
fiefs and these were treated like minor daimyo.[18] Most of
the hatamoto and gokenin were permanently domiciled at the
shogun's capital where they were employed as soldiers or
officials in the central bureaucracy. The services of the
gokenin and most of the hatamoto were rewarded by stipends in
rice and money from the bakufu treasury rather than by grants
of land. Their relationship to the shogun thus tended to be
more bureaucratic than feudal in nature.[19]

Territorially, the Tokugawa state was divided into the
public domains directly controlled by the Tokugawa shogun and
a number of greater and lesser fiefs held by daimyo and other
vassals. The shogunal or public domains (tenryō) embraced about
a fifth of the territory of the realm and included about a third
of the population.[20] They contained all the important cities of
the empire--Edo, the seat of the central government; Kyoto, the
imperial capital; and Osaka (with Sakai), the great trading
center. While most of the shogunal holdings were concentrated
in central Honshu, they were also distributed among 48 of Japan's
68 provinces, extending as far as Kyushu in the extreme west.[21]

The annual productive capacity of the shogunal domains
was about 4 million koku of rice during most of the Tokugawa
period, although the yield for the whole country increased
from about 24 million koku in 1722 to 30 million in 1864.[22]
The actual income derived from the domains in taxes was about
35 per cent of the rice yield, or roughly 1.4 million koku.[23]
This rice tax constituted the bulk of the shogunate's regular
revenues, and with this limited and relatively fixed income
the shogunate undertook to direct the affairs of the whole
country instead of taxing the daimyo regularly in accordance
with a national revenue system. The productive capacity of
the domains of the daimyo totaled 17,550,104 koku in 1722 and
increased to 22,499,497 koku in 1842, while the fiefs of the
hatamoto and gokenin were assessed at 2,641,910 koku in 1722
and 3,065,580 koku in 1864.[24]

The bakufu had a dual role. On the one hand it functioned
as the central government of the country as a whole, while on
the other it administered the affairs of the Tokugawa domain and
feudal household. Its administrative machinery was essentially
an extension and elaboration of the simple patrimonial bureaucracy of a typical feudal lord.[25] Under the shogun, assisting
and advising him in the conduct of affairs and in matters of
high policy, particularly the relations of the shogunate with
the  imperial court and the daimyo, was a sort of cabinet consisting of from four to five senior councilors (rōjū or "elders"),
sometimes presided over by a chief minister called the Great
Councilor (tairō or "great elder"). A lesser group of executive
officers who dealt primarily with the affairs of the hatamoto
and gokenin was composed of four to five junior councilors
(waka-doshiyori or "young elders").

Acting as the eyes and ears of the two groups of

councilors were censors (<u>metsuke</u>) whose chief functions were
to keep watch on bakufu feudatories and officials, and to report
on cases of subversive activities on the part of the former and
maladministration or malfeasance in office on the part of the
latter.  Those responsible to the senior councilors were called
Great Censors (<u>ōmetsuke</u>) and were especially concerned with
daimyo affairs.

Also among the more important administrative and judicial
offices of the central bureaucracy were the commissioners of temples
and shrines (<u>jisha</u> <u>bugyō</u>), the finance commissioners (<u>kanjō</u> <u>bugyō</u>),
and the Edo city magistrates (Edo <u>machi</u> <u>bugyō</u>).  The temple and
shrine commissioners, usually two in number, reported directly
to the shogun. They controlled the secular affairs of the
religious institutions of the country and the people residing
in the domains attached to them.  The finance commissioners
numbered four, two handling the finances of the bakufu and the
other two performing administrative and judicial functions.
They supervised the forty or so <u>daikan</u> or intendants who collected
the revenues and administered justice in the shogunal domains,
and judged lawsuits between  inhabitants of these territories.
The two Edo city magistrates were the municipal administrators
and judges of Edo as well as the police authority.  Two incumbents
usually held this office; they rotated their turns of duty each
month as did, in fact, all the higher offices of the administration
including the <u>rōjū</u>.  Other city magistrates were installed in
the principal bakufu cities and towns throughout the country.
In the cities of Osaka and Kyoto, they functioned under the
authority of the Keeper of Osaka Castle (Osaka <u>jōdai</u>) and the
Kyoto Deputy (Kyoto <u>shoshidai</u>), who guarded these municipalities
and the surrounding country as the shogun's direct representatives.

The temple and shrine commissioners, the finance commissioners

and the Edo city magistrates, assisted by the Great Censor
and others, formed the Supreme Court of Justice (hyōjōsho).
The proceedings of this court were supervised by one of the
senior councilors. It was primarily a court of appeal for the
bakufu domain, but it also exercised jurisdiction over important
matters outside this sphere, such as dissension within a daimyo's
household.

Such was the composition at the top levels of what might
be called the public bureaucratic administration of the Tokugawa
shogunate. There were, in addition, two other important offices
directly responsible to the shogun, which were concerned primarily
with affairs connected with the shogun's palace and court. One
of these was the office of Grand Chamberlain (sobayōnin), who
often wielded great political power because of his close association with the shogun and his control over the five or six chamber-
lains (sobashū),who acted as the medium of communication between
the shogun and the senior councilors. The other important office
was that of the Masters of Ceremony (sōshaban), some twenty or
more in number, who arranged the details of shogunal audiences
with the daimyo and hatamoto. They also performed services as
shogunal envoys (jōshi). These palace officials often came to
be the real policy makers of the shogunate.


4.  The Tokugawa Daimyo

The exact origin of the term "daimyo" (lit., "great
names") is obscure, but in its earliest usage it is generally
believed to have meant great (dai) holders of myō or myōden
("name [-bearing] rice-land"), which were privately owned
parcels of land newly opened to cultivation or acquired from
previous owners. These lands were given distinguishing names,

usually personal but sometimes descriptive or fanciful, in
order to individualize or to commemorate them.[26] With the
advent of the feudal ages the term came to refer to prominent
military families who possessed extensive land holdings--not
necessarily myōden--and controlled large numbers of retainers.
It was originally used merely to indicate relative wealth
and power, but in Tokugawa times it became restricted in meaning
to feudal lords, who were direct vassals of the shogun and who
were granted fiefs with an officially rated productive capacity
of at least 10,000 koku.[27]

The daimyo of the Tokugawa period were the territorial
rulers of self-contained political units called han which were
at once minor states and fiefs.[28] As chiefs of state the daimyo
were empowered to govern their realms without external inter-
ference, except when bakufu interests were affected. Though
during the first fifty years of Tokugawa rule the policy of
the bakufu toward the daimyo was often extremely rigorous and
minatory, it later became relatively lenient.[29] The baron's
power over his territory could be revoked for a serious in-
fraction of law, but it was otherwise almost completely autonomous in its internal administration.

Like the shogun, each daimyo ruled his domain in the
dual capacity of public ruler and feudal suzerain. As an
autocrat, the daimyo usually transcended his legitimate
authority as a suzerain. He treated his vassals as subjects
and recognized no sanction against himself from them. Though
his support came primarily from the income of the land which
he set aside for his own use, it was possible, when necessary,
for the lord to levy assessments at will upon the fiefs of
his vassals, and to curtail the stipends of his retainers.[30]
As was the case for the nation as a whole, the centralization

of power within the han was furthered by the practice of
collecting the samurai class at the castle town of the lord
to serve as garrison troops, administrative officials, or
merely as idle courtiers. Forcing all vassals to maintain
residences at the lord's capital was a device employed by
the daimyo as well as by the bakufu.[31]

Two other institutions employed by the daimyo to
enhance his power are described by Professor Asakawa as
follows:

(a) The baron [i.e., the daimyo] reserved for himself
domains under his direct control which he governed
through agents revocable at will. Only the remainder
of his barony he granted to sub-lords and religious
institutions. (b) The old custom of subinfeudation
was further obviated by a system of rewarding the
services of some vassals and officials. not with pieces
of land, but with quantities of rice distributed out of
the baronial granary. This system greatly added to the
flexibility of the administration of the han and to the
autocratic power of the baron.[32]

a. Obligations of the Daimyo

At every change of incumbent in the shogunacy, the
daimyo were required to submit written oaths swearing personal
fealty to the new shogun. In these documents each daimyo
promised to observe the laws of the shogunate, to take part
in no seditious activity against the shogun, and to serve him
faithfully. Implicit in the daimyo's obligation of service
was the duty of maintaining peace and order in his territory,
of keeping his domain prosperous and administering it with

20

justice, as well as the duty of attending upon and paying homage to the shogun.[33] Maladministration was regarded as dereliction of duty and was punishable by the bakufu.[34]

The daimyo had no regular financial obligations to the bakufu. The income that they derived from their domains in the form of taxes was entirely under their control and was used for their own support and the expenses of their own administration. Seasonally, and on special ceremonial occasions such as coming of age, marriage, succession, investiture, and funeral in the shogun's household, however, the daimyo presented gifts to the bakufu. Presents were also customary when the daimyo reported to the shogun for audience at Edo. These offerings were all prescribed by minute regulations as to type and amount in the time of Iemitsu (i.e., between 1623 and 1651), and were thereafter virtually compulsory.[35] But they were not considered taxes as such; they were rather a form of ritual tribute, a survival of the customary manner of exchanging civilities between lord and vassal throughout the feudal ages.[36]

Though the daimyo paid no fixed taxes to the central government, at the behest of the bakufu they were obligated to provide materials and manpower for the construction and maintenance of such public buildings and works as the shogunal and imperial palaces, bakufu castles and fortifications, dikes, levees, and roads. This obligation was known as tetsudai ("assistance"). The early Tokugawa shogun forced the daimyo to "assist" not only in building up the city and castle at Edo, but in constructing or enlarging the Tokugawa castles at Kyoto, Nagoya, and elsewhere in the bakufu territories, using this means not only to strengthen their own military position but to weaken their rival lords financially. These undertakings were usually performed by groups of daimyo, who were each assigned their share according to the size of their fiefs, but at times they were imposed on individual daimyo as punishment for infractions of the laws of Edo. Later they lost their punitive character and became less frequent, but whenever bakufu castles, riparian works,and other public installations were damaged, through floods, fire, or other causes, the daimyo were ordered to contribute to the cost of reconstruction and repair. These impositions, like the presentation of gifts, were sanctioned by feudal custom and had been enforced by feudal suzerains since Kamakura times. Hideyoshi had set the immediate example for the Tokugawa in their use for political ends.[37]

In addition to the _tetsudai_, the daimyo as vassals of the shogun owed military and administrative services. The paramount military obligation was service in war. The Tokugawa policy was to eliminate the possibility of war, internal or external, but the regime was formally organized on a war footing. Each daimyo was expected to maintain his military strength and to be ready to mobilize his quota of fully equipped troops at the order of the supreme commander, the shogun.[38] Peacetime military service consisted primarily of guard duty. The daimyo were called upon to provide guard troops for such places as the imperial palaces, the Osaka and Sumpu castles, the port of Nagasaki, and various coastal defense stations. When in Edo, they furnished guardsmen for the thirty-six outer gates of Edo castle.[39] They were frequently called upon to provide a military escort for the shogun when he traveled, and part of the police force in the shogun's capital or on his highways at some of the barriers (_sekisho_) where travelers to and from Edo were regulated and inspected.[40] Some daimyo were required to take over and administer parts of the bakufu domain or

another daimyo's fief,when for some reason it had been confiscated by the bakufu.[41]  They were often given responsibility
also for sponsoring and providing the expenses for religious
and other ceremonial observances of the shogun's court.  These
duties were originally performed mainly by the _fudai_ daimyo,
whose feudal relationship to the Tokugawa family was more
genuine than that of the "outside" or _tozama_ lords.  In time,
however, as the _fudai-tozama_ distinction became less meaning-
ful, both categories were treated alike.[42]

The key offices in the shogun's government were entrusted
to vassals of daimyo rank, but in accordance with the policy
laid down by the founders of the regime, the _tozama_ were
generally excluded from service in the central administration.[43]
Since the number of offices in the central bureaucracy normally
opened to those of daimyo rank was limited, and since these
tended to be filled only by members of certain families, very
few, even of the _fudai_,  could aspire to positions in the
bakufu.[44]

In addition to military and administrative  obligations,
all daimyo owed the service of attendance upon the shogun.  This
was the theoretical _raison_ d'être for the _sankin kōtai_.  When
in Edo the daimyo were obliged to appear for audience at the
shogun's court on regular monthly audience days (usually the 1st,
15th and 28th of each month) and on various other special occasions
to pay homage to the shogun.[45]

b.  Classification of the Daimyo

The daimyo were classified according to various
principles of grading which determined their obligations and
privileges as vassals of the shogun, their ceremonial precedence

and treatment at his court, and, indeed, every aspect of their
public life.[46] The first and most important classification
was made on the basis of the feudal relationship of the daimyo
to the shogun. There were three categories: (1) the shimpan
or "related feudatories," (2) the fudai or "hereditary vassals,"
and (3) the tozama or "outside lords." The shimpan (also
known as the kamon or "family" daimyo) were collateral members
of the Tokugawa house, all descended from Ieyasu. They consisted of the sanke or the Tokugawa houses of Owari, Kii, and
Mito, and their cadet branches; the house of Echizen and its
cadets; and a few other offshoots of the main Tokugawa house.
The sanke were lineal descendants of the seventh, eighth,
and ninth sons of Ieyasu, while the house of Echizen was descended from Ieyasu's second son, Matsudaira Hideyasu (1574-
1607). The shimpan numbered five in 1614, increasing to 23
by 1866.[47] The fudai or "hereditary" daimyo were members of
those families who had been vassals of the Tokugawa since
before Sekigahara, and who had possessed at the time, or were
subsequently promoted to, fiefs of 10,000 koku. It was generally
from among the fudai, who had the earliest ties of loyalty to
the Tokugawa family, that the key offices of the Edo bureaucracy
were filled. The tozama or "outside" daimyo were the lords who,
formerly equals of Ieyasu, recognized his overlordship only at the
time of or after the battle of Sekigahara. It is sometimes represented that the tozama were all enemies of Ieyasu, but this
is not true--for many were his strongest allies, without whose
valuable aid the Tokugawa victory could not have been achieved.
Because of their formerly independent status and their ancient
lineage and because they possessed most of the larger domains
of the realm, the tozama were accorded an elevated social
status and rank in the feudal hierarchy. They enjoyed a greater

degree of autonomy, but, as stated before, in accordance
with the balance of power principle of the Tokugawa, they were
as a rule excluded from any part in the bakufu administration.

Of the total of 195 daimyo in 1602, the second year
after Sekigahara, the number of tozama daimyo was 119, while
the fudai numbered 72.  The remaining four daimyo were shimpan.
In 1614 the tozama had been reduced to 115 houses and the fudai
increased to 82.  In the course of the ensuing two and a half
centuries, the tendency was for the fudai to multiply and
by the middle of the nineteenth century (1853), there were 145
fudai to 97 tozama.

A second principle of division was based on the koku daka,
or the assessed productive capacity of each lord's domain as expressed in koku of rice.  Hideyoshi between 1587 and 1595 had
initiated a general survey of the agricultural land in Japan
and had instituted on a national scale the practice of register-
ing all fiefs in terms of their annual taxable capacity (taka),
in koku of hulled rice, rather than by area.  This uniform
system of measuring feudal holdings made possible, among other
things, more efficient centralized control, since it simplified
all grants, changes, and transfers of fiefs, greatly increasing
the power of the suzerain over his vassals.[48]

Under the Tokugawa the taka of a vassal's fief became
the measure of status.  Since to be classed as a daimyo one had
to possess lands granted or confirmed by the shogun which yielded
at least 10,000 koku, daimyo were often referred to in Tokugawa
regulations as "mangoku ijō," or "ten thousand koku and above."
On the basis of this official rating, which was called omotedaka
("public aggregate"), the military and other obligations of the
daimyo to the shogunate were determined. The omotedaka represented
the total taxable capacity of a fief and was thus, theoretically,

a measure of the income of the lord. In practice, however, since the omotedaka of a lord was usually fixed at the time of the original grant or confirmation of his fief and revised only rarely on the basis of a new survey, the official figure was rarely representative of the real income (naidaka) of a fief. Aside from seasonal fluctuations in crop yield, there might be permanent accretions due to the opening up of new lands or the introduction of improved methods of agriculture. An extreme example is the case of the Tsugaru han of Hirosaki (Mutsu) which, while rated at 100,000 koku, actually had expanded the productive capacity of its holding to as much as 200,000-300,000 koku.

A third principle of division was according to the type of holding, based partly on the extent of the territory and partly on the kind of headquarters possessed. The highest grade was called kunimochi or kokushu ("lord of a province"). Although it technically included those lords whose fiefs consisted of one or more provinces, several daimyo who actually held less than a province, such as Date of Sendai (Mutsu), Hosokawa of Kumamoto (Higo), and Nabeshima of Saga (Hizen), were also called kunimochi or kokushu. The term kunimochi had been since Muromachi times more an honorary than a descriptive designation,and in the Edo period it came to be a purely formal status distinction. The kokushu category included seventeen tozama and three kamon daimyo, who were, with one or two exceptions, the ranking daimyo in wealth.

Below the twenty "lords of provinces" was a second category which included three tozama lords who were known as jun-kokushu ("quasi-kokushu") or kunimochi-nami ("rank equivalent to kunimochi"). Next in descending order was the rank of jōshu or "lord of a castle." Beneath these were the daimyo who had

no fortified headquarters, but who were given rank equivalent
to that of a lord of a castle and were called jōshu-nami or
jōshu-kaku. The fifth and lowest category was called mujō
("castleless"); these daimyo were also variously referred to as
jinya-mochi ("possessors of field residences") or ryōshu ("lords
of domains").

As courtiers of the shogun the daimyo were classified
according to a further system of categorization which was based
on the names of the assembly halls in the shogun's palace where
the daimyo were seated when attending court. In order of precedence,
these were: (1) the ōrōka or Great Corridor, (2) the tamari-no-ma
or Antechamber, (3) the ōbiroma or Great Chamber, (4) the teikan-
no-ma or Willow Chamber, (6) the gan-no-ma or Wild Geese Chamber,
and (7) the kiku-no-ma or Chrysanthemum Chamber. The ōrōka was
normally limited to the three cadet houses of the Tokugawa (sanke),
although at times certain other collaterals, the most important
fudai, and even an outside lord such as Maeda of Kaga, would
have the privilege of being seated in it. The tamari-no-ma
was reserved for five of the leading kamon and six fudai. The
ōrōka and tamari-no-ma daimyo came to serve as an advisory body
to the bakufu, often wielding considerable influence. Occupants
of the ōbiroma included the kokushu and jun-kokushu daimyo and
several of the more important collaterals. The teikan-no-ma
was reserved for the cadet branches of the house of Echizen
and fudai of middle rank. The yanagi-no-ma was exclusively
for the tozama not in the ōbiroma class, while the gan-no-ma
and the kiku-no-ma were for the lesser fudai.

In 1866 the distribution of the three classes of daimyo
by chambers was as follows:

| Chamber | Shimpan | Fudai | Tozama | Total |
|---------|---------|-------|--------|-------|
| ōroka | 3 | 0 | 0 | 3 |
| tamari-no-ma | 5 | 6 | 0 | 11 |
| ōbiroma | 11 | 3 | 24 | 38 |
| teikan-no-ma | 4 | 60 | 0 | 64 |
| yanagi-no-ma | 0 | 0 | 73 | 73 |
| gan-no-ma | 0 | 40 | 0 | 40 |
| kiku-no-ma | 0 | 36 | 0 | 36 |
| Total | 23 | 145 | 97 | 265 |

The practical effect of all these complex categories and classifications was, of course, to divide the body of feudal lords into artificial compartments separated by barriers of ceremony and protocol. As at Versailles where Louis XIV collected his grands seigneurs, the Tokugawa daimyo were made courtiers of the shogunal court at Edo. Extreme attention was paid to protocol. Relative rank determined precedence at the shogun's palace, on the highways to and from Edo, and in the daimyo residences. All of this meant that easy intercourse among the daimyo was almost impossible, and that mutual jealousies and rivalries were kept alive and fostered.

Chapter II

THE ORIGINS AND DEVELOPMENT OF THE SANKIN KŌTAI

1.  The Meaning and Derivation of the Term

Sankin kōtai may be freely rendered as "attendance upon the shogun by turns." Sankin,[1] which means "reporting for audience" or "reporting for service" (depending upon the character used to represent the syllable kin), referred to the act of journeying to Edo to attend the shogun's court. The system called for the return of one group of daimyo to the provinces at the same time another group relieved it at the capital, and kōtai,[2] meaning "to alternate" or "to rotate in shifts," referred to the return journey. As far as can be determined, the combined term sankin kōtai was not used before the time of the third Tokugawa shogun, Iemitsu, who in 1635 first instituted the alternation of tours of duty at Edo.

The term sankin alone, however, appears in Japanese literature as early as the thirteenth century. For example, in the annals of the Kamakura shogunate, the Azuma kagami, an order of the bakufu, dated 1251, refers to the sankin duty of the members of the hyōjōsho (the Supreme Court of the bakufu).[3] Among the legislative measures of the Ashikaga shogunate (1336-1573), there appears in 1429 a ruling to the effect that guardsmen must sankin according to schedule.[4] The term was applicable to any obligatory appearance by an inferior before his lord or patron to perform services. Troupes of actors fulfilling a scheduled engagement to perform before an aristocratic patron, for example, were said to <u>sankin</u>. Among the warrior classes, however, the word denoted the personal attendance of vassals on their immediate suzerains to perform military, ceremonial, or administrative duties at their lord's seat.

It is to be noted that Tokugawa documents often had the word <u>sankin</u> written with the character for <u>kin</u> which meant "to have an imperial audience," instead of with the alternative character which meant "to render service."  The latter  usage was more traditional in Japan, but the former had better connotations from the Tokugawa point of view, since it derived directly from the Chinese classics.[5]  In the <u>Chou li</u> and the <u>Li chi</u>, for example, it is defined as the "autumnal visits of the feudal princes to the Son of Heaven."[6]  It also appears in the <u>Shu ching</u> with reference to the audiences granted by the Emperor Shun (traditional dates:  B.C. 2317-2208) to the nobles of the empire when he confirmed them in their fiefs.[7]

Though this borrowing of terminology from the Chinese classics may suggest Chinese origins for the institution of the <u>sankin kōtai</u>, there is little evidence that Ieyasu or his immediate successors consciously sought to model their system on the practices of ancient Chinese feudalism. Rather, it is likely that the Tokugawa writers who used the alternative character for <u>kin</u> were merely indulging in their propensity toward giving native institutions Chinese labels to enhance the dignity and prestige of the Tokugawa court.  The Tokugawa scholars and statesmen thought of the regime, ideally at least, as a Confucian state; hence there was a constant attempt to identify their offices, institutions, and principles of government with those described in the Confucian classics.  The visit of a daimyo to Edo, for instance,

was sometimes referred to as <u>jusshoku</u> or "report of office"
(Chinese:  <u>shu</u> <u>chih</u>), a term borrowed from the <u>Book of Mencius</u>,
in which it is defined as follows:  "When the princes  attended
at the court of the Son of Heaven, it was called a <u>report</u> <u>of</u>
<u>office</u>, that is:  they reported the administration of their
offices."[8]  The term, however, was a mere euphemism, for in
actual practice, the Tokugawa daimyo were not normally
called upon to report the conduct of affairs within their
fiefs to the shogun.


## 2.  Pre-Tokugawa Origins

The <u>sankin</u> <u>kōtai</u> system is generally regarded as
an original product of Tokugawa statecraft and is usually
described as an instrument arbitrarily devised by the bakufu
for the exploitation of the daimyo.  In fact, the system
was the natural outgrowth of pre-existing institutions which
the founders of the Tokugawa  regime inherited and elaborated
to serve their own power interests.

The temporary attendance of feudal subordinates at
the seat of their suzerain had been customary among the
military class since ancient times, and such attendance was
always enforced whenever there was a strong central authority.
It had also been customary since early feudal times for
principal vassals to maintain permanent residences at their
lord's headquarters.  The practice of exacting hostages as
a proof of faith had even earlier origins.[9]  All of these
measures had been used in past regimes to consolidate
political power in a single center and to check the centri-
fugal forces inherent in any feudally organized society.

In the Heian period (796-1185), when suzerain-vassal

relations first arose among the private warriors and the
local military nobility in the provinces, the feudal household
usually consisted of warrior vassals living at or near the
residence of the lord and serving him in the capacity of
domestic retainers.[10] Thus Japanese vassalage strongly
tended to be familial in character, and participation in
the domestic affairs and ceremonials of the lord's household came to be an integral part of a vassal's obligations
to his lord.[11] As bodies of vassals coalesced into larger
groups and vassals became scattered over greater areas, the
coherence of the vassalage group was maintained by the obligation of vassals to attend the lord from time to time
and to render personal and domestic services in times of
peace as well as military service in time of war.

Thus, under the Kamakura regime (1185-1333), when
the Minamoto and later the Hōjō families assumed the
suzerainty of the warrior class throughout the entire realm,
it was customary for the gokenin or personal retainers of
the shogun to reside permanently at Kamakura or, in the case
of those installed in the provinces as shugo ("protectors"
or military governors) and as jitō, or stewards, to appear
frequently at the shogun's capital for service.[12]

According to the early Tokugawa philosopher-statesman,
Kumazawa Banzan (1616-1691), the Kamakura shogunate had a
regular system of obligatory attendance. In his Daigaku wakumon
he states:

> Provincial rulers had to pay homage at Kamakura once in
> three years, one-third of them each year. They were not
> allowed to travel to the capital in the sowing or harvest-
> ing seasons. The time allowed for the journey varied
> according to their distance from Kamakura. They were

not to travel at the same time with others, nor in haste.[13]

Kumazawa also claimed that these triennial visits of the Kamakura lords to the shogun's court were fifty days in duration.[14]

     Although Kumazawa claimed that his description was based upon records of Kamakura customs preserved by the descendants of ancient Kamakura families, modern scholars have not been able to confirm the existence of such detailed rules. There is evidence, however, that Kamakura gokenin owed, in theory at least, some sort of fixed service of attendance at the shogun's capital. One of the feudal obligations of the Kamakura gokenin was the performance of "ōyuka service," or the service of attendance at the shogun's court at Kamakura. This was limited in duration to one month.[15] The shogun's vassals were also required to attend him on various occasions of special domestic and ceremonial importance, such as coming of age, marriage, and funeral.[16] They were further responsible for assisting in the religious festivals at Kamakura and for the building and repair of shogunal temples and palaces.[17]

     The principal duty of most Kamakura gokenin was periodical guard service at Kyoto and Kamakura. The ōban'yaku, or "grand guard service," at the imperial city of Kyoto was in origin a public, rather than a feudal, obligation which had devolved upon the warrior class from pre-feudal times, when it was theoretically performed by able-bodied free male citizens of age serving in rotation for one year out of every three. In 1186 Yoritomo made this service incumbent on all his gokenin and reduced its duration to six months at a time. Later, under the Hōjō, the period of duty at Kyoto was further shortened to three months.[18] In 1275, a similar arrangement was instituted at Kamakura and those gokenin who resided in the

fifteen provinces of eastern Japan (Tōtomi and eastward) had
to serve as guardsmen for one month annually in rotation at the
shogunal capital.[19]

Important vassals who attended frequently at Kamakura
maintained mansions there for occupancy during their periods
of attendance.[20] That even those gokenin who were situated
in the remoter provinces of western Japan had such residences
in Kamakura is indicated by references to Kamakura yashiki
property in the transfer deeds and wills of the period.[21]
It was also the practice among the shugo and jitō to send
their sons to serve at the shogun's court and act as hostages
for their fidelity. In some cases families were also kept
at Kamakura.[22]

Thus in a rudimentary form the Kamakura shogunate
maintained control over its far-flung vassals by an arrangement in many ways analogous to the Tokugawa sankin kōtai system.
The obligations of the Kamakura gokenin at Kamakura and Kyoto
were perhaps less onerous and less rigorously enforced than
those imposed by the Tokugawa system on the daimyo, but
they had much the same limiting effect on local independence.
Indeed, one authority on Japanese feudalism, Professor Shimmi,
claims that the prolonged absences of the gokenin from their
fiefs, necessitated by their duties in the service of the
shogun, delayed the development of true feudalism on Japanese
soil.[23] For, as long as the central authority was able to
enforce the obligation of attendance at the capital, feudal
autonomy was necessarily impeded. The Kamakura regime was
not as strongly centralized as that of Tokugawa times, but
it was able for a century and a half to maintain effective
control over its warrior vassals and hence over the nation.

When the Kamakura shogunate finally fell in 1333, the
central authority of the shogun passed into the hands of the
Ashikaga family, after a brief restoration of nominal imperial
rule (1333-1336). The Ashikaga established their seat in the
old imperial capital of Kyoto and were the nominal suzerains
of feudal Japan from 1336 to 1573, but they never had a real
claim on the loyalty of a greater part of the warrior class
and were hence unable to maintain actual unified control
over the country for very long. In the civil wars and
anarchy which generally prevailed throughout this period,
particularly after the middle of the fifteenth century,
the country was split up into congeries of petty feudal
states under warring lords, who, defying all central authority,
were in continual strife with one another for land and power.
The vassalic obligations of these territorial lords or daimyo
to their chief suzerain, the shogun, were more honored in
the breach than in the observance.

The emerging feudal states or baronies of this period
came to be self-constituted political and economic units with
power concentrated in the hands of a single autocratic ruler.
The centralization of authority was reflected in the growth
of the castle town, a development furthered by progress in the
art of war and the separation of the warrior class from the
land. Especially after the middle of the sixteenth century
it became customary for the lord to collect his warrior vassals
near his castle in order to promote military efficiency and to
strengthen his control over his feudal subordinates. This
custom of separating the warrior class from their fiefs and
segregating them at the military and administrative seat of
the lord was a powerful contribution to centralized rule
within the baronies. When Nobunaga and Hideyoshi brought the

daimyo under their unified control, their daimyo vassals were made to conform to the same custom.  Under Nobunaga the daimyo built their residences at Azuchi in the province of Ōmi, where their chief built, between 1576 and 1579, a great fortress to serve as his military headquarters.[24]  Hideyoshi likewise collected his daimyo around his headquarters at Fushimi and Osaka, where he kept his watchful eye on them when they were not engaged in his campaigns in Kyushu, in the Kantō, and in Korea.[25]

According to Yamaga Sokō, Hideyoshi kept his daimyo in attendance at Fushimi or Osaka for three to five years at a time, allowing them to return to their fiefs only for periods of six months or a year.[26]  In addition, he required all the lords to submit the wives and children of their chief vassals and kinsmen as hostages to Osaka. These were rotated every seven months.[27]  Eventually the families of the daimyo themselves were retained as permanent hostages.  Hideyoshi also controlled the barons by weakening them financially. He burdened them with the costs of elaborate pageants, such as the famous tea ceremony of 1587 at Kitano. He used their resources to build his huge castles at Fushimi and Osaka as well as his luxurious palaces at Kyoto.  He further introduced the custom of exchanging extravagant gifts and purposely encouraged his barons to compete among themselves in luxury.[28]

The existence of these immediate precedents accounts in a large measure for the ease with which Ieyasu was able to impose the same type of controls on his rival barons after he had gained mastery over them.  After submitting to their new suzerain, the daimyo began almost spontaneously to come to pay homage, and many built their residences there and submitted hostages on their own initiative.

## 3.  The Establishment of the System

The sankin kōtai as a regularized and compulsory system
was formally established in the fourth decade of Tokugawa rule
when the third shogun Iemitsu (1623-1651) promulgated the laws
and issued the orders which rigidly defined the periodicity
and duration of the visits of the daimyo to Edo, fixed the
dates of their arrival and departure, and made it mandatory that
they all keep their wives and children in residence at the capital.
Long before the system was codified, however, its foundations
had been laid.  It may be said to have been in effective operation
by 1615, twenty  years before the first sankin kōtai law was
adopted.  By that time it had already become the general custom
for the daimyo to visit Edo at frequent intervals to pay homage
to the shogun.  The principal lords had all built their mansions
at the capital and had submitted hostages to Edo.  Conformity
to these practices was not yet enforced by statute, but the
power and prestige of the bakufu and the force of custom had
made compliance virtually universal.  Thus, when in 1632 Iemitsu
came to power in his own right, his task was largely to consolidate and systematize practices which had been observed
and accepted as normal for a generation.  His sankin kōtai
legislation merely elaborated existing arrangements and
standardized them as hard and fast rules.

The first of the great daimyo to visit Edo after
Sekigahara was Maeda Toshinaga (1567-1614), lord of the three
provinces of Kaga, Etchū, and Noto, and next to Ieyasu himself,
the wealthiest (1,192,700 koku) territorial lord of the realm.[29]
Toshinaga was the son of Maeda Toshiie (1538-1599), one of
Ieyasu's colleagues on Hideyoshi's council of regents (go-tairō).
Having inherited his father's position on that council, Toshinaga

technically shared with Ieyasu the responsibility of administering the affairs of state on behalf of Hideyori,
Hideyoshi's successor.  In the civil war of 1600 Maeda had
sided with Ieyasu and had been rewarded by the latter with
the province of Nōto (215,000 koku).  The Maeda-Tokugawa
alliance had begun in 1599 when Toshinaga, to prove his
loyalty to Ieyasu, had sent his mother as hostage to the
Tokugawa chief.[30]  At that time Ieyasu betrothed his grand-
daughter--the infant child of his son, Hidetada--to Toshitsune
(1593-1658), Toshinaga's brother and heir-apparent.  In 1601
the Tokugawa bride (then two years old) was duly sent to
Kanazawa, the Maeda seat, and Toshitsune at his coming-of-
age ceremony that year received the ancient Tokugawa surname Matsudaira as a mark of favor.[31]

Thus, it was as a proud peer and honored  ally that
Toshinaga early in 1602 set out from Kanazawa for Edo.  His
primary object was to see his mother who was still detained
at the Tokugawa capital, but at the same time it is said
that he expected to obtain special recognition from Ieyasu
as the leading daimyo under the Tokugawa regime.[32]  Maeda
may have assumed that Ieyasu would follow Hideyoshi's
precedent in this respect and give him a place in the administrative councils of the central government.  Shortly
before Toshinaga's arrival, however, Ieyasu left Edo for
Kyoto, leaving his son, Hidetada, to receive the visitor.
This was a deliberate snub, according to Professor Mikami,
and was probably meant to show his displeasure at Maeda's
pretensions.[33]

Arai Hakuseki's Hankampu presents an interesting
account of Maeda Toshinaga's reception by Hidetada, which
claims to be based upon authentic records.[34]  Hidetada

greeted him personally at Itabashi on the outskirts of
Edo and escorted him in state into the city, but when
Toshinaga later appeared at the castle to pay his compliments,
he found himself treated not as an equal but as a subject
before a sovereign. Hidetada received the visitor seated
on a dais, while the proud lord of Kaga was relegated to an
inferior position and forced to perform humble obeisance
to his host. Toshinaga was greatly angered and mortified
by this humiliating treatment.[35] The Tokugawa were trying
to establish a relationship of superiority and inferiority
between themselves and the daimyo, who had been their equals
under Hideyoshi. The treatment of Maeda on his initial visit
to the new shogunate was undoubtedly meant to set a precedent
to be followed with other daimyo who came to Edo after him.[36]

Toshinaga's reception by Hidetada was otherwise
marked by a great show of hospitality. After the audience
Hidetada entertained him lavishly and presented him with
valuable gifts. During the rest of his stay at Edo, Toshinaga
was visited daily either by Hidetada or by one of the latter's
chief officials. When Toshinaga finally returned to his domain
via Kyoto and Osaka, where he saw Ieyasu and Hideyori, he
received a courteous letter from Hidetada thanking him for
being the first of the daimyo to come to Edo.[37]

This combination of flattery and humiliation was
typical of the technique which Ieyasu and Hidetada used to
establish their authority over the more powerful tozama lords.
They dispensed favors and honors to win the good will of the
daimyo and to encourage them to come to Edo, but at the same
time they lost no opportunity to impress the barons with their
autocratic power.[38]

The next major visitor to Edo was Date Masamune (1566-

1636), lord of Sendai (Mutsu--605,000 koku), who, like Maeda,
had been a leading ally of Ieyasu since before Sekigahara
and had fought for the Tokugawa cause in the north during
the civil war of 1600.   Though Date had been rewarded
with a mere 25,000 koku increase in his holdings for his efforts,
he was an assiduous supporter of the Tokugawa until the end
of his life.   Ieyasu had earlier strengthened his relations
with Date by contracting a political marriage between his
sixth son Tadateru (1593-1683), and one of Date's daughters.
In 1601 Date had gone to Fushimi to see Ieyasu and at that
time had been given land at Edo for a residence.[39]   The
following year, when his Edo mansion was completed, Date
came down from Fushimi to occupy it.[40]

The real influx of daimyo to the Tokugawa capital
began in 1603, the year that Ieyasu was appointed shogun
and Edo became officially the seat of the bakufu.   Even
before Ieyasu was invested as shogun at Fushimi on the
twelfth day of the second month, four of his leading
allies--Matsuura Shigenobu (1549-1614), lord of Hirado (Hizen--
63,200 koku); Hachisuka Yoshishige (1586-1620), lord of
Tokushima (Awa--186,000 koku); Hosokawa Tadaoki (1563-1645),
lord of Nakatsu (Buzen--399,000 koku); and Kuroda Nagamasa
(1568-1623), lord of Fukuoka castle (Chikuzen--523,100 koku)[41]--
had already visited Edo.   They were the vanguard of a steady
stream of western daimyo who during the spring of 1603 came
eastward to Edo to pay their respects to Hidetada, Ieyasu's
son and heir, who presided over the new shogunal court while
Ieyasu remained at Kyoto and Fushimi.[42]

Among the more prominent of the tozama lords who paid
homage at Edo during the first year of the shogunate were:
Uesugi Kagekatsu (1555-1623) of Yonezawa (Dewa--300,000 koku);[43]

Ikeda Terumasa (1564-1613) of Himeji (Harima--520,000 koku);[44]
Mōri Terumoto (1553-1625) of Nagato and Suō (319,000 koku);[45]
Asano Yoshinaga (1576-1613) of Wakayama (Kii--376,500 koku);[46]
Katō Kiyomasa (1562-1611) of Kumamoto (Higo--515,000 koku);[47]
and, for a second time, Date Masamune.[48] The following year
(1604) Fukushima Masanori (1516-1624), lord of Hiroshima (Aki--
498,300 koku);[49] Satake Yoshinobu (1570-1633), lord of Akita
(Dewa--200,000 koku);[50] and Yamanouchi Kazutoyo (1546-1605),
lord of Kōchi (Tosa--202,600 koku)[51] among others made their
initial visits to the Tokugawa court.

Since neither Ieyasu nor Hidetada attempted to compel
attendance by direct order, these early visits were made on
a **voluntary** basis. Some of the daimyo came to acknowledge
specific favors received by themselves or members of their
families at the hands of the Tokugawa. Ikeda Terumasa, for
instance, came to return thanks for the grant of the province
of Bizen to his second son, Tadatsugu (1599-1615).[52] He
himself had been granted land worth 370,000 koku, more than
twice his pre-Sekigahara holding of 150,000 koku. Similar
reasons may have prompted the visits of such generously
rewarded beneficiaries of Ieyasu as Fukushima, Kuroda, Katō,
and Yamanouchi, whose fiefs he had doubled after Sekigahara.[53]
Others made the journey at this time simply to curry favor
with the Tokugawa. This was especially the case with Uesugi,
Mōri, and Satake, who had opposed the Tokugawa cause in the
civil war and therefore had every reason to try to conciliate
their victorious rival.[54]

Another reason which brought the daimyo to Edo was
the obligation imposed upon them by the bakufu to assist on various
construction and engineering projects at the capital. One of
Ieyasu's first steps as shogun was to launch a giant program

of works designed to transform his rustic castle town into
a great metropolis worthy of its new importance as the
military and administrative capital of the empire.[55] He began
in 1603 by ordering large tracts of land reclaimed from the
bay, streets laid out, and moats and canals dug.  Sites were
provided both for the mansions of the feudatories and the
homes and shops of the townspeople, who were already flocking
to Edo in great numbers.[56]  In 1606 the construction of Edo
castle was begun, and soon an immense fortress more imposing
even than Hideyoshi's great citadel at Osaka had been built.
To assist in these undertakings, the leading daimyo were
assessed according to their income for labor, materials,
and transport.[57]  Wishing to outdo each other, they often
remained in Edo to supervise their allotted share.[58]

For these and similar reasons more and more daimyo
began to find it necessary to appear at Edo from time to
time.  It soon became customary, for the major daimyo at
least, to visit the capital at more or less regular intervals.

Ieyasu and Hidetada on their part did everything
they could to encourage the attendance of the daimyo at their
court.  To give the maximum of "face" to the proud tozama,
they welcomed them with great ceremony and entertained them
as honored guests.  Hidetada's reception of Ikeda Terumasa
in 1603 was typical.  He was greeted on arrival by Hidetada's
chief councilor and was furnished with the provisions for his
entire party during his stay.  After Ikeda presented gifts
and was received in audience, Hidetada personally served him
tea.  On departure he was given valuable gifts and accompanied
as far as Hakone by an escort of two bakufu officials.[59]

Courtesies of this type were customarily accorded all
tozama lords until Iemitsu's time.  In the case of visitors of

the highest rank, the shogun himself went out to the suburbs,
dressed and attended as if on a hunting trip, to meet them as
they arrived.[60]  Reception pavilions were built to welcome incoming lords near Shinagawa on the Tōkaidō, Itabashi on the
Nakasendō, and Senjū on the Ōshu kaidō, where the main highways
to Edo approached the city.  The shogun's gifts to the daimyo
were often quite valuable and usually included highly prized
swords, paintings, falcons, and horses, as well as rolls of
silk and pieces of gold and silver.[61]

As time went on, attendance at Edo became less and less
a matter of free will on the part of the daimyo.  In the eleventh
month of 1609 Hidetada ordered them all to appear in Edo that
winter and spend the New Year's season at court.[62]  This marks
the introduction of the compulsory element, for it was the
first time the shogun had demanded general attendance.  The
purpose of this order is not clear from the sources, but it
may have been an attempt to test the strength of the shogun's
authority over his daimyo vassals.  By this time the Tokugawa
power and prestige had developed to the point where the daimyo
could be treated openly as subjects.  In 1610, for instance,
they were ordered to send the families of their chief retainers
to Edo as hostages.[63]  In 1611 the tozama lords who happened
to be at Kyoto were summoned to the Nijō palace, the Tokugawa
headquarters in the imperial capital, and made to  swear an
oath of fealty to the shogun.  A similar step was taken the
following year at Edo.[64]  As open hostilities against Osaka
became imminent, daimyo such as Kuroda, Fukushima, and Katō
Yoshiaki, whose loyalty the bakufu had reason to suspect, were
arbitrarily detained as virtual prisoners at Edo.[65]

After the fall of Osaka in 1615, the final threat to
the supremacy of the Tokugawa was removed.  The bakufu was now

in a position to dictate its will unreservedly to the daimyo.
In the eleventh month of 1615, the first code of buke shohatto,
or laws for the military houses, was promulgated. Consisting of
thirteen articles, it contained among its chief provisions
strictures designed to curb the warlike spirit of the military
nobility, to regulate their conduct, and to weaken their
offensive power.[66] The sankin of the daimyo to Edo is referred
to in the ninth article as follows:

> Item. Rules for daimyo reporting for service (sankin).
> In the Shoku Nihongi (Chronicles of Japan continued)[67]
> it is recorded amongst the enactments:--"Except when
> entrusted with some official duty, no one is allowed
> at his own pleasure to assemble his whole clan within the
> limits of the capital, no one is to go about attended by
> more than twenty horsemen, etc." Hence it is not per-
> missible to lead about a large force of soldiers. For
> daimyo whose domains are assessed at below 1,000,000
> koku and above 200,000 koku the number of twenty horse-
> men[68] is not to be exceeded. For those whose domains
> are assessed at 100,000 koku and under, the number is to
> be in the same proportion. On occasions of official [i.e.,
> military] service, however, the number of followers is to
> be in proportion to the capacity of each daimyo.[69]

The purpose of this provision was simply to limit the
size of the retinues which accompanied the daimyo to Edo and
discourage the tendency for the lords to parade about the
capital with what amounted to small armies.[70] The attendance
of the daimyo is here taken for granted. The word sankin is
mentioned in the heading, but the law gave it no definition.
In the revised buke shohatto of 1629, reference to sankin is

44

missing altogether, although almost all other provisions of
the original code were repeated.[71]

Accordingly, no formal system may be said to have
yet existed under Ieyasu and Hidetada, but the absence of
specific legislation does not mean that there was no com-
pulsion or duress. Ieyasu, by manipulation rather than by
decree, had made it virtually impossible for any daimyo
to avoid paying frequent visits to do him homage at Edo,
Fushimi, and Sumpu.[72]

Though a brief visit to Edo at suitable intervals
sufficed during the time of the first two shogun, there is
evidence in the diary of Richard Cocks, chief of the English
Factory at Hirado from 1613 to 1621, that as early as 1616
Hidetada had already contemplated enforcing a prolonged detention of the daimyo at Edo. As quoted and paraphrased
by Peter Pratt, the diary states:[73]

> January 13th, 1616:--Certain "caveleros Japons" from Edo,
> came to see the English house at Firando [Hirado]. They
> report that the Emperor [i.e., the shogun] will have all
> the Kings (or Tonos) [daimyo] in Japan to goe for Edo,
> and there to remain for the space of 7 years, and to carry
> their wives with them, and live every one in his howse
> aparte with a servant of the Emperor's to be allwais in
> company with them, I meane with each one, to heare and
> see what passeth. This he doeth to prevent them from
> insurrections, and will not have sonns nor kynsmen, but
> the Kings themselves.
> On the 28th January the King of Firando[74] dined at the
> English house: he said he was to stay three or four
> years at Edo, which somewhat confirmed the above report.

Ieyasu's death a few months later (June 1, 1616) caused the abandonment of this plan, however, and Hidetada is reported to have "dispensed with the attendance of the Tonos at court for three years to come in order that they might 'take their ease for the panes they had taken in times past.'"[75]

In 1635 the tozama daimyo were divided into an eastern and western group which were ordered to alternate with each other their sojourn in Edo. The fourth month of each year was fixed as the time for arrivals and departures. The new arrangement was announced in the second article of the buke shohatto of that year as follows:[76]

Item. It is now settled that the daimyo and shōmyō [i.e., the greater and lesser lords] are to reside by turns at Edo. Sankin will be performed every year in summer during the course of the fourth month. Latterly the numbers of their followers have become excessive. This is at once a cause of wastefulness to the provinces and districts and of hardship to the people. Henceforward suitable reductions in this respect must be made. On the occasions of going up to Kyoto, however, shogunal instructions will govern. On occasions of official [i.e. military] service, the complement of each lord must be in accordance with their respective capacities (bungen).[77]

On the last day of the sixth month of 1635, Maeda of Kaga and twenty-five tozama daimyo of the eastern group were given leave to return to their domains, while fifty-five western tozama headed by Shimazu of Satsuma were ordered to remain in Edo.[78] The following day, the fudai daimyo were

called to the shogun's palace and informed that they were
to be exempt from the rotation system just announced.  They
were told that they would be allowed to stay in Edo and that
they should be prepared to repair quickly to the shogun's
palace whenever summoned.[79]

Seven years later, in 1642, new regulations were drawn
up.  This time the _fudai_ were brought under the system of
rotation, and, like the _tozama_, were made to divide their
time between the capital and their fiefs.[80]  In the fifth
month, sixty-nine of the _fudai_ were formed by lot into two
groups which were to alternate during the sixth month every
year.[81]  Four  months later the bakufu ordered nine other
_fudai_, similarly divided, to alternate during the eighth
month; while fourteen daimyo with fiefs in the Kantō area
were given a semiannual rotation schedule, seven of them
alternating with the other seven during the second and eighth
months of every year.[82]

These measures now obliged the great majority of the
daimyo to conform to a fixed schedule and finally established
the system.  The introduction of the alternation scheme can
be partly explained as a measure to relieve some of the
congestion at the capital, which was suddenly overcrowded
since the daimyo had all been ordered to establish their
families there.[83]  It can probably be understood best, however,
as simply another manifestation of Iemitsu's penchant for
regimenting and regularizing everything under his control.
Not even the slightest deviation from the established rule
was tolerated; when in 1636 Nambu Shigenao (1606-1664), lord
of Morioka (Mutsu--130,000 _koku_),reported late at Edo, he
was punished with three years house-arrest in his Edo
mansion.[84]

## 4. Residences and Family Hostages

The establishment of residences by the daimyo at Edo
also began shortly after Sekigahara on a voluntary basis, with
some of the earliest grants of land for this purpose going to
Date Masamune in 1601, Hosokawa Tadaoki (1563-1645), lord of
Nakatsu (Buzen--399,000 koku) in 1602, and Maeda Toshinaga.[85]
When Uesugi Kagekatsu made his initial visit to Edo in the
second month of 1603, Hidetada gave him a site for his residences just outside the Sakurada gate of Edo castle.[86]   In
the fifth month of that year Mōri Terumoto was similarly
favored.[87]   Mōri began building his Edo residence immediately
and completed construction by the eighth month.[88]   In 1604
Tōdō Takatora (1556-1630), lord of Imabaru (Iyo--203,000 koku),
proposed, with the support of Date Masamune, that all the daimyo
be called upon to maintain residences at the shogun's capital.[89]
This proposal was adopted, and already in 1607, when Father
Paez, the Jesuit Vice-Provincial,visited Edo, he was able to
report after describing the splendor of the shogun's palace:
"The principal lords had also built sumptuous residences, and
these immense and numerous edifices formed another city by
the side of that inhabited by the merchants and the people."[90]

As residences were established at the capital, some
of the daimyo began to  transfer their families from their
fiefs to their Edo mansions.  The practice of sending members
of daimyo families to Edo to serve as hostages began even before
Sekigahara.  Hideyoshi on his deathbed in 1598 had strictly
forbidden the giving or receiving of hostages among the daimyo,
but the custom was too deeply entrenched to be suppressed
by the order of a dead dictator, especially when he himself
had shown how the custom could be used to such good advantage.

Among those who submitted hostages to Edo before
Sekigahara were Tōdō Takatora,[91] Hori Hideharu (1575-1606),[92]
Asano Nagamasa (1546-1611),[93] Hosokawa Tadaoki, and Maeda
Toshinaga.[94]  In 1599 Asano, Hosokawa, and Maeda were accused
of plotting against Ieyasu by Masuda Nagamori (1545-1615), one
of Hideyoshi's councilors, who hoped thereby to alienate Ieyasu
and his potential allies.  Asano, who as a result had been
ordered confined to his fief in Kai, protested his loyalty
and sent his son, Nagashige (1588-1632), to Hidetada in Edo
as proof of his good faith.[95]  Hosokawa and Maeda likewise
submitted hostages to Ieyasu to disprove the charge of dis-
loyalty.  Hosakawa's third son, Tadatoshi (1586-1641),
arrived in Edo in the first month of 1600.  Maeda's mother
was first sent to Fushimi but was transferred to Edo in the
sixth month.[96]

After Sekigahara the flow of hostages to Edo began
almost at once. In 1601 Nabeshima Naoshige (1537-1619), lord
of Saga (Hizen--357,000 koku), and Mōri Terumoto sent their
sons to Edo.[97]  Date Masamune followed suit in 1602.[98]  When
in 1604 Sagara Nagatsune (1574-1636), a petty daimyo of Kyushu
(Hitoyoshi, Higo--22,100 koku),sent his mother from Fushimi to
Edo, Ieyasu singled him out for special honors and personally
presented him with a valuable sword.  Ieyasu also had the
bakufu provide 30 porters and 20 pack horses for the journey
and gave the mother a life pension of 50 rations a month.[99]
After 1605 several of the daimyo began to send their entire
families to live permanently at the capital.  Taking the
lead in transferring their domestic headquarters from their
fiefs to Edo were Asano Nagamasa and Tōdō Takatora.  Asano,
who had earlier turned over his fief to his son, Yoshinaga,
came with his family to Edo in 1605.  He was given a

new fief of 50,000 koku in Hitachi province for his support.[100]
Tōdō not only brought his own family to the capital in 1606,[101]
but prevailed upon his relative, Ikoma Kazumasa (1555-1610), lord
of Takamatsu (Sanuki--170,000 koku), to do likewise. Both were
duly rewarded by the shogun, who reduced their obligations to
the bakufu by half.[102]

In 1608 Tōdō, the ever-assiduous sycophant, proposed
that all the daimyo should send the wives and children of
their chief councilors (karō) to Edo to serve as shōnin or
sureties. He took the lead himself by submitting the children
of four of his chief retainers to Edo in 1609.[103] Tōdō is
usually credited with originating this practice, but Maeda
Toshinaga had actually established the precedent in 1600 when
he sent the sons of four of the karō of the Kaga han to accompany his mother to Edo.[104] It was only after 1610 that
the practice was actually enforced by bakufu order.[105]

The transfer of the wives and children of the daimyo
to Edo (as distinguished from the formal hostage system)
was left on a voluntary basis until 1634, when all fudai
daimyo were ordered to bring their families there.[106] By
that time the practice had come to be universally observed.
In 1624 Shimazu Iehisa (1576-1638), lord of Satsuma (729,500
koku), suggested that the residence of daimyo families at
the capital be enforced as a matter of state policy. In a
memorial to the bakufu he advised that the peace and tran-
quility of the realm was not properly secured by merely
requiring the daimyo to leave hostages when they returned
to their domains, and he offered to set the example for
others by bringing his own family to Edo. Receiving travel
expenses from a grateful bakufu, he did so the next year.[107]
Shimazu's lead was soon followed by many of those tozama who

had not already moved their families to Edo.[108]

      Ten years later, it was finally made compulsory by
bakufu order for all daimyo to keep their families in Edo.
Even before this, however, the bakufu made it extremely im-
politic for anyone to do otherwise. Among the charges of
improper conduct brought against Katō Kiyomasa's son, Tadahiro,
when his fief was confiscated in 1632, was that he had taken
his Edo-born son back to his domain without the bakufu's permission.[109]

Chapter III

STRUCTURE AND OPERATION OF THE SYSTEM

## 1. The Structure of the System

By 1651 when the third shogun, Iemitsu, died, the
basic features of the sankin kōtai system had been defined
by specific rules and had become an integral part of the
institutional structure of the Tokugawa regime. Though there
were certain modifications in detail from time to time, the
system, as it was established by Iemitsu in 1642, remained
essentially unchanged throughout the entire Tokugawa period.
The eighth shogun, Yoshimune (1716-1745), relaxed the system
for a brief period after 1722, but this was only a temporary
emergency measure. In 1862 the system was again relaxed, but
by this time the bakufu no longer had the power to maintain
it, and relaxing it was simply a graceful way to abandon it.

One of the main features of the system from 1642 to
1862 was the requirement that the wives and children of all
the daimyo were to be permanently domiciled at Edo, and that
all marriages between daimyo families had to be solemnized there.[1]
This rule was rigidly enforced by the careful inspection at the
sekisho or highway inspection stations of all travelers going
out of Edo. As much attention was paid to detecting any attempt
by the daimyo to smuggle their wives out of the capital as to
controlling the number of weapons being brought in, since both
"outgoing women and incoming guns" (de-onna ni iri-deppō) were
seen as the necessary first steps in any attack upon the
shogunate.[2]

While at the outset only the tozama and certain

groups of _fudai_ were subject to _kōtai_ or rotation, eventually
all daimyo--_shimpan_, _tozama_, and _fudai_ alike--were required
to conform to the system in principle. There were, however,
always daimyo who were exempt either permanently or on a
contingent basis and who remained in Edo. These were referred to as _jōfu_ or "retained at the capital." Most prominent among the permanent _jōfu_ was the Tokugawa house of Mito,
which was exempt from the system throughout the period. The
Mito lord was  not allowed to visit his domain except by special
permission from the bakufu. Contingent exemptions were granted
to daimyo officials of the bakufu during their tenure of office.[3]
Iemitsu in 1642 had exempted the _gan-no-ma_ daimyo,[4] a special
group of his favorites, from the _sankin kōtai_; these were _jōfu_
until 1686, when they were finally ordered to return to their
fiefs seminauually in rotation.[5]

Although the _sankin kōtai_ was primarily an obligation
imposed on the daimyo, there was a group of some thirty _hatamoto_,
called _kōtai yoriai_, who were also subject to the system. These
were petty vassals of the Tokugawa who, because they were related
by blood or had some other special connection with the shogunal
house, were given the same treatment and status as the daimyo.[6]

The schedules laid down by Iemitsu in 1642 specified
annual rotation for the great majority of the daimyo and semiannual rotation for the _fudai_ of the Kantō area. The _tozama_
were to make their annual trips to or from the capital during
the fourth month, and the majority of the _fudai_ during the
second and eighth months each year, while the Tokugawa lords
of Owari and Kii made annual journeys during the third month.[7]

The above schedules remained the general rule throughout the period, but there were also a number of variations and
exceptions. The Ii of Hikone (Ōmi) and a few other leading

fudai, for instance, made their journeys in the fifth month.
Others alternated during the seventh, eighth, tenth, eleventh,
and twelfth months for periods which were not always uniform
in duration.[8]

Certain daimyo in outlying areas with special responsibilities for defense had a reduced sankin obligation.  The Sō of
Tsushima reported for four months only once every three years,
coming to Edo in the eleventh month and departing in the
second month of the next year. Special dispensation was
probably granted because of the strategic importance of
the island of Tsushima vis-à-vis the continent and because
the long journey to Edo by sea and land involved special
hardships.[9]  For similar reasons the Matsumae daimyo of Yezo
(Hokkaidō) was required to come to Edo for a four month stay
only once every five years.[10]  Since the Kuroda of Chikuzen
and the Nabeshima, Gotō, and Ōmura families of Hizen were
responsible for the defense of Nagasaki, they too had their
duty of attendance limited to the winter period between the
eleventh and the second months, but each had to report every
other year.[11]

Among the kōtai yoriai there were some who reported
either in the sixth or fourth month of every other year,
others who reported in the twelfth month every year and
left during the fifth or eighth month of the following year,
and still others (those from Mino province) who either reported during the fourth month annually and left the following month, or reported for a single month once in five years.[12]

In addition to the established exceptions described
above, emergency temporary exemptions or postponements of
sankin duty were granted from time to time. These were
mainly of three kinds:  (1) to relieve the daimyo after

disastrous fires or earthquakes, (2) to reward extraordinary
services to the bakufu, and (3) to strengthen the defenses
of the country.

After the great Edo fire of 1657 which destroyed
most of the capital, fourteen daimyo were given leave, twenty-
two who were due to arrive during the fourth month were
ordered to postpone their visits for two months, and seventeen
were excused from attendance that year.[13] Similar concessions
were made to daimyo whose yashiki were destroyed in other
great disasters such as the conflagrations of 1721 and 1772,[14]
and the earthquake and fire in 1855.[15]

In 1760 Kanazawa, the seat of the Maeda han, suffered
a fire which destroyed the castle and over 10,000 dwellings.
As a relief measure the bakufu gave the Maeda lord a loan
of 50,000 ryō and relieved him of sankin duty that year.[16]
Two years later, when fire destroyed the Edo yashiki of the
Satsuma han, the lord was allowed to postpone his journey to
Edo and was granted a bakufu loan of 20,000 ryō.[17]

On the whole, however, the bakufu was reluctant to
permit deviations from the system even for such emergencies.
In 1721, for example, the main Edo yashiki of the Matsudaira
han of Aizu (Mutsu) was completely destroyed by fire, but
when permission to leave Edo was requested, the bakufu ruled
that only if all three of the han yashiki were destroyed and
there were absolutely no other quarters available could leave
be granted.[18]

Another illustration of the typical bakufu policy
with regard to these deviations from the established system
is afforded by the account in the Tokugawa jikki of the con-
troversy between Tokugawa Yorinobu (1602-1671), founder of
the Kii branch of the Tokugawa house, and Matsudaira Nobutsuna

(1596-1662), the Great Councilor who ordered the partial suspension of the sankin kōtai after the Edo fire of 1657.
Yorinobu criticized Matsudaira for inviting danger to the
bakufu by relaxing the system at a time when the capital was
in confusion as a result of the fire. He also censured the
minister for taking such a drastic step without consulting
himself and others. Matsudaira replied that such consultation
would have taken too long and would have defeated the purpose
of his action, which was to relieve as quickly as possible the
pressure on housing and food supply within the stricken city.
Since the daimyo concerned had lost their yashiki and their
grain stores and could neither shelter nor feed their multitude
of retainers, their presence was a liability. Furthermore,
Matsudaira argued, if trouble should develop, it could be
handled more effectively in the provinces than in the capital.[19]

On rare occasions, exceptional service in the interests
of the bakufu was rewarded by temporary suspension of sankin
duty. In 1673, for instance, Tsugaru Nobumasa, the daimyo of
Hirosaki, was relieved of duty at Edo that year because he
had aided the bakufu in suppressing an uprising in Yezo.[20]
In 1748, Sō of Tsushima was excused from making his scheduled
appearance the following year because he had accompanied the
Korean embassy to Edo.[21]

Since coastal defense was one of the major responsibilities
of the seaboard daimyo, sankin duty was suspended whenever there
was danger of foreign invasion. The earliest instance of this
type of exemption was the bakufu order in the second month of
1641 to Kuroda, Gotō, and Ōmura, the daimyo responsible for
the defense of Nagasaki, to remain in their fiefs instead of
coming up to Edo as scheduled.[22] The reason for this order
was the fear that the Portuguese, who had in 1639 been

56

expelled from Japan, would attempt reprisals for the execution
of the envoys whom they sent the following year from Macao
to request the reopening of trade relations.[23] Toward the
end of the Edo period, when the foreign threat again became
a problem on a much vaster scale, these exemptions for defense
purposes became more frequent and general.[24] Eventually, the
daimyo began to use their responsibility for coastal defense
as an excuse to avoid appearing in Edo and to flout the authority
of the bakufu.

The original scheme of alternation divided the _tozama_
daimyo geographically into a western and an eastern group,
who would spend alternate years in residence at the capital.
This meant that every other year, all the daimyo in whole
sections of the country would be absent from their domains.
While this arrangement was obviously to the advantage of
the Tokugawa, since it kept the _tozama_ of the east and west
apart, at the same time it left certain strategic areas
regularly unoccupied. Accordingly in 1642 the two daimyo
of Kaga and Echizen, Maeda and Matsudaira respectively, as
well as other pairs of daimyo whose fiefs constituted or
adjoined strategic locations, were ordered to alternate their
tours of duty at Edo so that one member of the pair would
always be present in his fief.[25] In 1714 the daimyo of
Yoshida and Kariya in Mikawa province and of Kakekawa and
Hamamatsu in Tōtomi province were also paired off and made to
report to Edo by turns.[26]

The following pairs of alternating fiefs were
eventually set up, all located in areas of strategic importance
to the bakufu:[27]

| | |
|---|---|
| Kanazawa, Kaga. | .Fukui, Echizen |
| Kukuoka, Chikuzen | .Saga, Hizen |
| Karatsu, Hizen. | .Shimabara, Hizen |
| Kishiwada, Izumi. | .Amagasaki, Settsu |
| Hamada, Iwami | .Tsuwano, Iwami |
| Yodo, Yamashiro | .Zeze, Ōmi |
| Yoshida, Mikawa | .Kariya, Mikawa |
| Kakekawa, Tōtomi. | .Hamamatsu, Tōtomi |
| Kuwana, Ise | .Nagashima, Ise |
| Takatsuki, Settsu | .Kameyama, Tamba |
|    (later Kōriyama, Yamato) | |
| Funai, Bungo. | .Usuki, Bungo |
| Ōmura, Hizen. | .Gotō, Hizen |

## 2. How the System was Regulated

While the **sankin kōtai** system had developed from
customary practices and was governed as much by tradition
and precedent as by statute, the Tokugawa molded the system
to their needs by statutory controls. A study of the legislation governing the system will therefore serve to clarify its
nature.

### a. Restrictions on Personnel

The legislation concerning the **sankin kōtai** system
was from the beginning concerned largely with the problem
of restricting the size of the daimyo retinues and the
population of the Edo **yashiki**. Its aims were: (1) to minimize
the danger of armed uprising by preventing the daimyo from
having too many men under arms when they came to Edo, and
(2) to reduce the congestion on the bakufu highways and in
the capital itself.

The first <u>buke</u> <u>shohatto</u> of 1615, it will be remembered, specified a limit of 20 horsemen for daimyo above the 200,000 <u>koku</u> class. In 1635, when the annual rotation of the <u>tozama</u> was introduced, the major emphasis was again on the problem of reducing excessive personnel in the daimyo trains.[28] The reasons given for urging reduction--that they were a burden upon the land and a hardship to the people--were to become oft-repeated platitudes. Subsequent <u>buke</u> <u>shohatto</u> all reiterate the same injunction against excessive personnel.[29] In addition to these general exhortations, the bakufu also issued frequent edicts and memoranda to compel the daimyo to reduce the size of their entourage on the road and their households in Edo.

In 1648 an attempt was made to set limits on the complement of warriors to be allowed each daimyo. The number of mounted retainers was restricted in proportion to the assessed income of each lord as follows:

| Number of horsemen allowed | Assessed income (in koku) |
| --- | --- |
| 5 | 20-30,000 |
| 7 | 40-60,000 |
| 10 | 70-90,000 |
| 15 | 100,000 and up |

The number of additional armed personnel on foot was to be reduced in conformity to these limits.[30]

In 1653, the bakufu issued the following order to the Edo representatives (<u>rusui</u>) of daimyo who were in their fiefs that year:

It has been reported that in recent years the daimyo have had excessive numbers of retainers when reporting [to Edo]. Since there is no need for [extra] numbers, daimyo will be attended as [specified] in former times.

Should an emergency need arise, personnel will be
recruited from nearby provinces. You will notify your
home fiefs to this effect.[31]

This order reflects the bakufu point of view that the daimyo
were bringing their retainers to Edo primarily for duty on
behalf of the bakufu and that, therefore, their numbers were
to be determined by the bakufu's needs. For the daimyo, on
the other hand, large retinues were a matter of prestige.
Hence the constant tendency to increase the number of attendants.
During the Genroku era (1688-1703) when extravagant display
was the dominant trend, bakufu attempts to legislate economy
and austerity apparently had little effect. Thus we can con-
clude from Kaempfer's description of the size and splendor
of the daimyo trains he witnessed during his visit to Japan
in the early 1690's.[32]

The bakufu tried to discourage large retinues by
restricting the transport facilities available to the daimyo
on the Tōkaidō. Ieyasu had early tried to encourage the
daimyo of western Japan to visit Edo by extending to them,
in 1602, the facilities of the post-station system he had
set up for his own use.[33]  By the middle of the seventeenth
century, however, the increasing demands upon men and horses at
the post stations were beginning to overburden the system.
Thus in 1660 regulations were issued which fixed load limits
for porters and pack horses and restricted the quota to 25
porters and 25 horses per daimyo per day. Large daimyo parties
were required to divide up into sections and travel a day apart.[34]
Subsequently frequent edicts were issued ordering observance of
load limits, quotas for men and horses, and traffic rules.[35]

One of the reasons for the large numbers of retainers
which the daimyo brought to Edo was the competition among the

lords to outdo one another in the size and splendor of the
guard contingent they were called upon to supply for manning
the numerous gates of Edo castle.  This was the chief opportunity
for martial display while they were in the capital.  Under the
sixth shogun, Ienobu (1662-1712), an attempt was made to reduce personnel in Edo by placing limits on the number of
guardsmen to be supplied.  In the fourth month of 1712, the
following memorandum was delivered to the representatives
of the several han:

> The number of retainers escorting the daimyo when they
> report [to Edo] has been determined by the law of Genna 1
> (1615).[36]  Yet, we learn that in recent years the numbers
> of attendants being brought to Edo and stationed here has
> been gradually increasing and that both the lords and
> their vassals are ruining themselves.  [This we cannot
> condone] nor, furthermore, do we feel that personnel
> left behind in the domains ought to be thus reduced in
> strength.  Henceforth care should be taken that the
> number of escorting troops be in accordance with the
> capacity (bungen) [of each daimyo].  Quotas will be
> announced in due course.[37]

Two months later regulations were issued defining
the number of personnel required by the bakufu for assign-
ment to guard duty at the seventeen (out of thirty-six) gates
of Edo castle which were entrusted to the daimyo.[38]  The
quotas established for the gate-guard were to determine the
size of the daimyo's contribution of man power for all his
public responsibilities at Edo.  The regulations stated:

> 1.  The number of guardsmen for the Ōte main gate and
> other gates of the shogun's castle will be in accordance

with the appended schedule.[39] Those [daimyo] charged
with guard duty will determine the numbers of retainers
to accompany them when they report [to the capital]
with this duty in mind. All additional personnel will
be reduced in accordance with capacity.

2. For performing all public duties whatsoever when
in the capital, including guard duty at Tōeizan and
Zōjōji,[40] the number of personnel to be supplied will
be calculated in proportion to the quota established
for the castle gate-guard detail.

3. Fire-watches for the castle and elsewhere will not
exceed twenty horse even for those daimyo in and above
the 200,000 koku bracket. The number of accompanying
troops will be proportionately limited.

4. All daimyo, whatever their rank, will, when they
report to the capital, adjust the number of their
attendants to their gate guard quota and bring along
the number appropriate to their status. Unnecessary
personnel will not be used. It is further ordered
that personnel remaining in the fiefs be left in proper
strength and that other preparedness measures not be
neglected.[41]

In the time of the eighth shogun, Yoshimune (1677-
1751), the bakufu made a similar attempt to establish more
or less definite statutory limits to the number of personnel
to be brought to Edo. In 1721 new regulations were announced
giving the maximum number of warrior retainers the daimyo
would be permitted to have in Edo.[42] These specified the
number of foot soldiers (ashigaru)[43] and petty attendants
(chūgen, ninsoku),[44] as well as mounted knights (bajō),[45]
as follows:

| Class of daimyo | Knights | Foot soldiers | Petty Attendants |
|---|---|---|---|
| 200,000 koku and above | 15-20 | 120-130 | 250-300 |
| 100,000 " " " | 10 | 80 | 145 |
| 50,000 " " " | 7 | 60 | 100 |
| 10,000 " " " | 3-4 | 20 | 30 |

These and subsequent efforts to restrict personnel
were of no avail in reducing congestion in Edo or on the highways, since they were apparently not heeded by the daimyo.
In the Enkyō era (1744-1747), for example, the Mōri han of
Chōshū (369,000 koku) had a total of 2,171 samurai and lesser
ranks stationed in Edo. Broken down by grades, these troops
consisted of 308 samurai, 188 ashigaru, 820 chūgen, and 875
men in the lesser grades of common soldiery.[46]

b.  Bakufu Reception of the Daimyo

The reception and treatment of the daimyo by the
bakufu when they reported to Edo and the formalities exchanged
between them throw light on the nature of the Tokugawa political
and social system. They reflect the suzerain-vassal relationship between the shogun and daimyo and the extreme emphasis
on status which characterized the social structure of the Edo
period.

When the sankin kōtai system was regularized under
Iemitsu, the customs and usages which governed the reception
of the daimyo at the capital were also institutionalized.
Under the first two shogun it had been the practice for the
bakufu to send officials of appropriate rank to the outskirts
of the capital to meet and welcome arriving lords and to see
them off on departure. In the case of great lords of
kokushu rank, the shogun himself would often greet the
incoming dignitary.[47]

Under Iemitsu, these courtesies were discontinued
and the shogun merely sent his envoys (jōshi) to the Edo
residence of certain major daimyo upon arrival and before
departure.[48] Tozama under 100,000 koku and all but a hand-
ful of the most important fudai and kamon reported and took
leave without special ceremony.[49] The top-ranking daimyo--
the sanke, the leading kamon, and all kokushu tozama--were
formally welcomed to the capital and given official permission
to leave by a rōjū or Senior Councilor acting as the shogun's
envoy. Less favored treatment was shown by the use of the
sōshaban (masters of ceremony)[50] or the tsukaiban (messengers)[51]
as envoys.

The formalities accorded the daimyo may be roughly
classified as follows:

Class A: Rōjū as envoy on arrival and before departure.

Class B: Rōjū before departure but sōshaban on arrival.

Class C: Sōshaban on arrival and before departure.

Class D: Tsukaiban on arrival and before departure.

Class E: Tsukaiban only on arrival or before departure.[52]

In general the tozama received more elaborate treatment than the fudai because, though completely subject to the
bakufu, they still retained, formally at least, some vestiges
of their original status as guests. To illustrate the
difference: Ii of Hikone (Ōmi--350,000 koku), the top fudai,
and Matsudaira of Kuwana (Ise--100,000 koku), a collateral of
the Tokugawa, received Class E formalities, whereas Date of
Uwajima (Iyo--100,000 koku) and Tachibana of Yanagawa (Chikugo--
119,600 koku), both tozama, received Class B and C treatments
respectively.[53]

Though the times of reporting to Edo and returning
to the fief were fixed by bakufu legislation, it was still

necessary to go through the formalities of requesting permission
each time to come up to the capital or to leave it.[54]

     After a daimyo of the higher ranks returned to his fief
from duty at the capital, it was customary for him to send one
of his chief retainers as a messenger back to Edo to report
his safe arrival home. The Sendai han, for instance, sent
vassals of over 10,000 koku income to perform this function.[55]
Again, the rank of the daimyo determined how the messenger
would be received at the shogun's court. There were three
categories. In the first or highest rank were those daimyo
whose messengers were admitted to audience with the shogun
each time. In the next category were those whose representatives
were accorded a shogunal audience only once, on the occasion
of a new daimyo's first visit to his fief. In the third
classification were the majority of the daimyo, whose messengers
saw only the rōjū.[56] The sanke were further honored by the
shogun with the sending of a bakufu official to follow them
to their fiefs to congratulate them on their safe homecoming.[57]

   c. The Exchange of Gifts

     An important feature of the formal relations between
the bakufu and the daimyo was the exchange of gifts. This
was a survival of the ancient practice, dating from prefeudal
times, of subjects presenting gifts of local produce to the
sovereign as tribute. Under feudalism such presentations were
a customary token of submission on the part of vassals to their
suzerain. Objects presented were usually horses, swords,
armor, silk and other textiles, tea, cakes, fruit, fish, candles,
paper, and the like. In the Tokugawa period the kinds and
amounts of offerings were minutely prescribed and the occasions

upon which they were to be presented were fixed by specific and detailed rules.[58] There were two categories of regular offerings or kenjō mono: (1) sampu kenjō, which were the presentations made by each daimyo when he arrived in Edo and reported to the shogun's castle for audience; and (2) toki kenjō, which included gifts presented on specified occasions throughout the year, whether the daimyo was in Edo or not.[59]

    The sampu kenjō, as distinguished from other gifts presented to bakufu officials and the shogun's family, were largely of token significance. The bakufu made no profit from these presents, since it granted gifts (hairyō mono) roughly equivalent in value when the daimyo took leave of the shogun and returned to their fiefs. A daimyo in the 10,000-koku bracket usually presented rolls of silk and a piece of silver "in lieu of a horse" (madai) when he reported to the shogun, and would receive upon departure a shogunal gift of perhaps five rolls of silk. A major daimyo, controlling a domain assessed at 600,000 koku or more, would usually present 50 pieces of silver, 50 bundles of cotton, and a horse, and would receive in return 100 pieces of silver and 30 rolls of silk. The following table shows the standard tribute presented by ten of the more important daimyo on arrival at the Edo court and the shogunal gifts bestowed in return on their departure:[60]

| Daimyo and Fief | Daimyo's Tribute | Shogun's Gifts |
|---|---|---|
| Maeda of Kanazawa (1,022,700 koku) | silver, 50 pcs.; silk, 20 rolls | silver, 100 pcs.; silk, 30 rolls; 1 falcon; 1 horse |
| Shimazu of Kagoshima (770,800 koku) | silver, 50 pcs.; silk, 20 rolls | silver, 100 pcs.; silk, 30 rolls; 1 horse |
| Date of Sendai (625,600 koku) | silver, 50 pcs.; cotton, 50 bales; 1 horse | silver, 100 pcs.; silk, 30 rolls |
| Tokugawa of Nagoya (619,500 koku) | silver, 50 pcs.; silk, 20 rolls | 3 falcons; 3 horses |
| Tokugawa of Wakayama (555,000 koku) | silver, 30 pcs.; cotton, 30 bundles | silver, 50 pcs.; silk, 20 rolls; 1 falcon; 1 horse |
| Hosokawa of Kumamoto (540,000 koku) | silver, 30 pcs.; silk, 10 rolls | silver, 50 pcs.; silk, 20 rolls; 1 horse |
| Nabeshima of Saga (357,000 koku) | silver, 30 pcs.; silk, 30 rolls; cotton, 30 bales | silver, 50 pcs.; silk, 20 rolls; 1 horse |
| Ii of Hikone (350,000 koku) | silver, 20 pcs.; cotton, 20 bales | 3 falcons; 1 horse |
| Ikeda of Okayama (305,200 koku) | silver, 30 pcs.; silk, 10 rolls | silver, 50 pcs.; silk, 20 rolls; 1 horse |
| Sō of Tsushima (100,000 koku) | cloth, 20 bolts; silk damask, 10 rolls; 5 tiger skins; ginseng, 5 kin (1.32 lbs); gold piece in lieu of horse | silver, 50 pcs.; silk, 20 rolls; 1 sword; 1 horse |

When the daimyo took leave of the shogun at the end
of his tour of duty in Edo or, in some cases, after he had
arrived back in his fief, it was customary for him to send
the shogun a courtesy gift. This too was prescribed by
regulation according to the status of the daimyo concerned.
It consisted of one to three varieties of fresh fish and
one or two casks of sake or rice wine, plus an additional
item which might be one of a number of commodities such as
rolls of silk, candles, silk crepe, bleached cloth, furs,
etc.[61]

The toki kenjō or periodic offerings were of two
types, seasonal and monthly. The seasonal offerings were
presented on certain festival occasions observed by the
shogun's court and were primarily of ceremonial significance.
On New Year's Day and on Hassaku (the first day of the eighth
month, the anniversary of the day Tokugawa Ieyasu first
occupied Edo Castle in 1590 as lord of the Kantō), the daimyo
each presented an ornamental wooden sword and a gold or silver
coin which represented the gift of a horse (madai). On the
third day of the New Year, it was customary to present an
ornamental stand called a haidai which was adorned with
figures and symbols of good fortune and long life. On three
other occasions jifuku or "seasonal garments" were presented:
two katabira (hempen gowns for summer wear) at the Tango
festival celebration (fifth day of the fifth month); and two
kosode (padded silk gowns for winter wear), at the Chōyō (ninth
day of the ninth month) and Seibo (21st day of the twelfth
month) celebrations.[62] The monthly offerings consisted primarily

of fresh, salted, dried, or pickled seafood, seasonal fruits
and vegetables, game fowl, and other special products of a
particular han. These naturally represented a great variety
of products, but they were all catalogued and published in
the bukan as the fixed and traditional tribute of each
daimyo.[63]

In addition to these regular gifts to the shogun, there
were presents to be given to his household and his officials.
The wives of the daimyo exchanged gifts with the women of the
shogun's inner apartments. These were also prescribed by
regulations. When there was a retired shogun also living
at the castle, the daimyo and their wives had to present
duplicate gifts to him and his household.[64] Presents to
the rōjū and other bakufu officials were also compulsory and
were presented upon arrival in Edo for sankin duty and upon
numerous other fixed occasions. Though these were originally
in the nature of private bribes, they came to be officially
recognized by the bakufu and enforced by order. In 1792, for
instance, the following order was issued:

> Lately it has come to our attention that the gifts
> prescribed for presentation to the sobashū and other
> officials concerned with public affairs by the daimyo
> upon arrival at the capital and on different other fixed
> occasions during the year, have fallen off in quantity,
> declined in quality, or have ceased altogether. These
> gifts are not merely personal courtesies but duty
> offerings to superior authorities. Hence abovementioned
> [lapses] must cease. Henceforth [each daimyo] will see that
> his gifts are in keeping with the established status of his
> house and that they are not of inferior quality.[65]

Although this prescribed tribute in its various forms
did not represent large amounts individually, the total burden
upon the daimyo of these obligations was tremendous.  The cost
of transporting the commodities from distant fiefs to the
capital and the fact that the presentations had to be made
regularly year after year made the obligations particularly
onerous.  The gift of fresh fish, for instance, involved the
trouble and expense of shipping them alive over long distances.[66]

To relieve the daimyo in critical times and to curb
excessive expenditures on their part, the bakufu from time
to time tried to limit the amounts of gifts to be presented.
After the great Edo fire of 1657, for instance, the bakufu
ordered a three-year austerity program.  The sampu kenjō
was limited as follows:  daimyo above 100,000 koku were
to present from ten to two sets of jifuku according to income,
one sword, and one piece of gold as madai or "horse money";
those between 50,000 and 90,000 koku were to present a sword
and one piece of gold; and those below 50,000 were to present
a sword and one piece of silver.  The seasonal gifts were
waived except for daimyo above 50,000 koku who were to present from five to two sets of jifuku, according to income,
at the year-end audience only.[67]

In 1709 following the death of the fifth shogun,
Tsunayoshi (1646-1709), whose rule was marked by ruinous
extravagance, all private gifts were prohibited, and the
monthly tribute was restricted to fish, shellfish, and fowl.
In 1722, thirteen years later, Yoshimune (1677-1751), the
eighth shogun, instituted a drastic economy program and
reduced the amount of monetary gifts to one-tenth and other
gifts to about one-third of the amounts presented up to this
time.  The monthly  gifts of local produce were limited in

amount, and except for wine and fish nothing produced outside
of the han was to be presented.  Only one set of jifuku was
to be presented on the three prescribed occasions, and private
gifts to officials were strictly prohibited.  Although similar
attempts were made in 1733, 1788, and 1841, they were largely
ineffective because the custom was too deeply entrenched.[68]

### d.  "Sankin" Routes

The routes used by the daimyo as well as the times
of travel both to and from the capital were also fixed by
bakufu regulations.  The main official routes were the
Tōkaidō, the Nakasendō (or Kiso Kaidō), the Nikkō Kaidō,
the Ōshū Kaidō, and the Kōshū Kaidō, which radiated from
Nihonbashi in the shogunal city to the provinces.  In addition
there were several lesser routes to points in the Kantō area--
for example the Mito Kaidō, a direct route to Edo, used by
the Tokugawa lord of Mito and other daimyo of the provinces
of Hitachi, Kazusa, Shimosa, and Awa.  The western daimyo
without exception had to use the Tōkaidō for their sankin
journeys, entering or leaving it at Kyoto via Osaka, which
was the eastern terminal of land and sea routes from Chūgoku,
and Shikoku.  The Tōkaidō was thus the most heavily traveled
and consequently the most carefully supervised route.  According
to a tabulation made in 1821, of 198 daimyo who left Edo that
year, 116 (or almost sixty per cent) used the Tōkaidō.[69]  The
following table shows the number of daimyo who used each of the
main routes and the months during which their journeys were made:

|  | Tōkaidō | Nakasendō | Ōshū Kaidō | Kōshū Kaidō |
|---|---|---|---|---|
| 1st month | 0 | 0 | 1 | 0 |
| 2nd month | 4 | 2 | 6 | 0 |
| 3rd month | 0 | 0 | 0 | 0 |
| 4th month | 67 | 8 | 17 | 0 |
| 5th month | 2 | 1 | 1 | 0 |
| 6th month | 39 | 16 | 18 | 1 |
| 7th month | 2 | 0 | 0 | 0 |
| 8th month | 2 | 3 | 8 | 0 |
| | 116 | 30 | 51 | 1 /198 |

According to a survey made by the bakufu officials in 1821, 245 daimyo, whose combined holdings were assessed at 18,367,000 koku, were subject to the sankin kōtai.[70] Since the size of a daimyo's retinue was supposed to conform more or less to the assessed worth of his fief, the following table provides an index to the actual volume of traffic on each road:[71]

| Route | Number of Daimyo | Assessed Worth (in koku) |
|---|---|---|
| Tōkaidō | 146 | 12,000,000 |
| Nakasendō | 30 | 2,158,000 |
| Nikkō Kaidō | 4 | 184,000 |
| Ōshu Kaidō | 37 | 2,858,000 |
| Kōshū Kaidō | 3 | 83,000 |
| Iwatsuki-dō | 1 | 20,000 |
| Mito Kaidō | 23 | 894,000 |
| Nerima-dōri | 1 | 170,000 |
| | 245 | 18,367,000 |

Certain daimyo ordinarily assigned to the Tōkaidō route had the privilege of traveling on either the Tōkaidō or the Nakasendō.[72] All others were required to use only their assigned routes.[73]

3.  The Sankin Journey

    a.  Preparation for Departure

        When the time for the regular journey to Edo approached,
elaborate advance preparations were made in each han.   In the
Honda han at Zeze (Ōmi--60,000 koku), for example, it was
customary to instruct the family temple to select an auspicious
day for the departure.   The lord then placed his traveling
gear in the custody of the chief retainer (karō) who was to
attend him on the journey and exchanged gifts with him.[74]
When the departure date had been fixed, it was posted at
the han headquarters along with a set of road orders for
his retinue.   These orders were detailed instructions to
regulate the conduct of the daimyo's followers and to insure
order, discipline, and efficiency when on the road.   Proper
behavior toward the personnel of other daimyo and toward
bakufu officials was stressed.[75]   Pilgrimages were made to
temples and shrines in the domain or in the vicinity.   The
lord held audiences with the officials who administered han
affairs, calling upon them to render faithful and diligent
service in his absence.[76]

        Advance arrangements, meanwhile, had to be made all
along the route for lodgings, meals, and transportation.   One
or more retainers were, therefore, sent ahead several days
before the departure of the main party to reserve inns and pack
horses at the post towns and to hire boats and ferry-men at
river crossings.   The task of reserving inns was a difficult
one, since all such facilities were usually in great demand
at the same time.   The inns at the post towns used by the
daimyo, bakufu officials, and others of proper rank were known
as honjin or main hotels.   Since the honjin were limited in number,
a priority system was followed.   The three branch houses of

the Tokugawa family and high ranking bakufu officials enjoyed
preference whenever there was more than one applicant for
lodging on a given date. Other daimyo were accommodated
according to rank. If the honjin were all filled, waki
honjin or annexes were used to take care of the overflow.
In addition, arrangements also had to be made to billet
retainers in inns of a lower class which were called shita
yado.[77]

### b. The Daimyo Procession

The daimyo procession of Tokugawa times was a
decadent survival of the warlike columns of armed men who
accompanied their lord to battle or attended him on his
journeys in the days before the long Tokugawa peace. Although
in theory the daimyo trains were still military contingents
being brought up to Edo to guard the gates of the shogunal
castle and to perform other military services, these functions
had become purely formal and meaningless. Arms were carried
by the attendant samurai, but the spears, swords, guns, bows
and arrows became primarily objects of display. As tastes
grew more luxurious, particularly after the Genroku era
(1688-1703), weapons and the equipage of the trains were more
and more elaborately and expensively decorated. Their chief
function was to advertise the rank and position of the daimyo
on the road.

The type and number of weapons and equipment of the
retinue were all prescribed by rigid rules. The various
specifications were determined by the family rank of the daimyo,
his relationship to the shogun, the military achievements of
his ancestors, and special traditional prerogatives all of
which were carefully distinguished and defined by the bakufu.[78]

The weapons among the paraphernalia of a daimyo procession
were the swords worn by the samurai, long bows and muskets
carried by foot troops of lesser rank, and long-shafted
spears.  The heads of the spears were capped with distinctive
sheaths, usually made of black or white wool in various
shapes, which served as one of the chief means by which the
procession of a given lord was identified.[79]  The greater
barons had more ornately sheathed long spears which were
called date dōgu or, roughly, "display gear."  These functioned
as "pikes of state" and were purely for the sake of ornament.
Of various shapes and sizes, the sheaths were made of bear fur,
tiger skin, antelope skin, horse hair, or the tail feathers of
chickens or pheasants.  Halberds (uchimono) likewise sheathed
and decorated were the privilege of a high-ranking few.

Also serving primarily as parade ornaments and as
insignia of rank were the dai-gasa and the tate-gasa (also
called tsuma-ori gasa).  The former was merely a rain helmet
mounted on a pole and covered with a cloth bag which was
secured with a fancy cord.  The latter was a conventional
umbrella with a long handle.  It likewise was encased in a
wool or velvet bag.  Neither was meant for actual use.[80]

Another characteristic appurtenance was the hasami-
bako, a lacquered box, which was carried by means of a long
handle resting on the shoulder of a bearer.  The hasami-bako
was usually emblazoned on its sides and top with the daimyo's
crest.  It was a mark of high distinction to have the privilege
of displaying the crest in gold and to be allowed to have
hasami-bako either singly or in pairs carried near the head
of the procession.[81]

In addition to the hasami-bako, which was supposed to
contain the lord's clothing and personal accessories, there
were other receptacles for footgear, armor, raincoats, etc.,

which were again brought along more for show than for practical
use.[82]  Most of the actual luggage was carried in oblong chests
called <u>nagamochi</u> suspended on a pole between two porters.  It
was also a mark of distinction to be allowed to sport a
<u>chabentōki</u> ("tea-lunch kit"), a portable apparatus which provided
hot water for warming <u>sake</u> or brewing tea and contained the
necessary utensils for preparing and serving refreshments on
the road.[83]

The lord traveled in a palanquin of the type specified
for his rank.  Details of its construction and outside finish
were marks of social distinction.  The typical daimyo palanquin
for highway use was made of lacquered split bamboo.  The better
ones had hinged roofs to enable the user to get in and out
without bending over.[34]  Palanquins were also used by the
important vassals of the lord when they accompanied him on
the journey.

Saddle horses were also a part of the procession,
though they were rarely ridden.  At the head of the trains
of greater lords there might be one or more richly caparisoned
horses led by attendants on foot.  Behind the palanquins of
the lord and his chief retainers were their personal mounts.
The number of horses and the details of their gear (bridles,
saddles, and the like) were also determined by the quality and
rank of the daimyo.[85]

c.  <u>Size and Composition of the Retinue</u>

Since pageantry and display  were the chief purpose
of the daimyo procession, there was accordingly a constant
tendency for the daimyo to increase the size of his retinue
to enhance his prestige.[86]  In the early Tokugawa period
even a fairly humble daimyo, such as Matsuura of Hirado,

was accompanied by a train of 1000 men on his Edo journeys.[87]
Kaempfer, writing about what he saw during his return trip
from Edo to Nagasaki in 1692, reports that:

> ...the train of some of the most eminent of the Princes
> of the Empire fills up the road for some days.  According-
> ly tho' we travell'd pretty fast ourselves yet we often
> met the baggage and fore-troops, consisting of the
> servants and inferior officers, for two days together,
> dispers'd in several troops, and the Prince himself
> follow'd but the third day attended with his numerous
> court, all marching in admirable order.  The retinue
> of one of the chief Daimios, as they are called, is
> computed to amount to about 20,000 [sic] men, more or
> less, that of a Sjomio [shōmyō] to about 10,000 [sic];...[88]

Kaempfer's figures are undoubtedly exaggerated.
The German doctor made his observations in the Genroku
era, which was characterized by prodigious displays of
extravagance on the part of the daimyo, but even the
retinues of the largest and wealthiest of them did not
approach this figure.  According to the biography of Maeda
Tsunatoshi (1643-1724), the daimyo of Kaga (1,022,000 koku),
the retinue accompanying this top-ranking lord to Edo in
this period numbered about 4,000 retainers.[89]  Even allowing
for numerous porters, pack horse men, and miscellaneous transport personnel hired en route, the whole  train could not
have totaled as much as Kaempfer claimed.

Whatever the accuracy of his figures, Kaempfer's
minute description of the processions he met on the road
provides perhaps the best picture of the "pomp and magnificence"
of a daimyo's entourage in the flamboyant days of the Genroku
era.  Describing the processions of typical daimyo, not those

of the <u>sanke</u> or the lords of Kaga or Satsuma, he observed:[90]

> The trains differ but little, excepting only the coats
> of arms, and particular pikes, some arbitrary order
> in the march, and the number of led horses, Fassanbacks
> [hasami-bako], Norimons [norimono], Cangos [kago], and
> their attendants.
>
> 1. Numerous troops of fore-runners, harbingers, clerks,
> and other inferior officers begin the march, they being
> to provide lodgings, victuals, and other necessary things,
> for entertainment of their prince and master and his
> court. They are follow'd by,
>
> 2. The prince's heavy baggage, pack'd up either in
> small trunks,...and carried by horses each with a banner,
> bearing the coat of arms and the name of the possessor,
> or else in large chests covered with red lacker'd leather,
> again with the possessor's coat of arms, and carried upon
> men's shoulders with multitudes of inspectors to look
> after them.
>
> 3. Great numbers of smaller retinues belonging to the
> chief officers and noblemen attending the prince,
> with pikes, scymeters, bows and arrows, umbrellos,
> palanquins, led-horses, and other marks of their
> grandeur, suitable to their birth, quality, and office.
> Some of these are carried in Norimons, others in Cangos,
> others go on horseback.
>
> 4. The Prince's own numerous train, marching in admirable
> and curious order, and divided into several troops,each
> headed by a proper commanding officer. As, 1) Five, more
> or less, fine led horses, led each by two grooms, one on
> each side, two footmen walking behind. 2) Five, or six,
> and sometimes more porters, richly clad walking one by

one, and carrying Fassanbacks, or lacker'd chests, and
japan'd neat trunks and baskets upon their shoulders,
wherein are kept the gowns, cloaths, wearing apparel,
and other necessaries for the daily use of the Prince:
each porter is attended by two footmen, who take up his
charge by turns.   3)   Ten or more fellows walking again
one by one, and carrying rich scymeters, pikes of state,
firearms, and other weapons in lacker'd wooden cases
as also  quivers with bows and arrows.  Sometimes for
magnificence's sake, there are more Fassanback  bearers,
and other led horses follow this troop.   4)   Two, three,
or more men, who carry the pikes of state, as the badges
of the prince's power and authority, adorn'd at the
upper end with bunches of cock-feathers, or certain
rough hides, or other particular ornaments, peculiar
to such or such a Prince.  They walk one by one, and
are attended each by two footmen.   5)   A gentleman
carrying the Prince's hat, which he wears to shelter
himself from the heat of the sun, and which is covered
with black velvet.  He is attended likewise with two
footmen.   6)   A gentleman carrying the Prince's
Somberiro or umbrello, which is cover'd in like manner
with black velvet, attended by two footmen.   7)   Some
more Fassanbacks and varnish'd trunks, cover'd with
varnish'd leather, with the Prince's coat of arms upon
them, each with two men to take care of it.    8) Sixteen,
more or less, of the prince's pages, and gentlemen of
his bed-chamber, richly clad, walking two and two
before his Norimon.  They are taken out from among the
first quality of his court.   9)   The Prince himself
setting in a stately Norimon or Palanquin, carried by

six or eight men, clad in rich liveries, with several
others walking at the Norimon's sides, to take it up by
turns.   Two or three gentlemen of the Prince's bed-
chamber walk at the Norimon's side to give him what he
wants and asks for, and to assist and support him in
going in or out of the Norimon.   10) Two or three horses
of state, the saddles cover'd with black. One of these
horses carries a large elbow-chair, which is sometimes
cover'd with black velvet, and plac'd on a Nori-kake
of the same stuff.   These horses are attended each by
several grooms and footmen in liveries, and some are
led by the Prince's own pages.   11) Two Pike-bearers.
12) Ten or more people, carrying each two baskets of a
monstrous large size, fix'd to the ends of a pole, which
they lay on their shoulders in such a manner, that one
basket hangs down before, another behind them.   These
baskets are more for state, than for any other use.
Sometimes some Fassanback-bearers walk among them, to
increase the troop.   In this order marches the Prince's
own train which is follow'd by
5.   Six to twelve led-horse, with their leaders, grooms
and footmen, all in liveries.
6.   A multitude of the Prince's Domesticks and other
officers of his court, with their own very numerous
trains and attendants, Pike-bearers, Fassanback bearers,
and footmen in liveries.  Some of these are carried in
Cangos, and the whole troop is headed by the Prince's
high-steward carried in a Norimon.

By the second quarter of the eighteenth century most
of the daimyo were impoverished, and many were forced by economic

necessity to reduce the size of their train.  In the Kyōhō era (1716-1735), a Kyushu daimyo worth 100,000 koku had a retinue of only 219 persons, while a daimyo of 60,000 koku usually had 150 attendants.[91]  Maeda's retinue was reduced in 1747 to about 1500 persons.[92]  For the rest of the period, according to one authority, the average size of a daimyo procession ranged between 150 and 300 persons.[93]

Chapter IV

THE ECONOMIC EFFECTS OF THE SANKIN KŌTAI


The effectiveness of the sankin kōtai system as an
instrument of political control was greatly enhanced by the
financial burden it imposed on the daimyo. The maintenance
of elaborate establishments at Edo and the expenses of the
costly annual journeys to and from the capital imposed a
constant and ruinous drain on the han exchequers and resulted
in the chronic bankruptcy of the daimyo and the progressive
impoverishment of the entire feudal class. Since it affected
so deeply the fortunes of the most important segment of the
population, the operation of the system naturally had wide
repercussions on the economic life of the country as a whole.
The assembling of the political and social elite in a single
metropolitan center and the concentrated demand thus created
for goods and services inevitably stimulated trade, industry,
communications, and a money economy on a nation-wide scale.
Hardly a single aspect of the economy of Tokugawa Japan remained unaffected by the sankin kōtai system, and it may
well be considered the key to understanding the economic
history of the Tokugawa period. A full investigation of
this large subject, however, cannot be attempted here. We
shall concern ourselves in this chapter solely with the direct
impact of the system on the finances of the daimyo.

In order to demonstrate how the sankin kōtai system
and the enforced residence of the daimyo in Edo actually contributed to the financial impoverishment of the han, it is
necessary to explain (1) the financial organization of the han,

particularly the nature of its sources of revenue; (2) the
size and nature of the expenditures the system entailed; and
(3) the proportion of the han budget that was spent in Edo.

## 1. The Financial Organization of the Han

In Tokugawa times the economic wealth of a daimyo's
domain was customarily evaluated in terms of the assessed
productive capacity of the rice lands within its boundaries.
This capacity was expressed in koku of rice and was known as
its taka or "aggregate." The omotedaka or "public aggregate"
was the figure reported to the bakufu. It was purely nominal
and was used to define the formal status of the lord of the
han in the feudal hierarchy and to determine the magnitude
of his military and other obligations to the shogunate. This
official rating tended to remain fairly fixed from generation
to generation, although some adjustments were made on occasion.
The real productive capacity of the han at any given time
was known as its naidaka ("inside aggregate") or jitsudaka
("actual aggregate"). It reflected increased crop yields
resulting from improved agricultural techniques and from
increments of reclaimed land and was hence sometimes greatly
in excess of the assessment figure officially associated with
the han.[1]

Not all the productive capacity of the domain, however,
represented income to the han treasury. A greater part of the
barony was usually parceled out as fiefs among the vassals of
the lord of the han, leaving less than half of the han's productive land under his direct control. The lord's domain, known
as the kura-iri (lit., "to be put into the treasury"), was the
chief source of the revenues with which he supported his own
household, paid his officials and retainers, and met his

administrative and official expenses as a chief of state and
vassal of the shogun.

The primary source of ordinary revenue in a daimyo's
budget was the nengu, or annual land tax, which, while it
varied from han to han, was generally about fifty per cent
of the rice crop produced within his kura-iri.  This basic
income was augmented by numerous lesser taxes payable in
money or in kind, which were imposed upon the owners or users
of forest and meadow land, upon rivers and seacoasts, and upon
commercial and industrial enterprises.  Additional income
was also derived from han monopolies of important local industries, such as the manufacture of paper, indigo, lacquer,
sugar, salt, and textiles.  There were other means available
to the lord to raise further revenue when circumstances demanded.
He could exact forced loans from wealthy merchants within his
han or demand contributions from his samurai retainers and
fief-holders.  He could issue paper money secured against
his reserves of rice and other consumable goods.  But these
were expedients which disrupted the economy of the han and
were resorted to only in times of financial crisis.[2]

The proceeds of the rice tax constituted the bulk
of the ordinary revenues of most of the han.  Money taxes constituted only a minor portion of the total regular revenues.
Hence the finances of the han depended almost entirely upon
the money realized from the sale of han produce in the markets
of the great bakufu cities.  That portion of the rice income
of the lord which was not consumed by his household at home
and in Edo, or paid out as allowances and stipends to his
retainers, or disbursed in kind for administrative expenses,
was regularly shipped to Osaka and Edo to be sold for cash.

Because the money income of most of the han was

dependent primarily on the rice surplus and was, therefore, sharply limited by the han's relatively inflexible productive capacity, it could not keep pace with the constantly mounting money needs of the times. As a consequence, the various daimyo were forced to call upon the financial assistance of merchant moneylenders early in the Edo period, and by the end of the first century of Tokugawa rule, few, if any, of the han were free of debt to the wealthy merchants of the big cities.

The financial situation of a typical fudai han at the beginning of the eighteenth century is succinctly summarized in the following report, written by an official of the Sakai han of Shōnai (Dewa--140,000 koku):

The productive capacity of my lord's [fief] is 51,000 koku over the official assessment of 140,000 koku, or a total of 191,000 koku. His actual rice income varies each year, but the average annual income [from the basic tax] for the last ten years has been roughly 210,000 hyō (84,000 koku).[3] Additional income in rice from miscellaneous taxes and other sources amounted to 27,000 hyō (10,800 koku) making his total annual rice revenue 237,000 hyō (94,800 koku). Of this amount 172,000 hyō (68,800 koku) was consumed each year by my lord's household, by his retainers in Edo and Shōnai, and by his fief-holders, leaving an average annual surplus of 65,000 hyō (26,000 koku). The proceeds [from the sale of this surplus] have varied from year to year according to the prevailing price of rice in a given year, but over a ten-year period have averaged about 16,000 ryō per year. An addition 8,900 ryō has accrued from miscellaneous money taxes. A special rice assessment (agemai) levied during this period on the incomes of han retainers in Shōnai and holders of fiefs has yielded

in money another 11,000 ryō. Cash revenues from the above
three sources total 35,900 ryō. As for outlays to be taken
care of by this income, living expenses and special needs
at Edo and Shōnai now total roughly 48,000 ryō per year.
There is thus a shortage of 12,000 ryō. Since, in addition,
there are interest payments of 15,000 ryō per year to be
paid on loans, the total annual deficit is 27,000 ryō.
Han indebtedness has been steadily increasing in recent
years, and now has reached a sum of about 80-90,000 ryō.[4]

The extremely unhealthy financial condition of the Shōnai
han reflected in this report was not unusual for the times, since
practically every han was deep in debt as a result of the extravagant spending which was universal during the Genroku era.
Even the wealthiest of the feudatories, the Maeda of Kaga
(1,022,700 koku), began to encounter financial difficulties
in this period.

Owing to a relative abundance of statistical data extending over most of the Tokugawa period, the financial history
of the Kaga han provides perhaps the best picture of the economic
trends within a majority of the feudatories of Tokugawa times.[5]
The Kaga han was the largest of the baronies, aggregating
1,022,700 koku in taka or assessed productive capacity, but
its sources of income were the same as those of all but a few
of the han and its pattern of expenditures was also typical.
A description of its financial arrangements and a brief analysis
of its revenues and expenditures will thus be useful.

As was the case with the Shōnai han and most other baronies,
the actual productive capacity (naidaka) of the Kaga han was somewhat greater than its official capacity (omotedaka). New rice
lands developed by the han in the course of the Tokugawa period

totaled in taka over 330,000 koku, the greater part of which--
about 260,000 koku--was added by the beginning of the eighteenth
century.[6] Thus the actual productive power of the Maeda territories was approximately 1,300,000 koku for most of the period.
Since land aggregating about 800,000 koku in taka was assigned
to vassals and religious institutions as fiefs, the kura-iri,
or lord's domain, measured in taxable capacity about 500,000
koku.[7] The tax ratio after the end of the seventeenth century was roughly 5:5--fifty per cent to the lord and fifty
per cent to the cultivator--in the Kaga han as well as elsewhere.[8] Thus,barring crop failures and other disasters, the
annual rice income of the han was roughly 250,000 koku.

Ordinarily about one-half of the 250,000 koku income
from the rice tax was disbursed as grain in the form of rice
donations, allowances and stipends to retainers (40-60,000
koku), payments to salt workers (20-30,000 koku) and supplies
for the lord's households in Kanazawa and Edo, or used to re-
plenish the reserve stores in the han granaries (60,000 koku).
The remaining one-half was converted into cash by selling it
in the han or in the rice markets of Edo and Osaka, with Osaka
receiving by far the bulk of the surplus rice earmarked for
sale.[9] Proceeds from the rice sold at Osaka constituted about
one-half of the ordinary cash income of the han. The other
half came from the sale of rice at home and at Edo, from
taxes collected in money, and from the receipts of the han
salt monopoly.

The expenditures of the han were generally divided
for budget purposes into three categories:  (1) home requirements, (2) Kamigata (Osaka and Kyoto) requirements, and (3)
Edo requirements.  The home allotment was primarily devoted
to expenditures connected with the conduct of the han

administration, although it also included the cost of the
sankin journey and other items not consumed within the han.
It usually constituted about thirty per cent of the total
han budget.  The budget for Edo expenses was always the largest
of all the categories since it included the cost of maintaining
the yashiki at the capital, where everything had to be purchased
with money at inflated prices.  The requirements of the home
budget were usually met by the income from sources in the han
(e.g. local rice sales, the receipts from the salt monopoly,
and taxes remitted in money).  But the expenses at Edo, Osaka,
and Kyoto consistently exceeded the amounts realized from the
sale of the rice surplus at Edo and Osaka.

The income and expenditure figures of the Kaga han
at different times in the middle and late Tokugawa period
illustrate  part of what has been stated in general terms
above.  According to a report dated 1767, the income from
the han rice tax was 250,000 koku, which after payments of
allowances and stipends would leave a net of only 60,000
koku.  By augmenting this with assessments upon fiefholders,
it was estimated that 88,000 koku would be available for sale
at Osaka yielding at the market rate of .06 kamme of silver
per koku, a cash income of 5280 kamme which would be available
for outside expenditures.  These expenditures were expected
to be 6000 kamme for Edo requirements, 500 kamme for Osaka
requirements, and 3516 kamme for interest payments (on outstanding debts totaling 29,943 kamme).  A deficit of 4,376
kamme was therefore anticipated.[10]

That this was a chronic situation may be seen by
comparing the above with the following figures, which give
the estimated revenues and requirements (exclusive of payments on interest and principal of debts) for the years 1791,
1803, 1835, and 1848:[11]

| Year of estimate | Income (kamme) | Requirements (kamme) | | | | Deficit (kamme) |
|---|---|---|---|---|---|---|
| | | Home | Edo | Osaka-Kyoto | Total | |
| 1791 | 7,162 | 3,609 | 5,746 | 1,000 | 10,355 | -3,193 |
| 1803 | 6,475 | 3,140 | 3,998 | 235 | 7,373 | -898 |
| 1835 | 9,750 | 5,162 | 5,860 | 700 | 700 | -1,972 |
| 1848 | 8,215 | 6,500 | 4,000 | 1,000 | 11,500 | -3,285 |

## 2. The Expenses of the Sankin Journey and the Edo Residences

### a. Sankin Expenses

The actual expenses of the journeys to and from Edo
varied with the size of the han retinues and their distance from
the capital. They also varied for a given han from period to
period according to the state of its finances at a given time.
Owing to the paucity of actual data for a sufficient number
of han, a complete picture of sankin expenditure cannot be presented, but a few examples of the amounts spent by various han
should serve to indicate the general picture.

Beginning with the major han, we have as the first
example the Tokugawa han at Wakayama (Kii-555,000 koku), one
of the three branch houses (sanke) of the Tokugawa family
itself. This han had a money revenue of about 340,000 ryō
in the early nineteenth century. In 1831 the lord spent 8,650
ryō to make the 365-mile journey from Wakayama to Edo (a distance of 146 ri). Travel allowances to attending samurai came
to 4,280 ryō, making the total cost of the one-way journey
12,930 ryō. In other words, about 3.8 per cent of the han's
cash income was directly devoted to defraying the cost of
attendance at Edo.[12]

The leading tozama feudatory, the Maeda han of Kaga,
had a money income of 6,475 kamme silver (about 107,900 ryō

gold) in 1803. The annual cost of the lord's journey to Edo
was estimated in the budget of that year to be 339 kamme
(5,770 ryō),[13] or 5.2 per cent of the han income.

The Shimazu han at Kagoshima (Satsuma--770,800 koku)
was the most distant (411 ri) of all the han from Edo. Its
sankin journeys usually required about fifty days of travel
and were therefore quite expensive. The cost of a one-way
trip to the capital, according to a calculation made in 1801,
was 850 kamme (14,167 ryō).[14] The han's exact money income
for this period can only be roughly estimated, but a very conservative estimate, based upon incomplete data, would place
its cash revenue at the beginning of the nineteenth century
somewhere in the neighborhood of 9,000 kamme (roughly 150,000
ryō).[15] If this approximate figure is used, we find that the
sankin journey of the Satsuma lord consumed about 9.4 per cent
of his cash income.

Another Kyushu feudatory, the Nabeshima han of Saga
(Hizen--357,000 koku), is said to have spent as much as 1750
kamme (29,167 ryō) for a single journey in the time of the
lord Narinao (1780-1830), who was notorious for his extravagance and neglect of the economic welfare of his domain.[16]

Among the smaller han, the sankin costs and percentages
of the Matsudaira han at Takasaki (Kōzuke--82,000 koku) and the
Itakura han at Matsuyama (Bitchū--50,000 koku) are perhaps
representative. The Matsudaira han had a naidaka of 95,000
koku and a cash income in 1833 of 33,500 ryō. The expenses
of the lord of this fudai han for the journey to Edo were
900 ryō and travel allowances to his retinue have been estimated at 450 ryō. The total travel expense thus came to
about 1,350 ryō or about 4 per cent of the han's cash income.[17]
The Itakura han, also a fudai feudatory, had a cash income

in 1852 of 17,000 ryō.  Its sankin expenses for that year
were 2,000 ryō or 11.8 per cent of its income.  In 1856, as
part of a stringent economy program, it reduced these expenses
to 1500 ryō, and since its income that year was 19,000 ryō, the
amount spent for travel was 8 per cent.[18]

Though these few examples hardly suffice for precise
conclusions about the percentage of han income consumed by
the sankin obligation, it may tentatively be assumed that
similar percentages obtained in the majority of the han during
the last decades of the Edo period.

An important part of the expenses of a lord's journey
was the cost of hiring boats and porters for crossing the
numerous water barriers on the route to and from the capital.
In 1852, the lord of the Inaba han at Yodo (Yamashiro--102,000
koku) made his regular journey to Edo, accompanied by 130
samurai.  The entire procession, including spear-bearers,
palanquin bearers, sandal-bearers, and 173 porters hired for
the whole trip, totaled several hundred persons. The numbers
of boats or ferry porters required at the various water crossings
on his route, the Tōkaidō, were as follows:

| Crossing | Boats | Porters |
|---|---|---|
| Kuwana - Atsuta | 25 | -- |
| Arai - Maisaka | 44 | -- |
| Tenryūgawa | 15 | 1990 |
| Ōigawa | -- | 2996 |
| Abegawa | -- | 2040 |
| Okitsugawa | -- | 1990 |
| Fujikawa | 11 | -- |
| Sakawagawa | -- | 2395 |

The expense account for this trip also mentions the hiring of
200 extra porters and 45 lantern-bearers for crossing the Hakone
pass.  Since darkness overtook the party here, 8,863 candles
and 350 pine torches had to be purchased.  These expenses and
expenditures for food and lodging for the 125-ri journey cost
the han several thousand ryō.[19]


b.    The Expenses of the Edo "Yashiki"

The han yashiki or residential estates of the daimyo
in Edo numbered over 600 in all and are said to have occupied
practically one-half of the total metropolitan area of the
capital.[20]  Each daimyo normally had three yashiki apiece,
which were designated as the kami ("upper" or main), the naka
("middle"), and the shimo ("lower") yashiki.  Most of the larger
han possessed more than the usual three estates.  The Ikeda han
of Tottori (Inaba), for instance, owned ten yashiki, the Mōri
of Chōshū had nine, while the Tokugawa of Kii and the Date of
Sendai each had eight.[21]

The bakufu had detailed regulations limiting the area
to be allotted to each daimyo according to his status.  Those
in the 10-20,000 koku bracket were to have only 2,500 tsubo
(about 2 acres), while those with incomes of 100-150,000 koku
were to content themselves with 7,000 tsubo (5.7 acres).[22]
Actually these limits were often ignored, and estates ten times
the regulation size were not unknown.  The Date of Uwajima
(Iyo--100,000 koku) and the Matsudaira of Matsuyama (Iyo--150,000
koku), for example, had holdings of 86,278 and 71,460 tsubo
respectively, the former with five separate estates and the
latter with seven.[23]

In the Kyōhō era (1716-1736), thirty daimyo had yashiki

holdings totaling between 10,000 and 60,000 tsubo in area, eighteen had property of between 50,000 and 100,000 tsubo, and three possessed estates which covered from 100,000 to 300,000 tsubo.[24] Maeda, the greatest of the feudatories, headed the list. This magnate had only four yashiki, but they covered an area of 328,222 tsubo or about 267 acres.[25] Besides these holdings, which were granted to the daimyo by the shogun, many of the lords possessed additional properties in Edo purchased or rented from the townspeople or peasants.[26]

The typical daimyo yashiki was a compound or an enclosure containing the lord's mansion and numerous outbuildings. A long row of barracks usually served as an outer wall and provided quarters for the daimyo's troops as well. An idea of the impressive size and elaborateness of some of the estates may be obtained from the following details describing the "middle" and "upper" yashiki of the Tokugawa lord of Wakayama (Kii). The "middle" yashiki of this han, located in the Akasaka section of Edo, covered an area of 136,970 tsubo (about 112 acres).[27] Although the yashiki was extremely large-- 31 chō, 20 ken (about 2.1 miles) in circumference--it was almost entirely enclosed by two-storied tile-roofed outer barracks. The main buildings within the enclosure were the mansions of the lord and his family, and in beauty and grandeur they were said to have rivaled the palaces of the shogun himself. Surrounding the lord's mansions were a great number of other buildings, such as residences for the lord's staff, various offices, storehouses, stables, a school (gakumonjo), a military gymnasium (budōjō), a falcon house, quarters for servants and petty retainers, and even a prison. The total area covered by the buildings alone was reportedly 18,200 tsubo (about 14 acres). The "upper" yashiki of the same family in Kōjimachi was 24,548

tsubo (about 20 acres) in size, and like the Akasaka estate,
was enclosed by the same tile-roofed outer barracks. The inner
buildings consisted of the lord's apartments, inner barracks,
gymnasium, and servants' quarters. The outer and inner barracks
of these two yashiki were the living quarters of the lord's retainers and their families. It has been estimated that the
barracks in the two yashiki could accommodate about a thousand
families.[28]

Each of the other han maintained similar establishments
at Edo, although usually on a more modest scale. Generally,
the "upper" yashiki was the most imposing and was used as
the official capital residence of the lord, his immediate
family, chief officials, and retainers. The "middle" yashiki
was ordinarily the residence of the lord's heir and his household. The third or "lower" yashiki was primarily used as a
retreat, and was often occupied by the retired lord, when
there was one. It was not built up as extensively as the
other sites, two or three small buildings amid garden-like
surroundings being the typical arrangement.[29]

Because of the fires which swept Edo every few years,
most of the han had their yashiki wholly or partly destroyed
several times during the Tokugawa period.[30] The main yashiki
of the Date han of Sendai was burned down about ten times,
the Akasaka yashiki of the Kii Tokugawa about eight times.
The Oda han of Kashiwabara (Tamba--20,000 koku) had to rebuild
its main yashiki sixteen times and its "lower" yashiki six
times because of fires.[31]

A few examples should suffice to give some idea of the
outlays involved in building the sometimes palatial mansions
and the numerous structures which occupied the Edo estates of
the daimyo. During the Tempō era (1830-1844) when the Akasaka

yashiki of the Kii Tokugawa was destroyed by fire, the cost
of replacing the main residence of the lord alone was said
to have amounted to the princely sum of 120,000 ryō--more than
a third of the han's annual cash revenue.[32]  When the Date han
of Sendai lost its main yashiki during the Kyōhō era (1716-1736),
it was also forced to expend 120,000 ryō to rebuild it, although
because of the han's straitened financial situation, the new
construction was more modest in scale and simpler in design
than before.[33]  In 1730 the Maeda han of Kaga had to raise
a sum of 24,900 ryō by forced loans to rebuild its main Edo
residence.[34]  The Mōri han of Chōshū during the An'ei era (1772-
1781) spent 3,054 kamme of silver (about 50,900 ryō) to replace
its main yashiki.[35]  To cite an example of one of the smaller
han, the Nambu of Hachinohe (Mutsu--20,000 koku) in 1704 sent
the relatively large sum of 5,000 ryō to Edo to rebuild their
main yashiki there.[36]

The figures given above represent the costs of rebuilding
only the principal yashiki of the han mentioned.  It may be
assumed that comparable sums were also needed from time to time
to repair or rebuild the secondary yashiki as well.  Since
building materials and labor had to be sent from the han or
procured on the inflated Edo market, the burden upon the han's
financial resources must have been extremely heavy.  Thus the
Shokkaben, a Tokugawa treatise on economics, states:  "When
in the fires of the Eastern Capital (Edo), the (han) yashiki
are destroyed, two or three years' income of the fief are
expended."[37]  A similar point is made in the Temmei roku,
a dissertation on political economy written in 1856, which
says:  "The conflagrations in Edo yashiki are felt in the
farthest corners of the whole country."[38]

The Edo yashiki were actually miniature communities

which housed a considerable staff of functionaries, warriors, and domestics in addition to the lord and his family. The temporary population included the kimbanshi or "samurai on guard duty," who were assigned to duty in Edo on a rotation basis, and those others who accompanied the lord to and from the capital. The permanent yashiki population consisted of members of the lord's family and their attendants, the yashiki officials, administrative personnel, garrison troops, and menials. The temporary residents as a rule left their families at home, but the permanent yashiki personnel had theirs with them.[39]

The yashiki population which each han had to support at the capital ranged in number from a hundred or so for the smallest feudatories, to as many as several thousand for the larger han. The Ii han of Hikone (Ōmi--350,000 koku), for example, is said to have had about 5,000 people in Edo during the Genroku era (1688-1703). During the same period, the Maeda han maintained a regular yashiki staff of about 1,000 retainers and their families, which meant a permanent population of about 4,000 people in Edo. Since another 4,000 retainers accompanied the lord to and from the capital, there were as many as 8,000 han personnel in the Maeda yashiki in the years when the lord was in residence.[40]

About fifty years later during the Enkyō era (1744-1748), the permanent Edo population of the Kaga han almost tripled when the number of its retainers stationed at Edo increased from 1,000 to 2,750.[41] Since this probably meant a corresponding increase in family dependents residing in Edo, it is likely that the population of the Maeda yashiki was over 10,000 persons even when the lord was not in residence. The Mōri han of Chōshū (369,000 koku) must also have supported a comparable

number of persons in Edo at this time, for in 1746 it had 2,171
retainers on its rolls there.[42]  At the end of the Tokugawa period,
the Kii Tokugawa had a total yashiki population of 5,000-6,000
persons, 4,000 of whom were permanent personnel and their
families.[43]

As for the smaller han, the Itakura han of Matsuyama
(Bitchū--50,000 koku) is estimated to have had about a thousand
people in Edo dependent upon the han treasury during the latter
part of the Tokugawa period.  The Mizuno daimyo, who were residents of Matsumoto (Shinano--50,000 koku) from 1642 to 1777,
supported an Edo population of about 1,300 during the Kyōhō era
(1716-1734).[44]

About one-third to one-half of the han's Edo expenses
went for the support of these relatively numerous dependents.
Outlays for stipends and allowances constituted a good part of
these expenses, since Edo personnel were entitled to special
allowances while they were in the capital.  The Maeda (Kaga)
han in 1747, for example, earmarked 3,000 out of a total of
6,000 kamme for all Edo expenses to support its Edo personnel.[45]
The much smaller Okabe han of Kishiwada (Izumi--53,000 koku)
in the An'ei era (1772-1780) similarly devoted 2,160 ryō
out of a 6,660-ryō Edo budget for rice allowances to its yashiki
personnel.[46]

## 3.  Sankin Kōtai Expenditures

The expenses of the sankin journey, plus the costs
of maintaining the Edo yashiki and supporting the great
numbers of personnel stationed there permanently or temporarily,
clearly constituted a ruinous drain on the resources of the han.
The Tokugawa economist Kaiho Seiryō (1755-1818) claimed that

half the expenditures of all the han were devoted to their needs in Edo.[47] Another Tokugawa scholar, Gamō Kumpei (1768-1813), in a memorial to the bakufu written about 1807 asserted:

> Since all the daimyo have their households in Edo, they
> each have built several mansions there. They fill them
> with many male and female attendants, who lead rootless and
> useless lives. The number of these attendants generally con-
> stitutes one-fifth of the number of their kind in the han;
> while the consumption in money and grain (in Edo) amounts
> to seven-tenths of the total expenditures of the han.[48]

Date Kenji, in his study of the amount of consumer expenditure by the daimyo in Edo, has gathered together some illuminating data on what proportion of their total money expenditure was regularly disbursed by the various han in Edo and elsewhere as a direct or indirect result of the sankin kōtai system.[49] Taking five representative fudai han and five representative tozama han, he has demonstrated how from about 60 to as much as 84 per cent of their total cash outlay went to defray the expenses of the sankin journey and to maintain han establishments in the shogun's capital. Date chose as examples of typical fudai feudatories the Sakai han of Shōnai (Dewa-- 140,000 koku), the Makino han of Nagaoka (Echigo--74,000 koku), the Okabe han of Kishiwada (Izumi--53,000 koku), the Itakura han of Matsuyama (Bitchū--50,000 koku), and the Tozawa han of Shinjō (Dewa--68,200 koku).

According to a financial report made in 1707, the average annual expenditure of the Sakai han over a five-year period from 1702 to 1706 was 39,680 ryō, of which 32,500 ryō or 82 per cent was spent in Edo and only 7,180 ryō, or 18 per cent, was used to defray home expenses.[50] Another report, dated 1723, gave the han's total budget as 32,200 ryō, of which 25,600 ryō or 79 per cent was for Edo expenses and 6,600 ryō, or 21 per cent, was for home expenses.[51]

Similarly, the Makino han, according to figures for the fiscal year of 1864-1865, spent (out of a total of 34,550 ryō) the sum of 27,400 ryō, or 79.3 per cent, in Edo; 1,300 ryō, or 3.8 per cent, in Ōsaka; and 5,850 ryō, or 16 per cent, in Nagaoka, the han seat.[52]

The total expenditures of the Okabe han of Kishiwada for the year 1776 were estimated at 9,360 ryō. Of this amount, 7,860 ryō was devoted to Edo or sankin expenses, itemized as follows: 2,160 ryō for stipends payable at Edo, 3,000 ryō for Edo expenses, 1,500 ryō for guard expenses at Edo, and 1,200 ryō for the cost of the lord's journey to Edo. Expenses in Kishiwada consumed only 1,500 ryō. The ratio between home and outside expenses thus was about 16 per cent for Kishiwada, and 84 per cent for Edo and the sankin journey.[53]

According to a report made in 1850 by a treasury official of the Itakura han of Matsuyama, the han's cash expenditures (exclusive of interest payments on debts) totaled 19,000 ryō. Of this amount 3,000 ryō, or 16.7 per cent, were for Matsuyama expenses; 1,000 ryō, or 5.5 per cent, were for Osaka and Kyoto expenses; and 14,000 ryō, or 77.8 per cent, were for Edo expenses.[54] Similar percentages are shown for the Tozawa han of Shinjō: out of 15,645 ryō expended in the year 1855, about 77 per cent went to Edo.[55]

Expressed in tabular form, the percentages for these five han are:[56]

| Fudai Han | Date of Data | Home Expenditures (per cent) | Outside Expenditures (per cent) | | |
|---|---|---|---|---|---|
| | | | Edo | Kyoto-Osaka | Total outside |
| Sakai Shonai, Dewa (140,000 koku) | 1702-1706 | 18.0 | 82.0 | 0.0 | 82.0 |
| Makino Nagaoka, Echigo (74,000 koku) | 1864-1865 | 16.9 | 79.3 | 3.8 | 83.1 |
| Okabe Kishiwada, Izumi (53,000 koku) | 1776 | 16.0 | 84.0 | 0.0 | 84.0 |
| Itakura Matsuyama, Bitchū (50,000 koku) | 1850 | 16.7 | 77.8 | 5.5 | 83.3 |
| Tozawa Shinjō, Dewa (68,200 koku) | 1855 | 23.0 | 77.0 | 0.0 | 77.0 |
| Average percentages: | | 18.1 | 80.0 | 1.9 | 81.9 |

While the above information is not entirely satisfactory for purposes of generalization because the figures are not for the same time period, the data still tend to support the general conclusion that by the middle of the nineteenth century the average fudai han was spending from 70 to 80 per cent of its annual cash expenditures in Edo.

For purposes of comparison, the expenditures of the five tozama han selected by Date as typical of the "outside" feudatories have been tabulated in terms of percentages of their total budgets as follows:[57]

| Tozama Han | Date of Data | Home Expenditures (per cent) | Outside Expenditures (per cent) | | |
|---|---|---|---|---|---|
| | | | Edo | Kyoto-Osaka | Total outside |
| Maeda Kanazawa, Kaga (1,022,700 koku) | 1747 | 31.0 | 59.0 | 10.0 | 69.0 |
| Yamanouchi Kōchi, Tosa (242,000 koku) | 1830-1843 | 25.4 | 62.3 | 12.3 | 74.6 |
| Arima Kurume, Chikugo (210,000 koku) | 1814 | 28.0 | 40.0 | 32.0 | 72.0 |
| Tsugaru Hirosaki, Mutsu (100,000 koku) | 1816 | 36.5 | 63.5 | 00.0 | 63.5 |
| Satake Akita, Dewa (205,800 koku) | 1745 | 24.0 | 72.0 | 4.0 | 76.0 |
| Average percentages: | | 29.0 | 59.3 | 11.7 | 71.0 |

The tozama han, according to these figures, appear to have spent a smaller percentage of their total expenditures in Edo than did the fudai. The difference may be partially accounted for by the fact that the fudai were less rooted in their fiefs than the tozama. They were more frequently moved from fief to fief by the shogunate, and many of them spent much of their time in Edo as members of the administration. Nevertheless, the difference was actually less than the figures would indicate. The Osaka-Kyoto expenditures of the daimyo were necessary to raise funds and purchase goods to maintain and supply the han establishments in Edo. Osaka outlays went largely to defray the expense of marketing the surplus rice and other products of the han and to pay interest on debts

incurred by the han.[58] The Kyoto account was almost exclusively
for purchases of clothing and furnishings for the lord and his
household at Edo. Thus the Osaka and Kyoto expenditures may
be regarded as expense deriving from the sankin kōtai. If all
non-home accounts are, therefore, combined and the percentages
of outside expenditures are compared, the difference between
the tozama and fudai figures is appreciably reduced. Furthermore, the home accounts of the Maeda, Arima, and Tsugaru han
included items which ought properly to be counted as outside
expenses, such as money for the sankin journey, travel allowances
for samurai assigned to duty at the shogun's capital, and the
cost of goods to be forwarded to Edo.[59]

It is thus apparent that both fudai and tozama han had
to devote as much as 70 to 80 per cent of their total normal
expenditures to expenses connected with the sankin kōtai
obligation. In addition, frequent extraordinary outlays not
provided for in the estimates of the han were required for
rebuilding the Edo yashiki after fires, for marriages and
funerals within the daimyo's family, for entertaining the
shogun when he visited them at their mansions, and for special
assessments levied by the bakufu. Because of the heavy demands
normally imposed by the sankin kōtai system upon their resources,
daimyo had very little surplus to absorb these emergency costs
and their only recourse was to go deeper and deeper into debt
to the merchants of Edo and Osaka. Economy programs, efforts
to increase production, and special taxes and assessments on
the samurai, peasants, and merchants of the han were all
attempted, but these expedients offered no permanent solution.

The basic dilemma of the daimyo lay in the fact that the
greater part of their money income was derived from that portion
of the han rice tax they could convert into cash. Only a few

exceptional han like the Satsuma barony had other sources of cash revenue extensive enough to make a difference.[60]  Since total rice production could be increased very little, the cash income of the daimyo tended to be fixed, while their cash requirements, on the other hand, were subject to no restrictions.  Inflationary forces, generated by the expanding economic life of the Tokugawa period, raised the cost of living in general; and the standards of consumption of the daimyo and their dependents were inevitably elevated by their life in an urban environment.  Money became the principal medium of exchange in the cities and its influence began to penetrate into the countryside, gradually destroying the self-sufficient economy which had once prevailed there.

Chapter V

CONTEMPORARY CRITIQUES OF THE SYSTEM


The ruinous inroads of the <u>sankin kōtai</u> on the finances
of the daimyo and its unsettling effects on Tokugawa society
made it a target of criticism by some of the leading scholars
and statesmen of the period.  Most of the critics were Confucianists who approached the subject from a conservative
point of view.  None questioned the basic validity of a system
which called upon the daimyo to report to the shogun's capital
for homage and service.  They focused their attention on what
they regarded as the evil side effects of the system, namely
the impoverishment and weakening of the feudal ruling class.
This was also a matter of grave concern to members of the bakufu
itself, and reforms of the system were considered from time to
time by the Tokugawa authorities.  But in the last analysis
no one in power was willing actually to tamper with an institution that had come to be regarded as a sacred legacy of
the founders of the regime.

So long as the shogunate was reluctant to change the
system, the scholarly critics' arguments and proposals for
reform were futile and literally academic.  Their commentaries
on the <u>sankin kōtai</u> are worth examining, however, because of
the light they throw on how contemporary observers viewed the
system and evaluated its impact on Tokugawa society.


1.  The Views of Kumazawa Banzan

Kumazawa Banzan (1619-1691) was one of the earliest
critics of the <u>sankin kōtai</u> system.  After an administrative

career as the chief minister of the Ikeda han (Bizen--315,000 koku), Kumazawa, at the age of forty, gave up statesmanship for scholarship and spent the latter half of his life as a teacher of Chinese classics and as a writer.[1] He wrote many books on the classics, on morals, and on political economy. The most famous of his works is the Daigaku wakumon,[2] a treatise written as a memorial to the bakufu in which he expounds his views on public policy and the problems of the day.[3] It is in this work that Kumazawa criticizes the sankin kōtai system and urges its fundamental reform as part of a comprehensive scheme to revitalize the economic and political life of his times.

The essence of Kumazawa's scheme was to rehabilitate the rural areas and to return the warrior class to the soil, where it and the peasantry could mingle and become one as they had been in ancient times. As an initial step, he advocated relieving the daimyo of some of the burden of their enforced sojourn at Edo by reducing the frequency and duration of attendance at the shogun's court. A model for the Tokugawa authorities to follow, he said, was the example of the Hōjō regents of the Kamakura shogunate who "established the rule that the daimyo were to sojourn at Kamakura for only fifty days once every three years, but even then admonished them against excessive spending while there, lest the wealth of the provinces be squandered in Kamakura."[4] Adoption of the Kamakura system, he argued, would not endanger the supremacy of the bakufu and would in fact strengthen its position:

In the Kamakura period there were daimyo of great parts and many powerful figures who gave just cause for apprehension, but even so, without the retention of hostages and with only a fifty day period of required residence at the capital once every three years, nothing untoward occurred. The Hōjō ruled for nine generations, the house of Ashikaga for fourteen. Even though the tenth [Ashikaga] of the line and his successors were shogun in name only and were forced to live in exile, no one ever raised his hand against the shogun. Why then in this age when the daimyo all have their mothers, wives, and children in Edo as hostages and there are none to cause anxiety should [the bakufu] hesitate to accept the divine favor which is theirs and keep looking for some calamity? If the bakufu should reduce the period of attendance at the capital, it would be regarded gratefully as a boon and win greater esteem and devotion. Further, it would not be a bad thing if daimyo unable to go up to Edo because of financial difficulties were to be released from the obligation upon petition. Such magnanimity...would be the basis of benevolent government.[5]

Kumazawa opposed the theory that the impoverishment and consequent weakening of the daimyo were to the advantage of the bakufu, pointing out that:

If the daimyo are bankrupt and the samurai are impoverished, their exactions from the people are heavier and the farmer suffers. If the peasantry is impoverished, the merchants and artisans likewise will suffer. In addition, great numbers of unemployed samurai (rōnin) will be produced and will be exposed to hunger and cold. Thus society as a whole will be afflicted with poverty and the heavens will cease to favor the shogun....The impoverishment of the daimyo is, therefore, the worst of evils for the shogunate. To regard it as an advantage to the bakufu is ill-advised statecraft.[6]

      Kumazawa wanted to relax the <u>sankin kōtai</u> system as
part of an overall program which aimed at nothing less than
the complete revolutionizing of the current social and political organization.  It was not enough, he believed, merely to
reduce the period of attendance at the capital.  Nothing
would be gained if the daimyo and their retainers were simply
returned to the provinces to indulge in idleness and extravagant
living.  The warriors should be settled on the land and restored
to their former position as farmer-soldiers (<u>nōhei</u>).  The economy
of the rural areas should be revitalized by a land program which
would redistribute and equalize peasant holdings.  The public
authorities--the bakufu and the daimyo--should use their resources
to pay off the debts and mortgages of the peasants.  Fields which
had been sold should be returned to their original owners, if the
seller had less land than the buyer. This done, the next step
would be to settle the warrior class on the land among the people
they ruled, instead of keeping them segregated in castle towns.[7]

      The resettlement of the parasitic warrior class on the
soil, Kumazawa argued, would not only relieve much of the tax
burden of the oppressed peasantry, who had to support the warriors
in idleness, but would also give the samurai once again a meaning-
ful role in society.  The peasants would be less exploited when
their relations with their rulers became more direct and intimate
and when the latter were made to treat the former as their hereditary charges, with whose fortunes they would be concerned for
generations to come.  Since the samurai would use their own
peasants to meet their military service obligations, they would
no longer have to maintain many retainers; and released from
ceremonial and official duties at the lord's court, they would
be encouraged to develop frugal and worthwhile habits.

Kumazawa's ideal farmer-soldier would occupy himself in over-
seeing his lands and looking after the welfare of his villeins,
in hunting and fishing "unmindful of the elements," and in
cultivating the military and literary arts.  He would thus
become a useful citizen and a "tower of strength" on behalf
of his lord.[8]

If, as he proposed, the daimyo  were required to spend
only fifty or sixty days every three years at Edo, Kumazawa
calculated that a lord with an assessed revenue of 100,000
koku or a net income of 10,000 koku[9] would need less than 3000
koku for his triennial expenses at Edo.  Since he would need
to lay away only 1,000 koku annually for Edo expenses, he
would have an ample 9,000 koku each year for his other needs.
This would alleviate the existing situation, in which the
lord's entire income was insufficient to meet his obligations
primarily because his Edo expenses were so great.  If he
borrowed, he became a slave of the usurers with disastrous
consequences for his retainers, since the debt-ridden lord
would be forced sooner or later to cut their stipends or to
discharge some of them altogether.[10]

Kumazawa's proposed reform of the sankin kōtai also
called for the return of the wives and children of the daimyo
to the provinces.  This, he pointed out, would cut down the
lords' expenses, since only one mansion in Edo instead of
several would then need to be maintained.  The capital would
also be cleared of unnecessary buildings and the newly available land could then be used for rice fields.[11]

Once the military class had been returned to the
land and the economy of the countryside had been restored,
Kumazawa proposed that the rice tribute of the peasant be

reduced from fifty per cent to ten per cent of the crop.
This he felt was sufficient for the needs of the ruling class,
if proper economies were practiced. The central government
might if necessary collect a two per cent tax on the rice
income of the daimyo and levy other taxes on miscellaneous
income. Any emergency deficit could be met by contributions
from the daimyo, who, since they would have been relieved of
a greater part of their duties to the central government,
could now afford to pay a little more tribute without diffi-
culty.[12]

As an economic theorist Kumazawa was, like the physio-
crats of eighteenth-century Europe, a believer in the supremacy
of the natural order. A society based on the natural self-
sufficient economy of earlier times was his ideal. He believed the ills of the times were due to urbanization and
the separation of the warrior class from the soil, which
resulted in the proliferation of materialistic wants and
impoverished the whole society while it also demoralized
and debauched it. His economic and social doctrines were
conservative enough and were probably shared by most contemporary Tokugawa theorists and statesmen, but his reform program
was far too radical to suit the authorities.

Kumazawa's proposals for the reform of the sankin kotai
system fell upon deaf ears, for the bakufu was unwilling to
accept his premise that the daimyo could be controlled by
benevolence rather than by force. His views, however, continued to influence the thinking of subsequent advocates
of reform, including Ogyū Sorai, the shogun Yoshimune, and
Yokoi Shōnan.

## 2.  The Views of Ogyū Sorai

Ogyū Sorai (1666-1728) has been described as "one of
the most capable, versatile and interesting figures among
Japanese Kangakusha" or scholars of Chinese philosophy.[13]
He was one of the leading lights of the kogakuha or School
of Ancient Learning, a school of Japanese Confucianism which
based its philosophy on the original texts of Confucianism
and directed it to the task of bettering society.[14]  Like
Kumazawa Banzan, he felt the cardinal evils of the day to be
the growing influence of money in the economic life of the
nation, the rising power of the townsmen (chōnin) over the
samurai class, and the consequent corruption and disordering
of society.  The best known of Ogyū's works is the Seidan
(Political discourses), which--like Kumazawa's Daigaku
wakumon--was presented originally as a memorial (in 1722)
to the bakufu.[15]

Ogyū was more favorably situated than Kumazawa for
the role of scholar-adviser to the shogunate.  He not only
lived under a more receptive administration, but actually
held an official post as a teacher in the employ of the bakufu.
He had the ear of the shogun Yoshimune, whose policy it was to
encourage the advice of the Confucianists when it promised to
yield practical solutions to the problems of government.[16]
Ogyū's Seidan was at once a broad discussion of state policy
and a blueprint for a detailed program of social reform.  One
of his major recommendations was the settling of the samurai
on the land away from the cities, and it is in connection
with this proposal, as in Kumazawa's case, that the sankin
kōtai system was discussed. Ogyū did not question the use-
fulness of the system as an instrument of government, but he
felt that since it impoverished the daimyo and rendered them

110

incapable of meeting their military and other obligations to the bakufu, it was defeating its own purposes. "In the early days of the bakufu," he wrote, "it was the best policy to weaken the daimyo and to encourage expenditures. Now since the daimyo are in severely straitened circumstances, the wisest policy is to see that they are kept solvent so that they can continue to perform the sankin kōtai."[17]

The enforced residence of the daimyo at Edo, Ogyū said, was instituted by Ieyasu as a check against insurrection. If, however, the daimyo continued to be impoverished, eventually the bakufu might have no choice but to suspend the sankin system altogether. Even if it did so, the accumulated power and prestige of Edo would discourage rebellion and the bakufu could probably maintain order for some time. Nevertheless, Ogyū warned, if the most important laws were thus to be set aside, it would create a precedent which would weaken respect for all law and eventually lead to anarchy.[18] Thus the system had to be maintained, but at the same time something had to be done to relieve the distress of the daimyo. Ogyu argued that although economy and frugality might be urged, such urgings were futile unless certain objective conditions which prevented the daimyo from practicing economy were corrected. These conditions, in his view, were: (1) the urbanization of the daimyo, and indeed of the whole military class; and (2) the extravagant standards of consumption and display which governed the lives of the daimyo in Edo.

Ogyū characterized the life of the military class of his times as ryoshuku seikatsu (lit., "inn life"). This term, which he used to describe the unsettled life of the feudal classes when separated from their fiefs, appears in many of his writings and was adopted by other Tokugawa writers as well. In the Seidan he explains it thus:

The life of the military nobility congregated in Edo is
like the life of people living in inns. So also is the
life of a daimyo's retainers who reside in the castle towns
of their lords, for though they are "home" with respect
to Edo, they are actually not living on their own holdings.
Life at Edo and in the castle towns is like inn life
because everything one needs--food, clothing, shelter
and even a pair of chopsticks--must be bought with money.[19]

In another work, the Taiheisaku, he wrote:

The manifold ills of the country today may all be traced
to the excessive concentration of people in Edo. Since
the daimyo and the hatamoto are collected in Edo, theirs
is the life of travelers staying at an inn. Travelers
living in inns cannot get along for a single day without
buying things; hence, money becomes all-important. Never
in any age since the foundation of the country has money
been so indispensable to life as during the last one
hundred years.[20]

The consequence of this state of affairs, said Ogyū,
was that the entire military class from the samurai to the
bakufu itself was being made bankrupt. The daimyo and their
subordinates, when on duty in Edo, were selling their entire
year's rice incomes in order to get the cash to purchase goods
and services, and to indulge in the pleasures of the city. Even
if the daimyo were not personally profligate, he pointed out,
they were forced to spend more and more of their substance at
Edo because of the high costs of living in the metropolis.[21]
Further, since the shogun and his dependents procured their
supplies in the same market, the bakufu treasury also suffered.
This meant that the benefits of the sankin kōtai really accrued

to the merchants of Edo, who prospered while the country as
a whole was impoverished.[22]

Ogyū described the daimyo as victims of a tyrannous
regimen of rules and conventions deriving from status or
kaku. Kaku prescribed a minimum of expenditures for every
rank of daimyo and made economizing impossible. It governed
every detail of his social and private life, including the
dress he wore, the food he ate, the equipment he used, and
the quarters he inhabited. The treatment of a daimyo's
servants and retainers, the manner of exchanging correspondence,
gifts, and messengers, the etiquette of his wife, and even the
details of his marriage, funeral, and other household ceremonials,
not to mention the size and equipment of his personal retinue
when he was about in the capital or traveling on the highways--
all were governed by kaku. These conventions, wrote Ogyū, were
neither sanctioned by the practices of the ancients nor imposed
by bakufu fiat. They were merely fashions of the day which
originated largely among the effete aristocracy of Kyoto and
were imitated by the daimyo, bewitched by the glamor of the
court nobility. These fashions had in the course of time
become crystallized into fixed standards which no daimyo would
think of flouting. So important had they become that a daimyo
would ruin himself and his dependents rather than deviate from
them.[23]

Ogyū's basic solution to these evils was, like that of
Kumazawa Banzan, to return the warrior class to the soil and
to revive the self-sufficient economy of the past. Each daimyo
was to be required to supply his needs with the products actually
raised or manufactured within the borders of his han, thus ob-
viating as far as possible the need for money purchases. All
his samurai dependents were to be given landed fiefs, where

they would reside except when they reported periodically to
their lord's castle for brief tours of duty. The number of
attendants which the daimyo were allowed to bring to Edo was
to be drastically reduced, as were their retinues within the
capital.[24] It was also necessary for the daimyo's private
as well as public expenses to be put under strict bakufu control. Merely to place limits on the latter was not enough,
so long as the demands of kaku kept draining the daimyo treas-
uries. The bakufu would have to use its authority to overcome
the sanctions of kaku and by detailed sumptuary legislation
scale down all personal and household expenditures to accord
with a daimyo's official rank and income.[25]

Though Ogyū attributed the impoverishment of the
daimyo mainly to the sankin kōtai, the only change that he
advocated in the system itself was a reduction in the length
of stay in Edo. He suggested that once the samurai were
settled on their own fiefs, the regular tours of duty at
Edo should be limited to one month or one hundred days in
duration.[26] He did not recommend, however, any change in
the frequency of sankin visits.

Ogyū's counsel was a more cautious version of Kumazawa's
recommendations and it apparently found favor with Yoshimune
for a while, but Sorai was not the only member of the shogun's
entourage of scholar-advisors, nor was he the most influential
one. That distinction probably belongs to Muro Kyūsō, whose
views we shall next discuss.


3. Muro Kyūsō's Advice to Yoshimune

Muro Kyūsō (1658-1734) was Ogyū Sorai's contemporary,
and like him, a scholar in the bakufu service.[27] Though less

brilliant than Ogyū, Muro enjoyed the personal trust and con-
fidence of the shogun Yoshimune, who frequently sought his
advice on administrative problems and economic policy.[28]
Muro often presented his views in the form of memoranda,
which were later compiled and published under the title
Kenkaroku.[29]

During the summer of 1722, when the bakufu was faced
with a serious deficit in the treasury, the revision of the
sankin kōtai system became one of the subjects of discussion
in a series of conferences which Yoshimune had with Muro.
According to Muro's account of these meetings,[30] Yoshimune
informed him that since the sankin kōtai system in its present
form was a source of excessive inconvenience and expense both
to the daimyo and the bakufu, he was contemplating its reform.
He pointed out that the system of biennial attendance kept
more than half the total number of daimyo constantly in Edo.
This not only constituted a great strain on the finances of
both the daimyo and the bakufu, but also led to the flooding
of Edo with too many merchants and artisans.  He was, therefore,
considering relaxing the system of biennial attendance so that
the sankin visits would be required only once every three or
five years.  Yoshimune then asked Muro to investigate what the
practice had been in ancient China and to comment on the contemplated change.[31]

In the memorandum which Muro finally submitted on this
matter, he advised strongly against making any change in the
existing system.  The reasons he gives for his position are
of interest, since they represent the point of view which
ultimately prevailed even during Yoshimune's fairly progressive
administration, and which held sway until the very end of the
bakufu period.  Muro argued as follows:

From the middle of the Ashikaga period the daimyo began
to act according to their own pleasure.  They ceased to
come up to Kyoto for audience and remained each in his
own domain.  As a result the power and prestige of the
shogun gradually atrophied.  In Keichō times (1596-1615)
and after, the power of the Tokugawa became so great and
compelling that the daimyo of the land rushed to Edo to
pay homage.  If at this time there had been more foresight,
the rules for sankin might have been more carefully laid
down.  But so great was the power of the bakufu that the
rule was established that the daimyo would report to Edo
for audience every other year and spend a year at a time
at the capital.  The daimyo have all conformed to this
arrangement and to this day have punctually and correctly
performed their services in rotation.  Moreover, since
their wives and children are in Edo, all have come to
regard Edo as their home.  They do not consider the
sankin onerous in the least.  Furthermore, this system
is the symbol of the authority and the foundation of the
safety of the bakufu.  It is part of the established order
of the realm.

If, therefore, the sankin rules are altered at this
time, the fabric of the state will suddenly be loosened.
The daimyo will come to look upon their sojourn in Edo
as something temporary and their stay in their domains
will assume greater importance.  When this happens the
tendency for the provinces to look up to Edo will gradually
disappear, and in time, the state will be weakened.[32]

Thus, Muro's argument was essentially that the sankin
kōtai had become a symbol as well as an instrument of power
and that, therefore, it should not be altered.  As for the

problems of the impoverishment of the daimyo and the deteriora-
tion of morals in Edo, the solution, he believed, was simply to
reduce the population of the capital city. He recommended that
the daimyo simply be ordered to cut down their Edo staffs by
one-third. He further proposed that the bakufu resettle its
own numerous retainers, particularly those who performed no
useful function in the administration, in the suburbs outside
Edo in groups of a hundred or two hundred families. The merchants and artisans of Edo were also to be transferred to
these new communities. Thus, Edo would be made less populous.
Muro argued that if these measures were taken, the samurai
purse would benefit, Edo morals would improve, and fires would
become less frequent.[33]

Muro's counsel did not deter Yoshimune from going ahead
with his plan to modify the sankin kōtai system, although some
writers suggest that he may have influenced the shogun to abandon
his original intention of altering the frequency of sankin visits
to once every three or five years.[34]

4. Yoshimune's Reform

After receiving Muro's memorandum, Yoshimune reportedly
chided him for his extreme conservatism. He insisted that the
real source of danger to the state was in the crowded condition
of Edo, and that this situation could not be solved by ordering
the daimyo to reduce their personnel. Speaking from personal
experience as a former daimyo[35] (Yoshimune was lord of the Kii
han before succeeding to the shogunacy), the shogun pointed out
that as long as a daimyo had to reside in Edo, he could not
get along without a certain minimum of personnel to staff his
establishment.[36]

Yoshimune had, therefore, made up his mind to go through with his plan. On the third day of the seventh month of 1722 his reform of the sankin kōtai was announced to the daimyo in the following order:

The number of gokenin who have been summoned into the service as hatamoto has gradually increased with each generation. The income of the shogunal treasury is also greater than in the past, but it has proven more and more inadequate each year to take care of disbursements for retainers' rice allowances (fuchi) and cash stipends (kirimai), and for other public expenses. Year after year there has been a deficit. The bakufu has managed in the past by drawing upon its stored rice and cash reserves. However, this year it has finally become unable to pay stipends and to meet the expenses of government. Accordingly, though this is something unheard of in the past, all those with fiefs yielding 10,000 koku and above (i.e. the daimyo) will be commanded to present rice [to the bakufu]. We take this shameful step since otherwise we have no alternative but to deprive several hundreds of our retainers of their allowances. Rice remittances will be assessed at the rate of 100 koku for every 10,000 koku of holding.

Izumi no Kami (Mizuno Tadayuki) has already been directed to study ways and means to increase tax revenues and to promote the development of new rice lands, but results cannot be expected for some years to come. In the meantime, the rice tribute (agemai) will be levied annually. Since as a consequence residence in Edo is to be reduced by a half a year, the daimyo are urged to use

the opportunity to take their ease in their domains.
In view of the fact that Edo is overcrowded and since
the period of residence at the capital is henceforth
to be of shorter duration, personnel in Edo must be
reduced as far as possible.[37]

Thus was imposed, as an emergency measure to relieve
the financial difficulties of the moment, what amounted to a
property tax upon the daimyo. This was the first time they
had been called upon to pay a direct tax to the shogunal
treasury. That the bakufu regarded this as a serious breach
of custom and an unworthy act on its part is clearly shown
in the apologetic wording of the order. It was as compensation
for this unprecedented levy that the bakufu offered the daimyo
a six-month reduction in their tour of duty at Edo. Although
this was not to be a permanent dispensation, it represented the
first reform of the sankin kōtai since the establishment of
the system.[38]

Under the modified system the old schedule of alternation dates for the daimyo--the fourth month for the tozama
and the sixth month for the fudai--was superseded, and the
third and ninth months were designated as rotation months
for both categories. The daimyo were divided into four
groups, each of which was to spend in turn six months out
of every twenty-four at the capital.[39] The heir-apparent
to each barony was allowed to visit his han while his father
was in attendance at Edo, but was required to report back to
the capital sixty days after his father returned to the fief.
Daimyo who were not yet of age were not permitted to leave
the capital, although they were to enjoy the privileges of
leave status--that is, exemption from guard duty and fire
watch--for the prescribed year and a half.[40]

The <u>agemai</u> tax yielded a total of 187,650 <u>koku</u> of rice per year, which, combined with the 5,000 <u>koku</u> contributed by the Tokugawa houses of Owari, Kii, and Mito, enabled the bakufu to raise about 54 per cent of the amount it needed to pay stipends and allowances.[41]   This still left a shortage, but by enforcing a strict retrenchment program, developing new rice lands, and instituting various economic reforms, the bakufu was able to weather the crisis and to nurse its finances to a healthier condition.   Aided by a succession of good harvests, the economic position of the bakufu rapidly improved.   In 1730, it was announced that as of the following year the <u>agemai</u> tax was to be suspended.   At the same time, it was ordered that the <u>sankin kōtai</u> system should revert to its original schedules.[42]

Muro, who had persisted in his opposition to the relaxing of the system, was thus finally vindicated.   Although the reform had benefited both bakufu and daimyo, it had meant a deviation from the "ancestral law" and hence could not be tolerated.


5.  <u>Nakai Chikuzan and Matsudaira Sadanobu</u>

Nakai Chikuzan (1730-1829), writing almost a full century after Kumazawa Banzan, renewed the attack on the <u>sankin kōtai</u> in a work known as <u>Sōbō kigen</u>.[43]   Like Kumazawa's <u>Daigaku wakumon</u> and Ogyū's <u>Seidan</u>, this was a discourse on politics addressed to the rulers of the state.   It was presented to the Tokugawa <u>rōjū</u>, Matsudaira Sadanobu,[44] in 1789 after the latter, during a tour of the Kyoto-Osaka region, had paid him a visit and requested his advice on state affairs. Living in Osaka, Nakai was relatively more sympathetic to the interests of the merchant class than were the scholars who lived in Edo closer to the center of bakufu authority. His arguments and proposals are refreshingly pragmatic.

Nakai first attacked the custom of keeping daimyo wives and children as hostages in Edo on practical and moral grounds. Hostages, he said, were a time-honored means by which good faith between allies or parties to a peace pact was expressed. However, historically, whenever there had been an advantage to be gained by breaking the agreement, hostages had always been sacrificed. Also, he argued, if hostages were killed, the onus would be borne by the side that did so rather than by the defaulting party, while, on the other hand, if the hostages were to be spared, there could be no object in holding them. Hence, he concluded, the keeping of hostages was more a liability than an advantage to the bakufu. Moreover, he contended, the detention of families in Edo was inhumane. The wives of the daimyo were doomed to spend their lives on alien soil, and since they were left behind in Edo every other year while the lords were in the domains, they spent half their lives as virtual widows. The family life of those retainers of the daimyo who were permanently assigned to duty as Edo was similarly disrupted. Sons, husbands, and fathers were forced to live away from their families, neglecting their aged parents and virtually abandoning their wives and children. Nakai strongly urged, therefore, that the families of the daimyo be allowed to return to their respective homes in the provinces.[45]

Nakai's chief criticism of the sankin kōtai system itself was that it was inequitable. He advocated that distant feudatories such as Satsuma should be required to come to Edo less frequently than those located near the capital, and he cited as precedents the systems of the ancient sage kings of China, who adjusted the frequency of audience visits to their

court according to the distance the vassal lord had to travel
from his domain. He dwelt at length on how the rigors of the
long journeys made by the lords and their retinues claimed many
lives each year and caused much suffering.[46]

Nakai's recommendation here was that the distance of
a daimyo's domain from Edo should determine the frequency and
duration of his periods of attendance at the shogun's court.
His elaborate scheme to equalize the burden of the sankin kōtai
was as follows:[47]

| Distance from Edo | Duration of attendance | Frequency |
|---|---|---|
| up to 50 ri | 50 days | every year |
| up to 100 ri | 100 days | every 2 years |
| up to 200 ri | 200 days | every 3 years |
| up to 300 ri | 300 days | every 4 years |
| over 300 ri | full year | every 5 years |

These reforms, Nakai claimed, would solve two of the crying
evils of the day: (1) the financial distress of the daiymo, and
(2) the overpopulation of the capital. He was not unaware of
the repercussions which the mass exodus of the daimyo and their
households from Edo would have on the economy of both Edo and
Osaka. He admitted that if the daimyo yashiki were depopulated
and the consuming population suddenly reduced, the artisans
and tradesmen not only of Edo but of Osaka and Kyoto would lose
their employment and general distress would result. The prosperity that Edo had long enjoyed would be no more.

Naki felt, however, that this prosperity was false and
unsound. "Sober reflection will show," he said, "that this
prosperity is largely excessive prosperity, which cannot be
regarded as true prosperity." It was, he believed, too dependent upon a population of transients who served no useful
function, took no part in government, and merely brought

congestion to the city. Consuming great quantities of food
and drink, these parasites kept the prices of daily necessities
high. Even in ordinary times they created a strain upon the
supply system, so that whenever food shipments from Osaka
were delayed, the city suffered immediate distress. Nakai
admitted that the bakufu's efforts to cut down the excessive
population of the capital may have had some beneficial results,
but he warned that if a foreign invasion should threaten and
the daimyo had to be sent home to prepare defenses, the bakufu
would have to face not only the foreign danger but a suddenly
disrupted internal economy as well. It would be far better,
therefore, to correct the evils of "excessive prosperity" by
a deliberate reduction of the Edo population before any crisis
should occur.[48]

Nakai's reform of the sankin kotai system was to be an
initial step in placing the economy of Edo on sounder foundations. He proposed that the yashiki vacated by the daimyo be
torn down or rented to merchants and artisans, who would be
encouraged to settle in Edo and develop local industries so
that the capital could become self-sufficient. Edo would be
rid of its boom-town characteristics. Profiteers, gamblers,
charlatans would be replaced by sober, industrious citizens,
and prices of commodities would be reasonable. To attain true
prosperity Edo must be transformed from a center of consumption
to one of production.[49]

Nakai's reform was not to be introduced overnight.
He outlined a timetable extending over a period of years
for the progressive relaxing of the sankin system. The most
distant of the daimyo would at first be allowed to spend two
years out of every three in their domains. Then nearer
groups in turn would have their sojourns in Edo reduced, until

after a decade or so the new arrangement would have been gradually and unobtrusively achieved. Nakai anticipated that not all the daimyo would take to his scheme. He wrote:

> Now among the daimyo and retired daimyo, there may be
> many who would say they prefer to stay in Edo and object
> to the new system. This attitude is the result of their
> addiction to evil habits. All requests to be allowed
> to continue in the old routine should be granted. There
> should be no compulsion by the authorities....The benefits
> of the new system will gradually become apparent and
> voluntary conformity will follow. In any case, it is the
> wiser policy to refrain from compulsion and to await the
> natural acceptance of the new order by the daimyo.[50]

Nakai's common-sense approach to the problem disregarded the basic function of the sankin kōtai from the bakufu point of view, namely that it served as a check on the daimyo. Equalization would have neutralized the effects of the sankin kōtai system as an instrument of daimyo control. So long as the nearby lords were the easiest to control and the distant most likely to prove troublesome, such a solution was not likely to be accepted. But Nakai was arguing as a philosopher seeking to attain social justice according to what he believed were the teachings of the ancient sages. For a Tokugawa writer, his views also reflect an unusual interest in the welfare of the merchant and artisan classes and an appreciation of their role in the economic life of the country.

It is not known whether Nakai's memorial actually influenced Matsudaira Sadanobu's views on the sankin kōtai. In one of Matsudaira's writings, however, there is evidence that he did consider a revision of the system which would allow the daimyo to reside in their domains for three-year stretches after spending three years in Edo.[51] This would have somewhat eased the burden of the hard-pressed daimyo by relieving them of the need to make their expensive journeys between home fief and capital every year. In the end, however, nothing was done.

The forces of conservatism were far stronger than the voices advocating reform. Moreover, after two centuries of Tokugawa rule, the daimyo themselves had come to accept the sankin kōtai as part of the natural order of things. As one of the defenders of the system wrote: "The feudal lords have come to feel that they were in an alien land when they visit their domains and actually look forward to their period in Edo."[52] This quotation comes from a work known as Sōbō kigen tekigi (Critique of the Sōbō kigen),[53] which was a vehement attack on the treatise by Nakai Chikuzan. Since its rebuttal of Nakai's attack on the sankin kōtai probably represents the dominant contemporary attitude on the subject, its arguments are worth summarizing. The author contended that the sankin kōtai was never a hostage system, arbitrarily imposed from above. Rather, he asserted, the daimyo had originally come to Edo of their own volition and had built their residences and settled their families there of their own accord.[54] His principal arguments against any reform of the sankin system were as follows: (1) since the daimyo had observed the practice of sankin kōtai for over two centuries without protest and had come to prefer their life in Edo to that of the provinces, a change in the system would mean upsetting a natural arrangement and would lead to the disruption of the Tokugawa policy, producing all manner of evil consequences; (2) the assembling of the daimyo in Edo to live among their peers and superiors

was necessary to maintain the sense of hierarchy and to foster
the spirit of obedience among the lords, who might otherwise
become tyrannical despots if left in their own domains; (3)
the sankin expenditures of the daimyo were not evil but good,
for they accrued to the benefit of the people and kept the
lords from wasteful and extravagant living.[55]

The commentaries on the sankin kōtai by the scholarly
critics discussed in this chapter were all based on the Confucian premise that the ideal state was a feudal order governed
by benevolence from above and supported by loyalty and obedience
from below. But while the Tokugawa state may have been Confucian
in theory and feudal in form, it was in fact a centralized dic-
tatorship resting on force. Because its form was feudal, a
system like the sankin kōtai was necessary to maintain centralized political control. Thus, all reform proposals which would
weaken its basic function as a control mechanism were bound to
be ignored or suppressed. It was not until the middle of the
nineteenth century, when outside forces rather than the daimyo
became the chief threat to the security of the bakufu, that
reform of the system became a matter of serious consideration.

## Chapter VI

## THE END OF THE SYSTEM

### 1. The Decline of the System

As noted in our discussion of the early history of
the sankin kōtai system, the attendance of the daimyo in Edo
and the establishment of yashiki at the Tokugawa capital represented an almost spontaneous response to the fact of
Tokugawa power. By Iemitsu's time, when the system was
written into law, the sanctions of custom had already insured
its general acceptance and observance. Despite the onerous
financial burden which the system imposed--a burden which
reached ruinous proportions as time went on--the daimyo for
the most part adhered faithfully to it. Deviations from the
statutes and regulations governing the system were usually
of the type that really served the original purposes of the
system, namely to weaken the daimyo and keep them subject to
centralized control. If, for instance, the daimyo failed to
adhere to their schedules, it was usually because they over-
stayed at the capital or refused to return to their fiefs at
all.[1]

Once the power of the bakufu began to weaken, however,
the system, too, began to decline. By the beginning of the
nineteenth century, the waning authority of the central government was reflected in an increasing number of late arrivals.
Cases of malingering became so numerous that the bakufu was
repeatedly forced to issue warning notices. Matsuura Kiyoshi
(1770-1841), lord of the Hirado han (Hizen--61,700 koku), writes
in his famous miscellany, the Kasshi yawa[2]: "In my youth

before I entered upon my duties [as a daimyo], there were cases
of daimyo remaining in the capital after having been granted
leave, but there were no cases where they stayed in their fiefs
beyond their allotted time. However, in recent years such
instances have gradually become more numerous." To illustrate,
Matsuura cites a notice dated the fifth month, 1805, from the
rōjū to the Edo representative of the daimyo, which stated:
"Too many daimyo have of late been failing to observe the
established schedules. The daimyo have often been reminded
that there should be no delays in performing the sankin kōtai.
While illness is unavoidable, if one is in any condition to
travel at all, he should try to report to the capital on time.
Each daimyo is to be notified to the above effect and their
councillors will be admonished from time to time."[3]

The same problem is dealt with in a bakufu edict
issued in 1841:

There have been frequent references in the past to the
fact that large numbers of daimyo have been failing to
report on time because of illness or have, though given
leave, continued to remain in the capital on the plea
of ill health. In recent years, moreover, there have
been a particularly large number requesting permission
to remain in the capital. Among them are some who have
not visited their fiefs for a long time. In addition,
there are still daimyo postponing their sankin visits.
We have repeatedly urged that, while illness cannot be
avoided, every effort should be made to report at the
established time, that overstaying one's period at the
capital should be avoided, and that in spite of being
ill, one should travel if at all in any condition to
do so. Hitherto, it has been the practice to allow

<u>sankin</u> deferments in case of illness and, after checking
the circumstances, to grant whatever was requested by
those pleading sick. Henceforth, however, there is no
telling what the shogun's orders in these cases will be.
This is not the place to broach such matters; they are
presented simply for your guidance.[4]

These and similar official pronouncements of the
time not only reveal the fact that the <u>sankin kōtai</u> schedules
were being rather widely flouted, but also indicate that the
bakufu was forced to adopt an almost supplicatory attitude
in dealing with violations. But the bakufu had no other recourse, since it no longer had the power to back its edicts
with force. Moreover, since the country was now being faced
with the threat of foreign encroachment, it was essential for
the sake of national unity that the daimyo be conciliated rather
than antagonized.

## 2. The Sankin Kōtai and the Problem of National Defense

The need that arose in the mid-nineteenth century for
the Tokugawa state to concern itself with the problem of de-
fending the nation against foreign aggression also gave rise
to a new look at the <u>sankin kōtai</u> system. For it was clear
that with the resources and energies of the daimyo being
dissipated by their <u>sankin</u> duties, they could not devote
themselves properly to their primary responsibility--that of
fortifying the coasts and building up their armament. Moreover, it became necessary for the sake of national safety and
national unity that the daimyo be treated less as captive
satellites and more as partners and allies.

The problem of national defense had been agitating

the minds of a few far-sighted men since the end of the
eighteenth century, when Russia's westward expansion to the
Pacific was first seen as a future menace to Japan.  Beginning
with Rin (Hayashi) Shihei (1754-1793), who as early as 1786 had
tried to warn his countrymen of the power of the West and of
the necessity for strengthening the nation's defenses,[5] a
number of forward-looking samurai scholars had been preaching
the need to prepare Japan militarily to meet the West on equal
terms.[6]  Though the bakufu was generally unreceptive toward
such suggestions, many of the leading daimyo were converted.

One such daimyo was Matsudaira Shungaku (1828-1890),
the lord of Fukui (Echizen--320,000 koku), who, because of
his close connections to the Tokugawa house both by birth
and adoption, was in a position to express unorthodox views
to the bakufu with relative impunity.[7]  His opportunity to
speak his mind came in 1853, when after Perry's initial visit,
Abe Masahiro (1819-1857),[8] the head of the rōjū, took the extraordinary and unprecedented step of inviting the daimyo to
submit their opinions on how the crisis should be met.[9]  Though
discussion of internal policy was not called for, Matsudaira
proposed among other things the relaxing of the sankin kōtai.
He memorialized the rōjū as follows:

> The daimyo in their present state of impoverishment are
> in no condition to contribute to the defense of the
> country.  It is of primary importance, therefore, that
> they be given relief and be allowed to build up the
> resources of their domains.  Since the expenses of
> the sankin kōtai and the cost of supporting their house-
> holds at Edo are tremendous, the first steps should be
> to relax their sankin kōtai duty by requiring it only
> once every three or four years and by permitting their

families to return home. If this is done, it will then be possible to perfect our military preparations.[10]

This first memorial was evidently unanswered, for early the following year, Matsudaira again brought up the subject in a second memorial:

As a result of the sankin kōtai and the tendency for the daimyo to summon great numbers of personnel from their fiefs, they are finding it difficult to meet their day-to-day expenses. Not only does this situation mean the exhaustion of the resources of the country, but it contributes to the weakening of its defenses. This misuse of defense manpower is the utmost folly. I, therefore, respectfully urge as I did in my petition of last fall, that the wives and children of the daimyo be sent back to their domains, that all offerings to the shogun throughout the year be suspended, that presents to bakufu officials also be stopped, and that the daimyo be required to attend court only once every three or four years. If this were done, not only would the bakufu benefit, but the daimyo would be most grateful. I further urge that all other conditions creating hardship for the daimyo be removed. For the impoverishment of the daimyo means the weakening of the Empire and is, therefore, a matter of gravest concern. If officials are going to be inconvenienced by being deprived of their perquisites in gifts, the bakufu might grant them extra allowances to make up their losses.[11]

Matsudaira, in the same memorial, predicted dire consequences for the bakufu and the nation if, in the face of the current situation, peacetime duties were not set aside and if the daimyo were to be made to come to Edo as before, while at the same time they were required to mobilize for defense each time foreign ships appeared. In his view this would "destroy all chances of recovering our national strength and would bring the bakufu to the brink of disaster." If it came to a showdown, he feared, it was even possible that the daimyo, alienated by their intolerable burdens, would not remain loyal. In any case, even if the daimyo "outdid themselves in loyalty," they would be incapable of rendering the assistance they should, because their resources would have been wasted away by their frequent exertions. Matsudaira urged that the bakufu, therefore, consult with the daimyo without delay and arrange to do away with all peacetime duties in favor of exclusively military services. Otherwise, there was to his mind "absolutely no hope for the restoration of bakufu power."

Abe's reply, dated the fourth day of the third month, 1854, was a polite rejection. He was impressed personally, he said, with Matsudaira's arguments, but he did not think that the proposal to alter the established system was expedient at the moment.[12]

Matsudaira was unable to move the bakufu on this occasion, but within a decade he was to find himself pushed by events into a position of power. In 1862, he and Tokugawa (Hitotsubashi) Keiki (1837-1903), later the fifteenth and last shogun,[13] were appointed by imperial order to head a reform administration at Edo as seiji sosai, or director-general of the government, and hosa, or shogunal adviser, respectively.[14] As the administrative head of the bakufu, Matsudaira, with the assistance of his counsellor, Yokoi Shonan (1809-1869), was now able to carry out the reforms he had suggested in his memorials.

Matsudaira's ideas on sankin kōtai reform were probably strongly influenced by Yokoi Shōnan, a free-thinking, practical-minded scholar originally from the Kumamoto han in Kyushu. Yokoi had begun his scholarly career as a student and teacher of Chinese philosophy, but, dissatisfied with the empty formalism of the official Chu Hsi school of Confucianism, he became the champion of an unorthodox school of thought which stressed political and social reform and practical studies. His ideas won a large following among the more open-minded and progressive samurai in his native province, and attracted the attention of Matsudaira Shungaku, who in 1849 offered him a post as adviser to the Echizen han. He refused the offer at first, but Matsudaira persisted until in 1857 Yokoi finally joined the group of able scholars whom Matsudaira had collected at Fukui.

In the interim, Yokoi traveled about the country observing conditions and developing his views. Gradually becoming convinced that Japan had to modernize itself if it was to survive, he interested himself in gunnery, navigation, and Western military science. He also developed various ideas for governmental reform. He was critical of the oligarchic and obscurantist family government of the Tokugawa, and thought that it should be liberalized by allowing men of ability from all the han, tozama as well as fudai, to have an opportunity to seek high office in the bakufu and by permitting wider discussion of public affairs.[15]

It is not known when Yokoi first began to advocate reform of the sankin kōtai system, but as early as 1855 he proposed in a letter to the karō, or chief elder, of the Tachibana han (Yanagawa, Chikugo) that: (1) the daimyo yashiki in Edo should be completely demolished and replaced by barracks or temporary shelters for occupancy by the daimyo while at the capital, and (2) the daimyo should perform their sankin journeys in battle array and stay only 100 days out of the year in Edo.[16]

The scheme which he later drafted for Matsudaira . Shungaku was essentially the same. When Matsudaira was made the seiji sōsai in 1862, he summoned Yokoi from Echizen to Edo to be his consultant. One of Yokoi's first tasks was to help draw up a reform program for Matsudaira, including the reform of the sankin kōtai. Yokoi's proposals for sankin kōtai reform called for: (1) abandoning the existing practice of keeping the daimyo in attendance at Edo as courtiers and quasi-hostages, and having the lords report in the future only for the purpose of discussing administrative matters with the bakufu; (2) moving the daimyo families out of Edo and returning them to the provinces; and (3) exempting the daimyo from guard duties for the bakufu.[17] This reform was to be the most important part of the many changes effected during Matsudaira's ten months in office as sōsai.[18]

Yokoi's role in the revision of the sankin kōtai was twofold, since he was the lobbyist for the plan as well as its draftsman. As such, he had the formidable task of winning over the conservative-minded officials of the bakufu. He is said to have won the support of one of the most prominent of the old-guard officials, Okabe Nagatsune, then holding the post of Great Censor (ōmetsuke),[19] with the following argument:

> If the sankin were completely suspended, it would be difficult to revive the sankin again. Hence, the sankin is to be converted into jusshoku, or "consultation." If the daimyo remain at the capital for about 100 days, reporting each day to the shogun to discuss affairs of state, the aims of the government will be thoroughly understood. In connection with the above change, the

wives of the daimyo will be allowed to return to the
provinces and useless equipment and troops will be
eliminated.[20]

The final acceptance of the reform scheme by the
bakufu conservatives was probably not won, however, by arguments stressing the benefits that would accrue, but by the
then irrefutable argument that no other course was possible.
This is illustrated by an anecdote retold by Sansom.  When
Yokoi showed bakufu official Ōkubo Ichiō (1817-1888)[21] a draft
of his reform program, Ōkubo balked at the proposal to relax
the sankin system.  Such a change, he said, would break down
the system upon which the Tokugawa depended.  Yokoi is said
to have retorted:  "Well, if the daimyo withdrew from Edo
without notifying the bakufu, what could be done to prevent
them?"  Ōkubo was obliged to reply, "Nothing!"[22]

## 3.  The Reform of 1862

On the fifteenth day of the intercalary eighth month,
1862, the shogun summoned the daimyo then present in Edo to
his palace and announced the program of reforms, including the
revision of the sankin kōtai, that he was ordering.  The daimyo
were told that the objects of the reforms were to expedite a
full scale rearmament of the nation and to promote national
unity. They were informed that henceforth the period of residence at the capital was to be reduced, so that they would
"have more time to give their people benevolent rule, cultivate
the literary arts, strengthen their military resources, give
thought to the economic welfare of their domains, and plan for
future eventualities."  Their free expression of opinion on
public affairs was invited.  A few days later, on the 23rd

of the same month, the revised <u>sankin</u> regulations were issued.[23]

Under the new system, the attendance of the daimyo at Edo was to be required only once every three years. For a great majority of the daimyo and the <u>kōtai yoriai</u>, the period of attendance was to be 100 days either in the spring, summer, fall, or winter. Only the <u>sanke</u>, and the <u>tamari-no-ma</u> daimyo, were to stay a full year each time. Sō of Tsushima, Kuroda of Chikuzen, and Matsuura of Hizen were to stay only one month each visit.

While in residence at Edo the daimyo were to appear at the shogun's palace from time to time to submit their ideas and advice on the national administration as well as inquiries and memorials on local problems and defense measures. They were also urged to discuss these matters among themselves.

The reform order also provided for the emergency withdrawal by the daimyo of personnel assigned to guard duty in Edo, the departure from Edo of <u>jōfu</u> daimyo when they requested it, the curtailing of daimyo gifts to the shogun, and the cutting down of <u>yashiki</u> personnel and expenses. As for the daimyo's wives and children, who for two centuries and more had never been permitted to leave the capital, the order stated that they might be removed to the provinces at will and that sons might, if desired, be left at the capital as observers.

The effect of this revolutionary decree is described in rather extravagant terms in the <u>Genji Yume Monogatari</u>, as follows:

In consequence, all the daimyo and <u>hatamoto</u> who owned lands sent their wives and children to their country residences, and in the twinkling of an eye, the flourishing city of Edo became like a desert, so that the daimyo allied to the Tokugawa family and the vassals of the shogunate of all ranks, and the townspeople, too, grieved and lamented.[24]

It is unlikely that the exodus of daimyo from Edo
was as sudden as this writer suggests, but it was the beginning of the end for the bakufu. The daimyo released from
their bondage to Edo began to assemble in Kyoto and to establish residences there. The influence of the Kyoto court,
which had already become strong enough to dictate orders to
the bakufu, became even more important as the powerful
Satsuma, Chōshū, and Tosa han of western Japan set up headquarters in the imperial city and began to plot actively against
the Tokugawa. Matsudaira and his colleagues in the reform
administration had not, of course, intended to destroy the
bakufu by this measure. It was their intention rather to
save it by making voluntary concessions to the daimyo. This
policy might have succeeded had the bakufu acted earlier,
while its power was still unchallenged. In 1862, reform
was too late and only hastened the fall of the regime.

In 1864, the bakufu, realizing its mistake, tried
to re-establish the system. A split between the leading
opponents of the Tokugawa had enabled the bakufu to rally
sufficient support to have the Chōshū han driven out of Kyoto.
Emboldened by its reviving fortunes, the bakufu in the ninth
month of 1864 announced that the old sankin kōtai system was
restored and that it was the shogun's will that the daimyo
attend again at Edo in accordance with their former schedules.
It was also decreed that wives and children would again be
required to return to the capital. Early the following year,
the daimyo were given direct orders to report to Edo, but the
tozama refused point-blank to comply and even the fudai made
excuses for delaying their visits. In addition, the Kyoto
court, asserting now its full prerogative as the supreme
source of authority, countermanded the bakufu order, stating

that the internal and external situation was such that the
daimyo could not be asked to return to the old system.[25]

Thus the sankin kōtai, which for over two centuries
had kept over 260 feudal lords in subjection, became a dead
letter. The system had always been based upon the real power
of the bakufu. When this power was no longer effective, it
was useless to try to preserve it. The system had been designed originally purely as an internal security measure, and,
as such, was eminently successful. It is doubtful whether the
Tokugawa could have maintained their supremacy for as long as
they did without it. When, however, the country was faced
with the necessity of consolidating its defenses and meeting
the problems created by the opening up the country to the
outside world, such a wasteful and one-sided arrangement as
the sankin kōtai system could not survive. It became irrelevant
to the central needs of the times. The breakdown of the system
was thus inevitable, once the self-imposed seclusion policy
was breached.

Since the control of the daimyo was the foundation
upon which the whole Tokugawa power system was based, the
collapse of the key mechanism of control meant the end of
the bakufu. Thus, though the Tokugawa shogunate did not
formally expire until 1867, the real end of Tokugawa rule
may be said to have come five years earlier, in 1862, when
the bakufu dealt itself a mortal wound by relaxing the sankin
kōtai and abandoning the system of daimyo hostages.

APPENDIX


Table of Daimyo Han as of 1853

(Source:  <u>Taisei bukan</u>)

| Daimyo | Seat of domain (province) | Assessed revenue (koku) |
|---|---|---|
| 1. Abe 阿部 | Shirakawa 白川 (Mutsu) | 100,000 |
| 2. Abe | Fukuyama 福山 (Bingo) | 110,000 |
| 3. Abe | Sanuki 佐貫 (Kazusa) | 16,000 |
| 4. Abe 安部 | Okabe 岡部 (Musashi) | 20,250 |
| 5. Akimoto 秋元 | Tatebayashi 館林 (Kōzuke) | 60,000 |
| 6. Akita 秋田 | Miharu 三春 (Mutsu) | 50,000 |
| 7. Akizuki 秋月 | Takanabe 高鍋 (Hyūga) | 27,000 |
| 8. Andō 安藤 | Iwakidaira 岩城平 (Mutsu) | 50,000 |
| 9. Aoki 青木 | Asada 麻田 (Settsu) | 10,000 |
| 10. Aoyama 青山 | Sasayama 篠山 (Tamba) | 60,000 |
| 11. Aoyama | Hachiman 八幡 (Mino) | 48,000 |
| 12. Arima 有馬 | Kurume 久留米 (Chikugo) | 210,000 |
| 13. Arima | Maruoka 丸岡 (Echizen) | 50,000 |
| 14. Arima | Fukiage 吹上 (Shimotsuke) | 10,000 |
| 15. Asano 淺野 | Hiroshima 廣島 (Aki) | 426,000 |
| 16. Asano | Hiroshima Shinden 新田 (Aki) | 30,000 |

| Status Categories | | | Distance from Edo (ri) | Sankin kōtai schedule (as of 1853) | |
| Chamber | Type of holding | Relation-ship | | Arrival | Departure |
|---|---|---|---|---|---|
| 1. gan | jōshu | fudai | 48 | 6th mo. odd yrs. | 6th mo. even yrs. |
| 2. teikan | jōshu | fudai | 194 1/2 | Retained in capital | |
| 3. gan | jōshu | fudai | 24 1/2 | 8th mo. every yr. | 2nd mo. every yr. |
| 4. kiku | mujō | fudai | 19 1/2 | 12th mo. every yr. | 8th mo. every yr. |
| 5. gan | jōshu | fudai | 18 | 8th mo. every yr. | 2nd mo. every yr. |
| 6. teikan | jōshu | fudai | 60 | 6th mo. odd yrs. | 6th mo. even yrs. |
| 7. yanagi | jōshu | tozama | 382 1/2 | 4th mo. even yrs. | 4th mo. odd yrs. |
| 8. gan | jōshu | fudai | 55 | Retained in capital | |
| 9. yanagi | mujō | tozama | 133 | 4th mo. odd yrs. | 4th mo. even yrs. |
| 10. gan | jōshu | fudai | 127 | 6th mo. even yrs. | 6th mo. odd yrs. |
| 11. gan | jōshu | fudai | 96 | 6th mo. odd yrs. | 6th mo. even yrs. |
| 12. ōbiro | kokushu | tozama | 292 | 4th mo. even yrs. | 4th mo. odd yrs. |
| 13. teikan | jōshu | fudai | 134 | 6th mo. odd yrs. | 6th mo. even yrs. |
| 14. kiku | mujō | fudai | 24 | 8th mo. every yr. | 2nd mo. every yr. |
| 15. ōbiro | kokushu | tozama | 231 | 4th mo. even yrs. | 4th mo. odd yrs. |
| 16. yanagi | mujō | tozama | 231 | Retained in capital | |

| | Daimyo | Seat of domain (province) | Assessed revenue (koku) |
|---|---|---|---|
| 17. | Date 伊達 | Sendai 仙臺 (Mutsu) | 625,600 |
| 18. | Date | Uwajima 宇和島 (Iyo) | 100,000 |
| 19. | Date | Yoshida 吉田 (Iyo) | 30,000 |
| 20. | Doi 土井 | Koga 古河 (Shimosa) | 80,000 |
| 21. | Doi | Kariya 刈屋 (Mikawa) | 23,000 |
| 22. | Doi | Ōno 大野 (Echizen) | 40,000 |
| 23. | Endo 遠藤 | Mikami 三上 (Ōmi) | 12,000 |
| 24. | Gotō 五島 | Gotō Fukue 福江 (Hizen) | 12,600 |
| 25. | Hachisuka 蜂須賀 | Tokushima 德島 (Awa) | 257,900 |
| 26. | Hayashi 林 | Kaibuchi 貝淵 (Kazusa) | 10,000 |
| 27. | Hijikata 土方 | Komono 薦野 (Ise) | 11,000 |
| 28. | Hitotsu-yanagi 一柳 | Ono 小野 (Harima) | 10,000 |
| 29. | Hitotsu-yanagi | Komatsu 小松 (Iyo) | 10,000 |
| 30. | Hōjō 北條 | Sayama 狹山 (Kawachi) | 10,000 |
| 31. | Honda 本多 | Okazaki 岡崎 (Mikawa) | 50,000 |
| 32. | Honda | Yamazaki 山崎 (Harima) | 10,000 |
| 33. | Honda | Izumi 泉 (Mutsu) | 20,000 |

| | Status Categories | | | Distance from Edo (ri) | Sankin kōtai schedule (as of 1853) | |
|---|---|---|---|---|---|---|
| Chamber | | Type of holding | Relation- ship | | Arrival | Departure |
| 17. | ōbiro | kokushu | tozama | 91 | 4th mo. odd yrs. | 4th mo. even yrs. |
| 18. | ōbiro | jun- kokushu | tozama | 278 | 4th mo. even yrs. | 4th mo. odd yrs. |
| 19. | yanagi | mujō | tozama | 275 | 4th mo. odd yrs. | 4th mo. even yrs. |
| 20. | gan | jōshu | fudai | 16 | 12th mo. every yr. | 8th mo. every yr. |
| 21. | gan | jōshu | fudai | 82 | 6th mo. odd yrs. | 6th mo. even yrs. |
| 22. | gan | jōshu | fudai | 141 | 6th mo. even yrs. | 6th mo. odd yrs. |
| 23. | kiku | mujō | fudai | 119 | Retained in capital | |
| 24. | yanagi | jōshu | tozama | 395 | 11th mo. odd yrs. | 2nd mo. even yrs. |
| 25. | ōroka | kokushu | tozama | 166 | 4th mo. odd yrs. | 4th mo. even yrs. |
| 26. | kiku | mujō | fudai | 21 | Retained in capital | |
| 27. | yanagi | mujō | tozama | 98 | 4th mo. even yrs. | 4th mo. odd yrs. |
| 28. | yanagi | mujō | tozama | 147 | 4th mo. odd yrs. | 4th mo. even yrs. |
| 29. | yanagi | mujō | tozama | 209 | 4th mo. even yrs. | 4th mo. odd yrs. |
| 30. | yanagi | mujō | tozama | 135 | 4th mo. odd yrs. | 4th mo. even yrs. |
| 31. | teikan | jōshu | fudai | 77 | Retained in capital | |
| 32. | teikan | mujō | fudai | 164 | 6th mo. even yrs. | 6th mo. odd yrs. |
| 33. | teikan | jōshu- kaku | fudai | 53 | Retained in capital | |

| | Daimyo | Seat of domain (province) | Assessed revenue (koku) |
|---|---|---|---|
| 34. | Honda | Tanaka 田中 (Suruga) | 40,000 |
| 35. | Honda | Zeze 膳所 (Ōmi) | 60,000 |
| 36. | Honda | Kambe 神戸 (Ise) | 15,000 |
| 37. | Honda | Iiyama 飯山 (Shinano) | 20,000 |
| 38. | Honjō 本庄 | Miyazu 宮津 (Tango) | 35,000 |
| 39. | Honjō | Takatomi 高富 (Mino) | 10,000 |
| 40. | Hori 堀 | Muramatsu 村松 (Echigo) | 30,000 |
| 41. | Hori | Shiiya 椎谷 (Echigo) | 10,000 |
| 42. | Hori | Susaka 須坂 (Shinano) | 10,053 |
| 43. | Hori | Iida 飯田 (Shinano) | 17,000 |
| 44. | Hoshina 保科 | Iino 飯野 (Kazusa) | 20,000 |
| 45. | Hosokawa 細川 | Kumamoto 熊本 (Higo) | 540,000 |
| 46. | Hosokawa | Kumamoto-Shinden 新田 (Higo) | 35,000 |
| 47. | Hosokawa | Udo 宇土 (Higo) | 30,000 |
| 48. | Hosokawa | Yatabe 谷田部 (Hitachi) | 16,300 |
| 49. | Hotta 堀田 | Sakura 佐倉 (Shimosa) | 110,000 |

| | Status Categories | | | Distance from Edo (ri) | Sankin kōtai schedule (as of 1853) | |
|---|---|---|---|---|---|---|
| Chamber | Type of holding | Relation-ship | | | Arrival | Departure |
| 34. gan | jōshu | fudai | | 48 | 6th mo. odd yrs. | 6th mo. even yrs. |
| 35. teikan | jōshu | fudai | | 120 1/2 | 6th mo. even yrs. | 6th mo. odd yrs. |
| 36. teikan | jōshu | fudai | | 101 1/2 | 6th mo. even yrs. | 6th mo. odd yrs. |
| 37. teikan | jōshu | fudai | | 64 | 6th mo. even yrs. | 6th mo. odd yrs. |
| 38. gan | jōshu | fudai | | 145 | 6th mo. odd yrs. | 6th mo. even yrs. |
| 39. kiku | mujō | fudai | | 97 | Retained in capital | |
| 40. yanagi | jōshu | tozama | | 107 | 6th mo. odd yrs. | 6th mo. even yrs. |
| 41. kiku | mujō | fudai | | 96 | Retained in capital | |
| 42. yanagi | mujō | tozama | | 58 | 6th mo. odd yrs. | 6th mo. even yrs. |
| 43. yanagi | jōshu | tozama | | 75 | 6th mo. even yrs. | 6th mo. odd yrs. |
| 44. teikan | mujō | fudai | | 22 | 12th mo. every yr. | 8th mo. every yr. |
| 45. ōbiro | kokushu | tozama | | 288 | 4th mo. odd yrs. | 4th mo. even yrs. |
| 46. yanagi | mujō | tozama | | 288 | Retained in capital | |
| 47. yanagi | mujō | tozama | | 292 | 4th mo. odd yrs. | 4th mo. even yrs. |
| 48. yanagi | mujō | tozama | | 26 | 6th mo. even yrs. | 6th mo. odd yrs. |
| 49. tamari | jōshu | fudai | | 13 1/2 | 5th mo. odd yrs. | 5th mo. even yrs. |

| | Daimyo | Seat of domain (province) | Assessed revenue (koku) |
|---|---|---|---|
| 50. | Hotta | Sano 佐野 (Shimotsuke) | 16,000 |
| 51. | Hotta | Miyagawa 宮川 (Ōmi) | 13,000 |
| 52. | Ichibashi 橋 | Ninshōji 西大路 (Ōmi) | 18,000 |
| 53. | Ii 井伊 | Hikone 彦根 (Ōmi) | 350,000 |
| 54. | Ii | Yoita 與板 (Echigo) | 20,000 |
| 55. | Ikeda 池田 | Tottori 鳥取 (Inaba) | 325,000 |
| 56. | Ikeda | Tottori-Shinden (Inaba) 新田 | 30,000 |
| 57. | Ikeda | Tottori-Shinden (Inaba) | 15,000 |
| 58. | Ikeda | Okayama 岡山 (Bizen) | 305,000 |
| 59. | Ikeda | Okayama-Shinden (Bizen) | 25,000 |
| 60. | Ikeda | Okayama-Shinden (Bizen) | 15,000 |
| 61. | Inaba 稲葉 | Yodo 淀 (Yamashiro) | 102,000 |
| 62. | Inaba | Tateyama 館山 (Awa) | 10,000 |
| 63. | Inaba | Usuki 白木 (Bungo) | 50,000 |
| 64. | Inagaki 稲垣 | Toba 鳥羽 (Shima) | 30,000 |
| 65. | Inagaki | Yamakami 山上 (Ōmi) | 23,043 |
| 66. | Inoue 井上 | Hamamatsu 濱松 (Tōtomi) | 60,000 |

| | Status Categories | | | Distance from Edo (ri) | Sankin kōtai schedule (as of 1853) | |
|---|---|---|---|---|---|---|
| | Chamber | Type of holding | Relation-ship | | Arrival | Departure |
| 50. | teikan | jōshu-kaku | fudai | 22 | 8th mo. every yr. | 2nd mo. every yr. |
| 51. | teikan | mujō | fudai | 119 | Retained in capital | |
| 52. | yanagi | mujō | tozama | 108 | 4th mo. even yrs. | 4th mo. odd yrs. |
| 53. | tamari | jōshu | fudai | 108 | 5th mo. even yrs. | 5th mo. odd yrs. |
| 54. | teikan | jōshu | fudai | 103 | 6th mo. even yrs. | 6th mo. odd yrs. |
| 55. | ōroka | kokushu | kamon | 180 | 4th mo. odd yrs. | 4th mo. even yrs. |
| 56. | yanagi | mujō | tozama | 180 | 4th mo. odd yrs. | 4th mo. even yrs. |
| 57. | yanagi | mujō | tozama | 180 | 4th mo. even yrs. | 4th mo. odd yrs. |
| 58. | ōbiro | kokushu | tozama | 173 | 4th mo. even yrs. | 4th mo. odd yrs. |
| 59. | yanagi | mujō | tozama | 173 | 4th mo. odd yrs. | 4th mo. even yrs. |
| 60. | yanagi | mujō | tozama | 173 | 4th mo. even yrs. | 4th mo. odd yrs. |
| 61. | gan | jōshu | fudai | 125 | 6th mo. even yrs. | 6th mo. odd yrs. |
| 62. | kiku | mujō | fudai | 36 | 8th mo. every yr. | 2nd mo. every yr. |
| 63. | yanagi | jōshu | tozama | 278 | 4th mo. even yrs. | 4th mo. odd yrs. |
| 64. | teikan | jōshu | fudai | 134 1/2 | 6th mo. even yrs. | 6th mo. odd yrs. |
| 65. | kiku | mujō | fudai | 120 | Retained in capital | |
| 66. | gan | joshū | fudai | 65 | 6th mo. even yrs. | 6th mo. odd yrs. |

| Daimyo | Seat of domain (province) | Assessed revenue (koku) |
|---|---|---|
| 67. Inoue | Shimotsuma 下妻 | 10,000 |
| 68. Inoue | Takaoka 高岡 (Shimosa) | 10,000 |
| 69. Ishikawa 石川 | Kameyama 亀山 (Ise) | 60,000 |
| 70. Ishikawa | Shimodate 下館 (Hitachi) | 20,000 |
| 71. Itakura 板倉 | Matsuyama 松山 (Bitchū) | 50,000 |
| 72. Itakura | Annaka 安中 (Kazusa) | 30,000 |
| 73. Itakura | Niwase 庭瀬 (Bitchū) | 20,000 |
| 74. Itakura | Fukushima 福島 (Mutsu) | 30,000 |
| 75. Itō 伊東 | Obi 飫肥 (Hyūga) | 51,080 |
| 76. Itō | Okada 岡田 (Bitchū) | 10,342 |
| 77. Iwaki 岩城 | Kameda 亀田 (Dewa) | 20,000 |
| 78. Kamei 亀井 | Tsuwano 津和野 (Iwami) | 43,000 |
| 79. Kanō 加納 | Ichinomiya 一宮 (Kazusa) | 13,000 |
| 80. Katagiri 片桐 | Koizumi 小泉 (Yamato) | 11,100 |
| 81. Katō 加藤 | Ōsu 大洲 (Iyo) | 60,000 |
| 82. Katō | Niiya 新谷 (Iyo) | 10,000 |

| | _Status Categories | | | Distance from Edo (ri) | Sankin kōtai schedule (as of 1853) | |
|---|---|---|---|---|---|---|
| | Chamber | Type of holding | Relation-ship | | Arrival | Departure |
| 67. | koku | mujō | fudai | 20 | 8th mo. every yr. | 2nd mo. every yr. |
| 68. | kiku | mujō | fudai | 19 | 8th mo. every yr. | 2nd mo. every yr. |
| 69. | teikan | jōshu | fudai | 103 1/2 | 6th mo. even yrs. | 6th mo. odd yrs. |
| 70. | gan | jōshu | fudai | 22 1/2 | 8th mo. every yr. | 2nd mo. every yr. |
| 71. | gan | jōshu | fudai | 186 | 6th mo. odd yrs. | 6th mo. even yrs. |
| 72. | gan | jōshu | fudai | 29 | 8th mo. every yr. | 2nd mo. every yr. |
| 73. | kiku | mujō | fudai | 173 | 4th mo. even yrs. | 4th mo. odd yrs. |
| 74. | gan | jōshu | fudai | 71 | 6th mo. odd yrs. | 6th mo. even yrs. |
| 75. | yanagi | jōshu | tozama | 343 | 6th mo. odd yrs. | 6th mo. even yrs. |
| 76. | yanagi | mujō | tozama | 180 | 4th mo. odd yrs. | 4th mo. even yrs. |
| 77. | yanagi | jōshu-kaku | tozama | 142 | 4th mo. even yrs. | 4th mo. odd yrs. |
| 78. | yanagi | jōshu | tozama | 247 | 4th mo. even yrs. | 4th mo. odd yrs. |
| 79. | kiku | mujō | fudai | 15 | 8th mo. every yr. | 2nd mo. every yr. |
| 80. | yanagi | mujō | tozama | 133 | 4th mo. odd yrs. | 4th mo. even yrs. |
| 81. | yanagi | jōshu | tozama | 231 | 4th mo. odd yrs. | 4th mo. even yrs. |
| 82. | yanagi | mujō | tozama | 230 | 4th mo. even yrs. | 4th mo. odd yrs. |

| Daimyo | Seat of domain (province) | | Assessed revenue (koku) |
|---|---|---|---|
| 83. Katō | Minakuchi (Ōmi) | 水口 | 25,000 |
| 84. Kinoshita 木下 | Ashimori (Bitchū) | 足守 | 25,000 |
| 85. Kinoshita | Hiji (Bungo) | 日出 | 25,000 |
| 86. Kitsuregawa 喜連川 | Kitsuregawa (Shimotsuke) | 喜連川 | 5,000 |
| 87. Koide 小出 | Sonobe (Tamba) | 園部 | 26,711 |
| 88. Kuchiki 朽木 | Fukuchiyama (Tamba) | 福知山 | 32,000 |
| 89. Kuki 九鬼 | Sanda (Settsu) | 三田 | 36,000 |
| 90. Kuki | Ayabe (Tamba) | 綾部 | 19,500 |
| 91. Kuroda 黒田 | Fukuoka (Chikuzen) | 福岡 | 520,000 |
| 92. Kuroda | Akitsuki (Chikuzen) | 秋月 | 50,000 |
| 93. Kuroda | Kururi (Kazusa) | 久留里 | 30,000 |
| 94. Kurushima 久留島 | Mori (Bungo) | 森 | 12,500 |
| 95. Kuze 久世 | Sekiyado (Shimoda) | 關宿 | 56,000 |
| 96. Kyōgoku 京極 | Marugame (Sanuki) | 丸亀 | 51,512 |
| 97. Kyōgoku | Tadotsu (Sanuki) | 多度津 | 10,000 |
| 98. Kyōgoku | Toyooka (Tajima) | 豊岡 | 15,000 |

| | Status Categories | | Distance from Edo (ri) | Sankin kōtai schedule (as of 1853) | |
|---|---|---|---|---|---|
| Chamber | Type of holding | Relation-ship | | Arrival | Departure |
| 83. teikan | jōshu | fudai | 109 | 6th mo. even yrs. | 6th mo. odd yrs. |
| 84. yanagi | mujō | tozama | 178 | 4th mo. odd yrs. | 4th mo. even yrs. |
| 85. yanagi | jōshu | tozama | 262 | 4th mo. even yrs. | 4th mo. odd yrs. |
| 86. no chamber | mujō | tozama | 36 | 12th mo. to celebrate New Year | every year |
| 87. yanagi | mujō | tozama | 131 | 4th mo. odd yrs. | 4th mo. even yrs. |
| 88. gan | jōshu | fudai | 142 | 6th mo. even yrs. | 6th mo. odd yrs. |
| 89. yanagi | jōshu | tozama | 137 | 4th mo. odd yrs. | 4th mo. even yrs. |
| 90. yanagi | mujō | tozama | 140 | 4th mo. odd yrs. | 4th mo. even yrs. |
| 91. ōbiro | kokushu | tozama | 298 | 11th mo. even yrs. | 2nd mo. odd yrs. |
| 92. yanagi | jōshu | tozama | 288 | 4th mo. even yrs. | 4th mo. odd yrs. |
| 93. gan | jōshu | fudai | 22 | 12th mo. every yr. | 8th mo. every yr. |
| 94. yanagi | mujō | tozama | 273 | 4th mo. odd yrs. | 4th mo. even yrs. |
| 95. gan | jōshu | fudai | 13 | 12th mo. every yr. | 8th mo. every yr. |
| 96. yanagi | jōshu | tozama | 184 1/2 | 4th mo. odd yrs. | 4th mo. even yrs. |
| 97. yanagi | mujō | tozama | 185 1/2 | 4th mo. even yrs. | 4th mo. odd yrs. |
| 98. yanagi | mujō | tozama | 153 | 4th mo. odd yrs. | 4th mo. even yrs. |

| | Daimyo | Seat of domain (province) | Assessed revenue (<u>koku</u>) |
|---|---|---|---|
| 99. | Kyōgoku | Mineyama 峯山 (Tango) | 11,144 |
| 100. | Maeda 前田 | Kanazawa 金澤 (Kaga) | 1,022,700 |
| 101. | Maeda | Toyama 富山 (Etchū) | 100,000 |
| 102. | Maeda | Daishōji 大聖寺 (Kaga) | 100,000 |
| 103. | Maeda | Nanukaichi 七日市 (Kōzuke) | 10,000 |
| 104. | Makino 牧野 | Nagaoka 長岡 (Echigo) | 74,000 |
| 105. | Makino | Komuro 小室 (Shinano) | 25,000 |
| 106. | Makino | Kasama 笠間 (Hitachi) | 80,000 |
| 107. | Makino | Tanabe 田邊 (Tango) | 35,000 |
| 108. | Manabe 間部 | Sabae 鯖江 (Echizen) | 50,000 |
| 109. | Masuyama 増山 | Nagashima 長島 (Ise) | 20,000 |
| 110. | Matsudaira 松平 (Echizen 越前 ) | Tsuyama 津山 (Mimasaka) | 100,000 |
| 111. | Matsudaira (Echizen) | Fukui 福井 (Echizen) | 320,000 |
| 112. | Matsudaira (Echizen) | Itoigawa 糸魚川 (Echizen) | 10,000 |
| 113. | Matsudaira (Echizen) | Matsue 松江 (Izumo) | 186,000 |
| 114. | Matsudaira (Echizen) | Hirose 廣瀬 (Izumo) | 30,000 |

| Status Categories | | | Distance from Edo (ri) | Sankin kōtai schedule (as of 1853) | |
|---|---|---|---|---|---|
| Chamber | Type of holding | Relation-ship | | Arrival | Departure |
| 99. kiku | mujō | fudai | 150 | 6th mo. odd yrs. | 6th mo. even yrs. |
| 100. ōroka | kokushu | tozama | 151 | 3rd mo. odd yrs. | 3rd mo. even yrs. |
| 101. ōbiro | jōshu | tozama | 166 | 4th mo. even yrs. | 4th mo. odd yrs. |
| 102. ōbiro | jōshu | tozama | 139 | 4th mo. odd yrs. | 4th mo. even yrs. |
| 103. yanagi | mujō | tozama | 29 | 6th mo. odd yrs. | 6th mo. even yrs. |
| 104. teikan | jōshu | fudai | 76 | Retained in capital | |
| 105. gan | jōshu | fudai | 41 | 6th mo. even yrs. | 6th mo. odd yrs. |
| 106. gan | jōshu | fudai | 28 | 6th mo. odd yrs. | 6th mo. even yrs. |
| 107. gan | jōshu | fudai | 145 | 6th mo. odd yrs. | 6th mo. even yrs. |
| 108. gan | jōshu | fudai | 134 | 6th mo. even yrs. | 6th mo. odd yrs. |
| 109. gan | jōshu | fudai | 95 1/2 | 6th mo. odd yrs. | 6th mo. even yrs. |
| 110. ōroka | jōshu | kamon | 171 | 4th mo. odd yrs. | 4th mo. even yrs. |
| 111. ōroka | kokushu | kamon | 130 | 4th mo. odd yrs. | 4th mo. even yrs. |
| 112. teikan | mujō | kamon | 96 | Retained in capital | |
| 113. ōbiro | kokushu | kamon | 223 | 4th mo. even yrs. | 4th mo. odd yrs. |
| 114. teikan | jōshu | kamon | 222 | 4th mo. even yrs. | 4th mo. odd yrs. |

| Daimyo | Seat of domain (province) | Assessed revenue (koku) |
|---|---|---|
| 115. Matsudaira (Echizen) | Mori 母里 (Izumo) | 10,000 |
| 116. Matsudaira (Echizen) | Kawagoe 川越 (Musashi) | 170,000 |
| 117. Matsudaira (Echizen) | Akashi 明石 (Harima) | 80,000 |
| 118. Matsudaira (Fujii 藤井) | Ueda 上田 (Shinano) | 53,000 |
| 119. Matsudaira (Fujii) | Kaminoyama 上山 (Dewa) | 30,000 |
| 120. Matsudaira (Fukamizo 深溝) | Shimabara 島原 (Hizen) | 70,000 |
| 121. Matsudaira (Hisamatsu 久松) | Matsuyama 松山 (Iyo) | 150,000 |
| 122. Matsudaira (Hisamatsu) | Kuwana 桑名 (Ise) | 110,000 |
| 123. Matsudaira (Hisamatsu) | Imabaru 今治 (Iyo) | 35,000 |
| 124. Matsudaira (Hisamatsu) | Tako 多古 (Shimosa) | 12,000 |
| 125. Matsudaira (Hoshina 保科) | Aizu 會津 (Mutsu) | 230,000 |
| 126. Matsudaira (Katahara 形原) | Kameyama 龜山 (Tamba) | 50,000 |
| 127. Matsudaira (Kii 紀伊) | Saijō 西條 (Iyo) | 30,000 |
| 128. Matsudaira (Kii) | Yata 矢田 (Kōzuke) | 10,000 |
| 129. Matsudaira (Matsui) | Tanakura 棚倉 (Mutsu) | 60,400 |
| 130. Matsudaira (Mito 水戸) | Takamatsu 高松 (Sanuki) | 120,000 |
| 131. Matsudaira (Mito) | Moriyama 守山 (Mutsu) | 20,000 |

| Chamber | Status Categories Type of holding | Relation- ship | Distance from Edo (ri) | Sankin kōtai schedule (as of 1853) Arrival | Departure |
|---------|-----------|----------|---------|---------|-----------|
| 115. teikan | mujō | kamon | 233 | Retained in capital | |
| 116. ōbiro | jōshu | kamon | 12 | 4th mo. odd yrs. | 4th mo. even yrs. |
| 117. ōrōka | jōshu | kamon | 141 | 4th mo. odd yrs. | 4th mo. even yrs. |
| 118. teikan | jōshu | fudai | 46 1/2 | Retained in capital | |
| 119. teikan | jōshu | fudai | 93 | 6th mo. even yrs. | 6th mo. odd yrs. |
| 120. teikan | jōshu | fudai | 301 1/2 | 6th mo. even yrs. | 6th mo. odd yrs. |
| 121. tamari | jōshu | kamon | 218 | 5th mo. even yrs. | 5th mo. odd yrs. |
| 122. tamari | jōshu | kamon | 94 | 5th mo. odd yrs. | 5th mo. even yrs. |
| 123. teikan | jōshu | fudai | 207 | 6th mo. odd yrs. | 6th mo. even yrs. |
| 124. kiku | mujō | fudai | 19 | 8th mo. every yr. | 2nd mo. every yr. |
| 125. tamari | jōshu | kamon | 65 | 4th mo. odd yrs. | 4th mo. even yrs. |
| 126. teikan | jōshu | fudai | 126 | 7th mo. even yrs. | 5th mo. odd yrs. |
| 127. ōbiro | jōshu | kamon | 205 | Retained in capital | |
| 128. ōrōka | mujō | kamon | 27 | Retained in capital | |
| 129. teikan | jōshu | fudai | 50 | 6th mo. odd yrs. | 6th mo. even yrs. |
| 130. tamari | jōshu | kamon | 179 1/2 | 5th mo. odd yrs. | 5th mo. even yrs. |
| 131. ōbiro | mujō | kamon | 56 | Retained in capital | |

| Daimyo | Seat of domain (province) | Assessed revenue (koku) |
|---|---|---|
| 132. Matsudaira (Mito) | Fuchū 府中 (Hitachi) | 20,000 |
| 133. Matsudaira (Mito) | Shishido 宍中 (Hitachi) | 10,000 |
| 134. Matsudaira (Nomi 能見 ) | Kizuki 杵築 (Bungo) | 32,000 |
| 135. Matsudaira (Ochi 越智 ) | Hamada 濱田 (Iwami) | 61,000 |
| 136. Matsudaira (Ōgyū 大給 ) | Nishio 西尾 (Mikawa) | 60,000 |
| 137. Matsudaira (Ōgyū) | Funai 府内 (Bungo) | 21,200 |
| 138. Matsudaira (Ōgyū) | Okudono 奥殿 (Mikawa) | 16,000 |
| 139. Matsudaira (Ōgyū) | Iwamura 岩村 (Mino) | 30,000 |
| 140. Matsudaira (Ōkōchi 大河内 ) | Yoshida 吉田 (Mikawa) | 70,000 |
| 141. Matsudaira (Ōkōchi) | Ōtaki 大多喜 (Kazusa) | 20,000 |
| 142. Matsudaira (Ōkōchi) | Takasaki 高崎 (Kōzuke) | 82,000 |
| 143. Matsudaira (Okudaira 奥平 ) | Oshi 忍 (Musashi) | 100,000 |
| 144. Matsudaira (Okudaira) | Obata 小幡 (Kōzuke) | 20,000 |
| 145. Matsudaira (Owari 尾張 ) | Takasu 高須 (Mino) | 30,000 |
| 146. Matsudaira (Sakurai 櫻井 ) | Amagasaki 尼崎 (Settsu) | 40,000 |
| 147. Matsudaira (Takiwaki 瀧脇 ) | Kojima 小島 (Suruga) | 10,000 |

| | Status Categories | | Distance | Sankin kōtai schedule | |
|---|---|---|---|---|---|
| Chamber | Type of holding | Relation-ship | from Edo (ri) | (as of 1853) Arrival | Departure |
| 132. ōbiro | mujō | kamon | 20 | Retained in capital | |
| 133. teikan | mujō | kamon | 25 | Retained in capital | |
| 134. teikan | jōshu | fudai | 263 1/2 | 6th mo. even yrs. | 6th mo. odd yrs. |
| 135. ōbiro | jōshu | fudai | 247 | 4th mo. odd yrs. | 4th mo. even yrs. |
| 136. teikan | jōshu | fudai | 80 | Retained in capital | |
| 137. teikan | jōshu | fudai | 262 1/2 | 6th mo. odd yrs. | 6th mo. even yrs. |
| 138. kiku | mujō | fudai | 86 | 6th mo. even yrs. | 6th mo. odd yrs. |
| 139. gan | jōshu | fudai | 93 | 6th mo. even yrs. | 6th mo. odd yrs. |
| 140. gan | jōshu | fudai | 72 | 6th mo. even yrs. | 6th mo. odd yrs. |
| 141. gan | jōshu | fudai | 22 | 12th mo. every yr. | 8th mo. every yr. |
| 142. gan | jōshu | fudai | 26 | 12th mo. every yr. | 8th mo. every yr. |
| 143. tamari | mujō | kamon | 15 | 4th mo. even yrs. | 4th mo. odd yrs. |
| 144. teikan | jōshu-kaku | fudai | 29 | Retained in capital | |
| 145. ōbiro | mujō | kamon | 95 | 4th mo. even yrs. | 4th mo. odd yrs. |
| 146. teikan | jōshu | fudai | 135 | 6th mo. even yrs. | 6th mo. odd yrs. |
| 147. kiku | mujō | fudai | 43 1/2 | 6th mo. odd yrs. | 6th mo. even yrs. |

| Daimyo | Seat of domain (province) | Assessed revenue (koku) |
| --- | --- | --- |
| 148. Matsudaira (Toda 戸田 ) | Matsumoto 松本 (Shinano) | 60,000 |
| 149. Matsumae 松前 | Matsumae 松前 (Ezo) | 10,000 |
| 150. Matsuura 松浦 | Hirado 平戸 (Hizen) | 61,700 |
| 151. Matsuura | Hirado Shinden 新田 (Hizen) | 10,000 |
| 152. Miura 三浦 | Katsuyama 勝山 (Mimasaka) | 23,000 |
| 153. Miyake 三宅 | Tawara 田原 (Mikawa) | 12,000 |
| 154. Mizoguchi 溝口 | Shibata 新發田 (Echigo) | 50,000 |
| 155. Mizuno 水野 | Yamagata 山形 (Dewa) | 50,000 |
| 156. Mizuno | Numazu 沼津 (Suruga) | 50,000 |
| 157. Mizuno | Tsurumaki 鶴牧 (Kazusa) | 15,000 |
| 158. Mizuno | Yūki 結城 (Shimosa) | 18,000 |
| 159. Mori 森 | Akō 赤穂 (Harima) | 20,000 |
| 160. Mori | Mikazuki 三日月 (Harima) | 15,000 |
| 161. Mōri 毛利 | Hagi 萩 (Nagato) [Chōshū] | 369,000 |
| 162. Mōri | Tokuyama 徳山 (Suō) | 40,010 |
| 163. Mōri | Fuchū 府中 (Nagato) [Chōshū] | 50,000 |
| 164. Mōri | Kiyosue 清末 (Nagato) [Chōshū] | 10,000 |

| Status Categories | | | Distance from Edo (ri) | Sankin kōtai schedule (as of 1853) | |
| Chamber | Type of holding | Relation- ship | | Arrival | Departure |
|---|---|---|---|---|---|
| 148. teikan | jōshu | fudai | 61 | 6th mo. odd yrs. | 6th mo. even yrs. |
| 149. yanagi | jōshu | tozama | 290 | 10th mo. even yrs. | 2nd mo. odd yrs. |
| 150. yanagi | jōshu | tozama | 319 | 11th mo. odd yrs. | 2nd mo. even yrs. |
| 151. yanagi | mujō | tozama | 319 | 4th mo. even yrs. | 4th mo. odd yrs. |
| 152. gan | jōshu | fudai | 184 | 6th mo. odd yrs. | 6th mo. even yrs. |
| 153. teikan | jōshu | fudai | 75 | 6th mo. odd yrs. | 6th mo. even yrs. |
| 154. yanagi | jōshu | fudai | 89 | 6th mo. even yrs. | 6th mo. odd yrs. |
| 155. gan | jōshu | fudai | 94 | 6th mo. odd yrs. | 6th mo. even yrs. |
| 156. teikan | jōshu | fudai | 29 1/2 | 6th mo. odd yrs. | 6th mo. even yrs. |
| 157. gan | jōshu- kaku | fudai | 16 | 12th mo. every yr. | 8th mo. every yr. |
| 158. teikan | jōshu | fudai | 21 | 6th mo. even yrs. | 6th mo. odd yrs. |
| 159. yanagi | jōshu | tozama | 155 | 4th mo. odd yrs. | 4th mo. even yrs. |
| 160. yanagi | mujō | tozama | 165 | 4th mo. even yrs. | 4th mo. odd yrs. |
| 161. ōbiro | kokushu | tozama | 271 | 4th mo. odd yrs. | 4th mo. even yrs. |
| 162. yanagi | jōshu | tozama | 253 | 4th mo. odd yrs. | 4th mo. even yrs. |
| 163. yanagi | jōshu- kaku | tozama | 280 | 4th mo. even yrs. | 4th mo. odd yrs. |
| 164. yanagi | mujō | tozama | 280 | 4th mo. odd yrs. | 4th mo. even yrs. |

| Daimyo | Seat of domain (province) | Assessed revenue (koku) |
|---|---|---|
| 165. Mōri | Saeki 佐伯 (Bungo) | 20,000 |
| 166. Morikawa 森川 | Oimi 生實 (Shimosa) | 10,000 |
| 167. Nabeshima 鍋島 | Saga 佐賀 (Hizen) | 357,000 |
| 168. Nabeshima | Ogi 小城 (Hizen) | 73,250 |
| 169. Nabeshima | Hasuike 蓮池 (Hizen) | 52,625 |
| 170. Nabeshima | Kashima 鹿島 (Hizen) | 20,000 |
| 171. Nagai 永井 | Takatsuki 高槻 (Settsu) | 36,000 |
| 172. Nagai | Kanō 加納 (Mino) | 32,000 |
| 173. Nagai | Shinjō 新庄 (Yamato) | 10,000 |
| 174. Naitō 内藤 | Nobeoka 延岡 (Hyūga) | 70,000 |
| 175. Naitō | Yunagaya 湯長谷 (Mutsu) | 15,000 |
| 176. Naitō | Murakami 村上 (Echigo) | 50,090 |
| 177. Naitō | Koromo 擧母 (Mikawa) | 20,000 |
| 178. Naitō | Takatō 高遠 (Shinano) | 33,000 |
| 179. Naitō | Iwamurata 岩村田 (Shinano) | 15,000 |
| 180. Nakagawa 中川 | Oka 岡 (Bungo) | 70,440 |
| 181. Nambu 南部 | Morioka 盛岡 (Mutsu) | 200,000 |

| | Status Categories | | Distance | Sankin kōtai schedule | |
|---|---|---|---|---|---|
| Chamber | Type of holding | Relation-ship | from Edo (ri) | (as of 1853) | |
| | | | | Arrival | Departure |
| 165. yanagi | jōshu | tozama | 266 | 4th mo. even yrs. | 4th mo. odd yrs. |
| 166. kiku | mujō | fudai | 12 | 11th mo. every yr. | 8th mo. every yr. |
| 167. ōbiro | kokushu | tozama | 290 | 11th mo. odd yrs. | 2nd mo. even yrs. |
| 168. yanagi | mujō | tozama | 313 | 4th mo. odd yrs. | 4th mo. even yrs. |
| 169. yanagi | mujō | tozama | 313 | 4th mo. even yrs. | 4th mo. odd yrs. |
| 170. yanagi | mujō | tozama | 347 | 4th mo. odd yrs. | 4th mo. even yrs. |
| 171. gan | jōshu | fudai | 132 | 6th mo. odd yrs. | 6th mo. even yrs. |
| 172. gan | jōshu | fudai | 97 | 6th mo. odd yrs. | 6th mo. even yrs. |
| 173. kiku | mujō | fudai | 136 | Retained in capital | |
| 174. teikan | jōshu | fudai | 293 | 6th mo. odd yrs. | 6th mo. even yrs. |
| 175. teikan | mujō | fudai | 53 | 6th mo. even yrs. | 6th mo. odd yrs. |
| 176. teikan | jōshu | fudai | 90 | Retained in capital | |
| 177. teikan | jōshu | fudai | 79 | 6th mo. even yrs. | 6th mo. odd yrs. |
| 178. gan | jōshu | fudai | 55 | 6th mo. even yrs. | 6th mo. odd yrs. |
| 179. kiku | mujō | fudai | 38 | On duty at Fushimi | |
| 180. yanagi | jōshu | tozama | 271 | 4th mo. odd yrs. | 4th mo. even yrs. |
| 181. ōbiro | kokushu | tozama | 139 | 3rd mo. odd yrs. | 3rd mo. even yrs. |

| Daimyo | Seat of domain (province) | Assessed revenue (koku) |
|---|---|---|
| 182. Nambu | Morioka (Mutsu) | 11,000 |
| 183. Nambu | Hachinohe 八戸 (Mutsu) | 20,000 |
| 184. Nishio 西尾 | Yokosuka 横須賀 (Totomi) | 35,000 |
| 185. Niwa 丹羽 | Nihonmatsu 二本松 (Mutsu) | 100,700 |
| 186. Niwa | Mikusa 三草 | 10,000 |
| 187. Oda 織田 | Tendo 天童 (Dewa) | 20,000 |
| 188. Oda | Kashiwabara 柏原 (Tamba) | 20,000 |
| 189. Oda | Shibamura 芝村 (Yamato) | 10,000 |
| 190. Oda | Yagimoto 柳本 (Yamato) | 10,000 |
| 191. Ogasawara 小笠原 | Kokura 小倉 (Buzen) | 150,000 |
| 192. Ogasawara | Kokura Shinden 新田 (Buzen) | 10,000 |
| 193. Ogasawara | Ashi 安志 (Harima) | 10,000 |
| 194. Ogasawara | Karatsu 唐津 (Hizen) | 60,000 |
| 195. Ogasawara | Katsuyama 勝山 (Echizen) | 22,777 |
| 196. Okabe 岡部 | Kishiwada 岸和田 (Izumi) | 53,000 |
| 197. Ōkubo 大久保 | Odawara 小田原 (Sagami) | 113,129 |
| 198. Ōkubo | Ogino 荻野 (Sagami) | 13,000 |

| Status Categories | | | Distance | Sankin kōtai schedule | |
| Chamber | Type of holding | Relation- ship | from Edo (ri) | (as of 1853) | |
| | | | | Arrival | Departure |
|---|---|---|---|---|---|
| 182. yanagi | mujō | tozama | 139 | Retained in capital | |
| 183. yanagi | jōshu-kaku | tozama | 169 | 4th mo. even yrs. | 4th mo. odd yrs. |
| 184. teikan | jōshu | fudai | 58 | 6th mo. odd yrs. | 6th mo. even yrs. |
| 185. ōbiro | jun-kokushu | fudai | 66 | 4th mo. even yrs. | 4th mo. odd yrs. |
| 186. teikan | mujō | fudai | 130 | Retained in capital | |
| 187. yanagi | mujō | tozama | 97 | 6th mo. even yrs. | 6th mo. odd yrs. |
| 188. yanagi | mujō | fudai | 136 | 4th mo. odd yrs. | 4th mo. even yrs. |
| 189. yanagi | mujō | tozama | 119 | 4th mo. odd yrs. | 4th mo. even yrs. |
| 190. yanagi | jōshu-kaku | tozama | 120 | 4th mo. even yrs. | 4th mo. odd yrs. |
| 191. teikan | jōshu | fudai | 266 | 6th mo. odd yrs. | 6th mo. even yrs. |
| 192. teikan | mujō | fudai | 266 | 6th mo. odd yrs. | 6th mo. even yrs. |
| 193. teikan | mujō | fudai | 160 | 6th mo. even yrs. | 6th mo. odd yrs. |
| 194. teikan | jōshu | fudai | 311 | 6th mo. odd yrs. | 6th mo. even yrs. |
| 195. teikan | jōshu | fudai | 144 | 6th mo. even yrs. | 6th mo. odd yrs. |
| 196. teikan | jōshu | fudai | 141 | 6th mo. odd yrs. | 6th mo. even yrs. |
| 197. teikan | jōshu | fudai | 20 | 8th mo. every yr. | 2nd mo. every yr. |
| 198. kiku | mujō | fudai | 20 | 8th mo. every yr. | 2nd mo. every yr. |

| Daimyo | Seat of domain (province) | Assessed revenue (koku) |
|---|---|---|
| 199. Ōkubo | Karasuyama 烏山 (Shimotsuke) | 30,000 |
| 200. Okudaira 奥平 | Nakatsu 中津 (Buzen) | 100,000 |
| 201. Ōmura 大村 | Ōmura 大村 (Hizen) | 27,970 |
| 202. Ōoka 大岡 | Nishi-Ōhira 西大平 (Mikawa) | 10,000 |
| 203. Ōseki 大關 | Kurokane 黒金 (Shimotsuke) | 18,000 |
| 204. Ōta 太田 | Kakegawa 掛川 (Tōtomi) | 50,037 |
| 205. Otawara 大田原 | Otawara 大田原 (Shimotsuke) | 11,400 |
| 206. Rokugō 六郷 | Honjō 本庄 (Dewa) | 20,021 |
| 207. Sagara 相良 | Hitoyoshi 人吉 (Higo) | 22,100 |
| 208. Sakai 酒井 | Himeji 姫路 (Harima) | 150,000 |
| 209. Sakai | Isezaki 伊勢崎 (Kōzuke) | 20,000 |
| 210. Sakai | Obama 小濱 (Wakasa) | 103,558 |
| 211. Sakai | Tsuruga 敦賀 (Echizen) | 10,000 |
| 212. Sakai | Katsuyama 勝山 (Awa) | 12,000 |
| 213. Sakai | Shōnai 庄内 (Dewa) | 140,000 |
| 214. Sakai | Matsuyama 松山 (Dewa) | 25,000 |
| 215. Sakakibara 木神原 | Takata 高田 (Echigo) | 150,000 |

| Status Categories | | | Distance from Edo (ri) | Sankin kōtai schedule (as of 1853) | |
| Chamber | Type of holding | Relation-ship | | Arrival | Departure |
| --- | --- | --- | --- | --- | --- |
| 199. gan | jōshu | fudai | 35 | 8th mo. every yr. | 2nd mo. every yr. |
| 200. teikan | jōshu | fudai | 268 | 7th mo. even yrs. | 6th mo. odd yrs. |
| 201. yanagi | jōshu | tozama | 350 | 11th mo. even yrs. | 2nd mo. odd yrs. |
| 202. kiku | mujō | fudai | 76 | 12th mo. every yr. | 8th mo. every yr. |
| 203. yanagi | mujō | tozama | 38 | 6th mo. odd yrs. | 6th mo. even yrs. |
| 204. gan | jōshu | fudai | 55 | Retained in capital | |
| 205. yanagi | jōshu | tozama | 37 | 6th mo. even yrs. | 6th mo. odd yrs. |
| 206. yanagi | jōshu | tozama | 140 | 4th mo. even yrs. | 4th mo. odd yrs. |
| 207. yanagi | jōshu | tozama | 351 | 4th mo. even yrs. | 4th mo. odd yrs. |
| 208. tamari | jōshu | fudai | 157 | 5th mo. even yrs. | 5th mo. odd yrs. |
| 209. kiku | mujō | fudai | 24 | 12th mo. every yr. | 8th mo. every yr. |
| 210. tamari | jōshu | fudai | 129 | 6th mo. even yrs. | 6th mo. odd yrs. |
| 211. gan | mujō | fudai | 124 | Retained in capital | |
| 212. kiku | mujō | fudai | 36 | 8th mo. every yr. | 2nd mo. every yr. |
| 213. teikan | jōshu | fudai | 124 | 6th mo. odd yrs. | 6th mo. even yrs. |
| 214. teikan | jōshu | fudai | 120 | 6th mo. even yrs. | 6th mo. odd yrs. |
| 215. teikan | jōshu | fudai | 72 | 6th mo. even yrs. | 6th mo. odd yrs. |

| Daimyo | Seat of domain (province) | Assessed revenue (koku) |
|---|---|---|
| 216. Sanada 眞田 | Matsushiro 松代 (Shinano) | 100,000 |
| 217. Satake 佐竹 | Akita 秋田 (Dewa) | 205,800 |
| 218. Satake | Akita Shinden 新田 (Dewa) | 20,000 |
| 219. Seki 關 | Niimi 新見 (Bitchū) | 18,000 |
| 220. Sengoku 仙石 | Izushi 出石 (Tojima) | 30,000 |
| 221. Shimazu 島津 | Kagoshima 鹿兒島 (Satsuma) | 770,800 |
| 222. Shimazu | Sadowara 佐土原 (Hyūga) | 27,070 |
| 223. Shinjō 新庄 | Asō 麻生 (Hitachi) | 10,000 |
| 224. Sō 宗 | Fuchū 府中 (Tsushima) | 100,000 |
| 225. Soma 相馬 | Nakamura 中村 (Mutsu) | 60,000 |
| 226. Suwa 諏訪 | Takashima 高島 (Shinano) | 30,000 |
| 227. Tachibana 立花 | Yanagawa 柳河 (Chikugo) | 119,600 |
| 228. Tachibana | Shimotedo 下手渡 (Mutsu) | 10,000 |
| 229. Takagi 高木 | Tannan 丹南 (Kawachi) | 10,000 |
| 230. Tamura 田村 | Ichinoseki 一關 (Mutsu) | 30,000 |
| 231. Tani 谷 | Yamaie 山家 (Tamba) | 10,082 |

| Status Categories | | | Distance | Sankin kōtai schedule (as of 1853) | |
| Chamber | Type of holding | Relation-ship | from Edo (ri) | Arrival | Departure |
|---|---|---|---|---|---|
| 216. teikan | jōshu | fudai | 53 | 6th mo. odd yrs. | 6th mo. even yrs. |
| 217. ōbiro | kokushu | fudai | 143 | 4th mo. even yrs. | 4th mo. odd yrs. |
| 218. yanagi | mujō | tozama | 143 | Retained in capital | |
| 219. yanagi | mujō | tozama | 192 | 4th mo. odd yrs. | 4th mo. even yrs. |
| 220. yanagi | jōshu | tozama | 149 | 4th mo. even yrs. | 4th mo. odd yrs. |
| 221. ōbiro | kokushu | tozama | 411 | 4th mo. even yrs. | 4th mo. odd yrs. |
| 222. yanagi | jōshu | tozama | 393 | 4th mo. odd yrs. | 4th mo. even yrs. |
| 223. yanagi | mujō | tozama | 36 | 6th mo. odd yrs. | 6th mo. even yrs. |
| 224. ōbiro | kokushu | tozama | 300 | 11th mo. ev. 3 yrs. | 2nd mo. foll. yr. |
| 225. teikan | jōshu | fudai | 78 | 4th mo. even yrs. | 4th mo. odd yrs. |
| 226. teikan | jōshu | fudai | 54 | 6th mo. even yrs. | 6th mo. odd yrs. |
| 227. ōbiro | jun-kokushu | tozama | 390 | 4th mo. odd yrs. | 4th mo. even yrs. |
| 228. yanagi | mujō | fudai | 75 | 4th mo. even yrs. | 4th mo. odd yrs. |
| 229. kiku | mujō | fudai | 135 | Retained in capital | |
| 230. yanagi | mujō | fudai | 115 | 4th mo. even yrs. | 4th mo. odd yrs. |
| 231. yanagi | mujō | tozama | 139 | 4th mo. odd yrs. | 4th mo. even yrs. |

| Daimyo | Seat of domain (province) | Assessed revenue (<u>koku</u>) |
|---|---|---|
| 232. Tanuma 田沼 | Sagara 相良 (Totomi) | 10,000 |
| 233. Tatebe 建部 | Hayashida 林田 (Harima) | 10,000 |
| 234. Toda 戸田 | Ōgaki 大垣 (Mino) | 100,000 |
| 235. Toda | Ōgaki Shinden 新田 (Mino) | 10,000 |
| 236. Toda | Utsunomiya 宇都宮 (Shimotsuke) | 77,850 |
| 237. Toda | Ashikaga 足利 (Shimotsuke) | 11,000 |
| 238. Tōdō 藤堂 | Tsu 津 (Iga) | 323,950 |
| 239. Tōdō | Hisai 久居 (Ise) | 53,000 |
| 240. Toki 土岐 | Numata 沼田 (Kozuke) | 35,000 |
| 241. Tokugawa 徳川 | Nagoya 名古屋 (Owari) | 619,500 |
| 242. Tokugawa | Wakayama 和歌山 (Kishū) | 555,000 |
| 243. Tokugawa | Mito 水戸 (Hitachi) | 350,000 |
| 244. Torii 鳥居 | Mibu 壬生 (Shimotsuke) | 30,000 |
| 245. Tōyama 遠山 | Naeki 苗木 (Mino) | 10,021 |
| 246. Tozawa 戸澤 | Shinjō 新庄 (Dewa) | 68,200 |
| 247. Tsuchiya 土屋 | Tsuchiura 土浦 (Hitachi) | 95,000 |

| | Status Categories | | Distance | Sankin kōtai schedule | |
| Chamber | Type of holding | Relation- ship | from Edo (ri) | (as of 1853) Arrival | Departure |
|---|---|---|---|---|---|
| 232. kiku | mujō | fudai | 55 | Retained in capital | |
| 233. yanagi | mujō | tozama | 160 | 4th mo. even yrs. | 4th mo. odd yrs. |
| 234. teikan | jōshu | fudai | 99 | 6th mo. even yrs. | 6th mo. odd yrs. |
| 235. kiku | mujō | fudai | 99 | Retained in capital | |
| 236. gan | jōshu | fudai | 26 | 6th mo. odd yrs. | 6th mo. even yrs. |
| 237. kiku | mujō | fudai | 20 | 8th mo. every yr. | 2nd mo. every yr. |
| 238. ōbiro | kokushu | tozama | 102 | 4th mo. even yrs. | 4th mo. odd yrs. |
| 239. yanagi | jōshu- kaku | tozama | 109 | 4th mo. odd yrs. | 4th mo. even yrs. |
| 240. teikan | jōshu | fudai | 36 | 12th mo. every yr. | 8th mo. every yr. |
| 241. ōroka | jōshu | sanke | 86 | 3rd mo. even yrs. | 3rd mo. odd yrs. |
| 242. ōroka | jōshu | sanke | 146 | 3rd mo. odd yrs. | 3rd mo. even yrs. |
| 243. ōroka | jōshu | sanke | 30 | Retained in capital | |
| 244. teikan | jōshu | fudai | 23 1/2 | Retained in capital | |
| 245. yanagi | jōshu | tozama | 84 | 4th mo. odd yrs. | 4th mo. even yrs. |
| 246. teikan | jōshu | fudai | 110 | 4th mo. odd yrs. | 4th mo. even yrs. |
| 247. gan | jōshu | fudai | 18 | Retained in capital | |

| Daimyo | Seat of domain (province) | Assessed revenue (koku) |
|---|---|---|
| 248. Tsugaru 津輕 | Hirosaki 弘前 (Mutsu) | 100,000 |
| 249. Tsugaru | Kuroishi 黒石 (Mutsu) | 10,000 |
| 250. Uchida 内田 | Omigawa 小見川 (Shimosa) | 10,000 |
| 251. Uemura 植村 | Takatori 高取 (Yamato) | 25,000 |
| 252. Uesugi 上杉 | Yonezawa 米澤 (Dewa) | 150,000 |
| 253. Uesugi | Yonezawa Shinden 新田 (Dewa) | 10,000 |
| 254. Wakebe 分部 | Ōmizo 大溝 (Ōmi) | 20,000 |
| 255. Wakizaka 脇坂 | Tatsuno 龍野 (Harima) | 51,089 |
| 256. Watanabe 渡邊 | Hakata 伯太 (Izumi) | 13,520 |
| 257. Yagyū 柳生 | Yagyū 柳生 (Yamato) | 10,000 |
| 258. Yamaguchi 山口 | Ushiku 牛久 (Hitachi) | 10,017 |
| 259. Yamanouchi 山内 | Kōchi 高知 (Tosa) | 242,000 |
| 260. Yamanouchi | Kōchi Shinden (Tosa) | 13,000 |
| 261. Yanagizawa 柳澤 | Kōriyama 郡山 (Yamato) | 151,200 |
| 262. Yanagizawa | Kurokawa 黒川 (Echigo) | 10,000 |
| 263. Yanagisawa | Mikkaichi 汨市 (Echigo) | 10,000 |

| | Status Categories | | Distance | Sankin kōtai schedule | |
|---|---|---|---|---|---|
| | | | from Edo | (as of 1853) | |
| Chamber | Type of holding | Relation-ship | (ri) | Arrival | Departure |
| 248. ōbiro | jōshu | tozama | 184 | 3rd mo. even yrs. | 3rd mo. odd yrs. |
| 249. yanagi | mujō | tozama | 186 | 4th mo. odd yrs. | 4th mo. even yrs. |
| 250. kiku | mujō | fudai | 26 | 12th mo. every yr. | 8th mo. every yr. |
| 251. teikan | jōshu | fudai | 134 | 6th mo. odd yrs. | 6th mo. even yrs. |
| 252. ōbiro | kokushu | tozama | 75 | 4th mo. even yrs. | 4th mo. odd yrs. |
| 253. yanagi | mujō | tozama | 75 | 4th mo. odd yrs. | 4th mo. even yrs. |
| 254. yanagi | mujō | fudai | 127 | 4th mo. even yrs. | 4th mo. odd yrs. |
| 255. tamari | jōshu | fudai | 160 | On duty at Kyoto | |
| 256. kiku | mujō | fudai | 139 | 6th mo. even yrs. | 6th mo. odd yrs. |
| 257. kiku | mujō | fudai | 113 | Retained in capital | |
| 258. kiku | mujō | fudai | 16 | 8th mo. every yr. | 2nd mo. every yr. |
| 259. ōbiro | kokushu | tozama | 235 | 4th mo. even yrs. | 4th mo. odd yrs. |
| 260. yanagi | mujō | tozama | 235 | Retained in capital | |
| 261. teikan | jōshu | fudai | 134 | 7th mo. odd yrs. | 6th mo. even yrs. |
| 262. teikan | mujō | fudai | 97 | Retained in capital | |
| 263. teikan | mujō | fudai | 92 | Retained in capital | |

| Daimyo | Seat of domain (province) | Assessed revenue (koku) |
|---|---|---|
| 264. Yonekura 米倉 | Kanazawa 金澤 (Musashi) | 12,000 |
| 265. Yonezu 米津 | Nagatoro 長瀞 (Dewa) | 11,000 |

| Chamber | Status Categories | | Distance from Edo (ri) | Sankin kōtai schedule (as of 1853) | |
| | Type of holding | Relation-ship | | Arrival | Departure |
|---|---|---|---|---|---|
| 264. kiku | mujō | kamon | 14 | 12th mo. every yr. | 8th mo. every yr. |
| 265. koku | mujō | fudai | 98 | On duty at Osaka | |

NOTES

## Abbreviations Used in the Notes

DNS — Dai Nihon shiryō (Japanese historical materials), comp. Tokyo Teikoku Daigaku Shiryō Hensansho (Tokyo Imperial University Historiographical Institute), 176 vols. (Tokyo, 1901-   ).

Kinreikō — Shihōshō (Ministry of Justice), Tokugawa kinreikō  6 vols. (Tokyo, 1931-1932).

Kokushi daijiten — Yashiro Kuniharu et al., eds., Daizōtei kokushi daijiten (Further revised and supplemented dictionary of Japanese history), 7th ed., 6 vols. (Tokyo, 1930).

KT — Kuroita Katsumi, ed., Shintei zōho kokushi taikei (Revised and supplemented compendium of Japanese history), 58 vols. (Tokyo, 1929-   ).

KZ — Katsu Kaishū, Kaishū zenshū (Complete works of Kaishū), 10 vols. (Tokyo, 1928).

NKS — Takimoto Seiichi, ed., Nihon keizai sōsho (Documentary series on Japanese economics), 36 vols. (Tokyo, 1914-1917).

Shokafu — Hotta Masaatsu, ed., Kansei chōshū shokafu (Kansei collated genealogies), modern printed ed., 9 vols. (Tokyo, 1918).

Taisei bukan — Izumodera Manjirō, Taisei bukan (Taisei military mirror), 3 vols. ([Edo], 1853).

TASJ — Transactions of the Asiatic Society of Japan.

## I. The Tokugawa Regime

1. Good analyses of the daimyo policy of the early Tokugawa may be found in Mikami Sanji, "Edo bakufu no jūyō naru seisaku" (Important policies of the Edo shogunate), Edo jidai shiron (Essays on Edo period history; Tokyo, 1915), pp. 31-65; and Kurita Motoji, Edo jidai jō (The early Edo period), Vol. IX of Sōgo Nihonshi taikei (Synthetic study of Japanese history; Tokyo, 1926), pp. 137ff., 260ff. For details on the post-Sekigahara settlement, see James Murdoch, History of Japan, 3 vols. (London, 1925-1926), II, 426-456.

2.  For example, the Asano at Fuchū (later Kōfu) in Kai
    province, the Nakamura at Fuchū (later Sumpu) in Suruga
    province, the Yamanouchi at Kakegawa in Tōtomi province, the
    Ikeda at Yoshida in Mikawa province, and the Fukushima at
    Kiyosu (later Nagoya) in Owari province were all transferred
    to larger but less strategically vital fiefs.  See Murdoch,
    II, 440; also see Matsudaira Tarō, Edo jidai seido no kenkyū
    (A study of the Edo period administrative system; Tokyo,
    1919), pp. 518-519.

3.  Ten thousand koku, or roughly 51,000 American bushels of rice,
    was the minimum size of holding--measured in terms of its
    estimated productive capacity--for status as a daimyo.

4.  The Tokugawa holdings, although mostly concentrated in central
    Honshu along the Pacific seaboard between Osaka on the west
    and Mito on the east, were scattered throughout 48 of the 68
    provinces.

5.  Matsudaira was the surname of a certain number of families
    related to the Tokugawa.  It was also granted as a special
    mark of high honor of eighteen of the leading daimyo, most of
    them tozama lords of kokushu rank. See E. Papinot, Historical
    and Geographical Dictionary of Japan (Yokohama, 1910), p. 355.

6.  Matsudaira Tarō, pp. 266-267.  See also Miura Kaneyuki,
    Hōseishi no kenkyū (Studies in legal history), new ed.,
    2 vols. (Tokyo, 1943-1944), II, 369.

7.  For text see Kinreikō, I, 90ff.; and Hagino Yoshiyuki et al.,
    eds., Nihon kodai hōten (Ancient Japanese laws; Tokyo, 1903),
    pp. 769ff.  For a full translation of this code in English
    see John Carey Hall, "Japanese Feudal Laws III--The Tokugawa
    Legislation," TASJ, 38.4:269-331 (1911).

8.  For an authoritative study of the effect of special assessments
    of the bakufu upon the finances of three of the leading daimyo
    houses--the Maeda, the Shimazu, and the Date--see Tsuchiya
    Takao, Hōken shakai hōkai katei no kenkyū (A study of the
    process of decay of feudal society), 2nd ed. (Tokyo, 1930).

9.  Kinreikō, I, 93; Hall, pp. 293-294.

10. The income of the imperial household under the Ashikaga
    shogun had been 3,000 koku.  Hideyoshi increased its regular
    income to 7,000 koku and augmented it with frequent gifts.
    Under the Tokugawa it was initially 10,000 koku, increasing
    by 1705 to 30,000 koku with additional revenues in cash.
    For further details on the revenues assigned to the emperor,

his relatives, and the court nobles, see Katsu Kaishū, Suijinroku (Records), Vols. III and IV in his collected works, Kaishū zenshū (hereafter abbreviated KZ), 10 vols. (Tokyo, 1928), III, 1ff. Cf. also Murdoch, II, 508-509.

11. Suijinroku, KZ, III, 1.

12. Murdoch, II, 510.

13. G.B. Sansom, The Western World and Japan (New York, 1950), pp. 178-179.

14. See Asakawa Kanichi, The Early Institutional Life of Japan: A Study in the Reform of 645 A.D. (Tokyo, 1903).

15. The full title of the office was sei-i tai shōgun (lit.: "barbarian-subduing generalissimo" or "commander-in-chief against the barbarians"). For the origins and history of the term see Kokushi daijiten, III, 1374-75. Cf. also Papinot, p. 550.

16. For a brief but authoritative description of Kamakura feudalism, see Asakawa Kanichi, "Some Aspects of Japanese Feudal Institutions," TASJ, 46.1:76-102 (1918).

17. Suijinroku, KZ, III, 159.

18. About thirty-three in number, they were called kōtai yoriai and performed the sankin kōtai like the daimyo. See Kokushi daijiten, pp. 529-530.

19. Thus Asakawa points out: "The rule of the Tokugawa Shogunate... was purely feudal neither in its governmental organization nor in its institutions of land." See Asakawa Kanichi, Documents of Iriki (New Haven, 1929), p. 335.

20. The population of Japan during the Tokugawa period was roughly 30 million during the eighteenth and nineteenth centuries. See Honjō Eijirō, The Social and Economic History of Japan (Kyoto, 1935), and Garret Droppers, "The Population of Japan in the Tokugawa Period," TASJ, 22.2: 269-331 (1894).

21. For a list of provinces with shogunal holdings, their yield, and the locations of the offices of intendants, see Ono Kiyoshi, Tokugawa seido shiryō (Historical materials on the Tokugawa administrative system; Tokyo, 1927), Pt. 2., pp. 226-237.

22. Suijinroku, KZ, III, 144ff.

23. Takekoshi Yosaburō, The Economic Aspects of the History of the Civilization of Japan, 3 vols. (New York, 1930), II, 306-311, gives tables showing the shogunate's annual revenue from taxes from 1716 to 1841. These show that the average annual output of the shogunal domain for this period of 126 years was 4,175,246 koku and that the average annual revenue actually received was 1,536,907 koku.

24. Suijinroku, KZ, III, 158-160.

25. For a detailed account in English of the administrative machinery of the Tokugawa, see Murdoch, III, 1-26. The "table of organization" of the Edo bureaucracy may be found in the Tokushi biyō (Handbook of Japanese history), comp. Tōkyō Teikoku Daigaku Shiryō Hensansho (Tokyo Imperial University Historiographical Institute; Tokyo, 1933), pp. 540-543.

26. Asakawa, The Documents of Iriki, pp. 103-104.

27. See Watanabe Yosuke, Daimyō hen (Volume on the daimyo), Vol. III of the Ruishū denki Dai Nihonshi (A biographical history of Japan), 15 vols. (Tokyo, 1934), pp. 4-7. For the history of the term "daimyo," see Kokushi daijiten, III, 1637-39.

28. The term "han" is often translated as "clan," but as Asakawa, among others, has pointed out, this usage is inaccurate and misleading since the Tokugawa han as an organization was not tribal but territorial in character, resembling closely the "feudal state" of Europe in the later stages of its development (Asakawa, The Documents of Iriki, p. 339, n. 3).

29. Under the first three shogun, daimyo domains were freely confiscated by the bakufu: 92 daimyo houses forfeited their lands for military opposition to the Tokugawa, 46 houses for the lack of a legitimate or satisfactory successor, and 59 houses for infractions of bakufu laws. Between 1600 and 1651 holdings totaling over 15 million koku in productive capacity were confiscated, while in the 66 years following 1651 total confiscations amounted only to about 2.1 million koku (Kurita Motoji, pp. 279ff., 476ff.).

30. When in financial distress, the Tokugawa daimyo customarily reduced stipends by one-half or more. This was called hanchi ("half-stipend") or, euphemistically, kariage ("loans").

See Honjō Eijirō, ed., <u>Nihon keizaishi jiten</u> (Dictionary of Japanese economic history), 2nd ed., 2 vols. (Kyoto, 1942), II, 1354.

31. In the Satsuma barony, the lord in 1612 ordered all his great vassals to leave their private domains and establish residences at Kagoshima, the lord's seat. See the Iriki-in genealogy in Asakawa, <u>The Documents of Iriki</u>, p. 396.

32. <u>Ibid.</u>, pp. 335-336.

33. For the text of a typical oath, see Matsudaira, pp. 269-270.

34. Watanabe, p. 28.

35. Takekoshi, II, 318-319.

36. Watanabe, p. 26.

37. Mikami, "Edo bakufu no jūyō naru seisaku," pp. 54-58.

38. Quotas for troops of various categories from mounted samurai, bowmen, musketeers, and pikemen down to members of the supply train were specified by uniform regulations. The military service quotas issued in 1633 and 1649 are given in the <u>Suijinroku</u>, KZ, III, 226-233. The 1649 quotas, which were standard for most of the Edo period, specified a minimum of 235 men for daimyo worth 10,000 <u>koku</u> to 2155 men for a 100,000-<u>koku</u> lord.

39. For details on the guard assignments and quotas of the daimyo at Edo, see Ono Kiyoshi, Pt. 1, pp. 7-11; Matsudaira, pp. 383-402.

40. The daimyo were responsible for the <u>sekisho</u> located within their domains. For details of <u>sekisho</u> locations and administration, see Ono Kiyoshi (section entitled "Sekisho sōran," paginated separately), pp. 1-24; Matsudaira, pp. 402-438; Hibata Sekko, <u>Edo jidai no kōtsū bunka</u> (Transportation culture of the Edo period; Tokyo, 1931), pp. 216-230. For a monograph on the subject, see Curtis A. Manchester, "The Development and Distribution of <u>Sekisho</u> in Japan," Ph.D. thesis (University of Michigan, 1946).

41. In 1860, some 708,400 <u>koku</u> out of 3,976,100 <u>koku</u>, or about 18 per cent of the total taxable capacity of the shogunal domain, was entrusted to 32 daimyo to administer on behalf of the bakufu (<u>Suijinroku</u>, KZ, III, 237).

42. Watanabe, p. 27.

43. There were cases, as Murdoch notes, of tozama being appointed senior councilors (rōjū) toward the end of the Edo period (Murdoch, II, 5).

44. The office of Great Councilor (tairō), for instance, was limited to the four leading fudai houses of Ii, Sakai, Hotta, and Doi; and senior councilors were selected from only among thirty-five families during the whole of the Tokugawa period. See Nakamura Kōya, "Daimyo no kenkyū" (A study of the daimyo), in Miyake hakase koki shukuga kinen rombunshū (Collection of monographs commemorating the 70th birthday of Dr. Miyake; Tokyo, 1929), p. 383.

45. See the calendar of ceremonial observances at the Edo court in the Tokushi biyō, pp. 657-712.

46. Information on the classification of the daimyo has been derived from Nakamura Kōya, "Daimyō no kenkyū," pp. 329-385; and the Koji ruien (Encyclopedia of ancient matters), revised popular ed., 60 vols. (Tokyo: Jingū Shichō [Office of Shrine Affairs], 1933-1936).    Pertinent sections in this latter work are found in the kan'i bu, Vols. 16 and 17 (1936 ed.).    Individual references have been omitted.  See also the Tokushi biyō, pp. 475-494: Watanabe, pp. 531-550; Honjō, Nihon keizaishi jiten, I, 975-991; or the Suijinroku, KZ, III, 234-262, for lists of daimyo giving data on their classification.  For Western material on this subject, see J.H. Gubbins, "The Feudal System in Japan under the Tokugawa Shoguns," TASJ, 15.2:133-141 (1887); and Maurice Courant, "Les clans japonais sous les Tokugawas," Annales du Musée Guimet, Bibliothèque de Vulgarisation, 15:1-82 (1904).

47. There is some confusion as to whether kamon was a generic term including the sanke or whether it refers only to the remainder of the collaterals.  The Koji ruien presents the former view, but the sanke are usually listed separately by most authorities.

48. Asakawa, The Documents of Iriki, p. 45, n. 2.

II.  The Origins and Development of the Sankin Kotai

1.  Sankin may be written 參覲 or 參勤.  The former is literally "to visit a superior for an audience"; the latter means to report to render services.

2.  Kōtai may be written 交代 or 交替.

3.  Azuma kagami (Kencho 3rd yr., 8th mo., 23rd day).  See KT, XXXIII, 487.

4.  Kemmu shikimoku tsuika (Shōchō 2nd yr., 8th mo., 20th day). Cited in Shimonaka Yasaburō, ed., Daijiten (Encyclopedia), 26 vols. (Tokyo, 1933), XII, 260.

5.  See Aoki Busuke, Shintei Dai Nihon rekishi shūsei (New revised composite history of Japan), 5 vols. (Tokyo, 1933), III, 263.

6.  Edouard Biot, Le Tcheou Li ou Rites des Tcheou (Paris, 1851), I, 424.  It appears in the Chǔ li section of the Li chi in the phrase:  Chu-hou pei-mien erh chien t'ien-tzu yüeh chin, which Couvreur translates as: "Les princes, le visage tourné vers le nord, saluent le fils du ciel: (en automne) cela s'appelle kin";S. Couvreur, Dictionaire classique de la langue Chinoise (Ho Kien Fou, 1911), p. 839. Cf. James Legge, The Lǐ Kǐ, A Collection of Treatises on the Rules of Propriety or Ceremonial Usages, in F. Max Müller, ed., The Sacred Books of the East (Oxford, 1885), XXVIII, 111.

7.  In the Shu ching, Shun tien, it is used in the phrase: nai jih chin ssu-yüeh ch'ün-mu, rendered by Couvreur, p. 839, as: "Chaque jour il donna audience aux chefs des quatre regions et aux gouverneurs des provinces." Cf. James Legge, tr., The Shoo King, in The Chinese Classics, 2nd ed., 7 vols. (Oxford, 1895), Vol. III, Pt. 1, p. 34.

8.  Legge, tr., The Works of Mencius, in The Chinese Classics, II, 159.

9.  See "Hitojichi," Koji ruien, XXIX, 783ff.; and in the Kokushi daijiten, IV, 2064.

10.  Shimmi Kichiji, Nihon ni okeru buke seiji no rekishi (The history of feudal military rule in Japan; Osaka, 1941), p. 140, n. 21.

11.  Asakawa, The Documents of Iriki, pp. 62-63.

12. See Kawakami Tasuke, "Toshi to shite no Kamakura" (Kamakura as a city), in Rekishi chiri (Historical geography), 3.4: 549 (1918).

13. Kumazawa Banzan, Daigaku wakumon, in NKS, I, 168.  Cf. English tr. by Galen M. Fisher, "Dai Gaku Wakumon, A Discussion of Public Questions in the Light of the Great Learning, by Kumazawa Banzan," in TASJ, second series, 16:343 (1938).

14. Kumazawa, NKS, I, 1515; Fisher, "Dai Gaku Wakumon...," p. 311.

15. Asakawa, The Documents of Iriki, p. 126, n. 22.

16. Ibid., pp. 17, 21, 62.

17. Ibid., pp. 123-124; Yamaga Soko, Buke jiki (Chronicle of the feudal military families), modern ed., 3 vols. (Tokyo, 1915-1918), III, 433.

18. See "ōban yaku" in Kokushi daijiten, I, 479-480; Asakawa, The Documents of Iriki, p. 126, n. 17.  Among the documents in the latter work is an order issued in 1198 by Shimazu Tadahisa, shugo of Satsuma, Hyūga, and Ōsumi,calling upon twenty-four gokenin of Satsuma in the name of the shogun to perform their customary knights' service as periodical grand guardsmen (ōban) at Kyoto (ibid., p. 107).

19. See "Kamakura ōban yaku" in Kokushi daijiten, II, 647.  For further details, see Ryo Susumu, Kamakura jidai no kenkyū (A study of the Kamakura period; Tokyo, 1945), p. 159.

20. Asakawa, The Documents of Iriki, pp. 63, 126, n. 28.

21. For several examples see Kawakami, p. 550.

22. Yamaga, III, 438.

23. Shimmi, p. 140, n. 21.

24. See Kokushi jiten (Dictionary of Japanese history), 4 vols. (Tokyo, 1940-1943), IV, 483.

25. Hideyoshi granted estates just outside the imperial city of Kyoto to his chief barons ostensibly for their convenience when they attended the emperor.  Ieyasu was granted such an estate in Ōmi province at Moriyama, a minor post-town on the Tōkaidō about twenty miles by road from Kyoto. See Hibata, pp. 376-377.

26. Yamaga, II, 434.

27. Asakawa, The Documents of Iriki, p. 325.

28. For an excellent description of the extravagances in which Hideyoshi indulged and which he encouraged among his subordinates, see G.B. Sansom, Japan: A Short Cultural History, rev. ed. (New York, 1943), pp. 436-439.

29. Mikami Sanji, Edo jidaishi (A history of the Edo period), 2 vols. (Tokyo, 1944), I, 24.

30. Cf. below, p. 48.

31. These details of the Tokugawa-Maeda relationship are taken from the genealogical history of the early Tokugawa daimyo families, the Hankampu, compiled by Arai Hakuseki (1675-1725) in 1701. See Arai Hakuseki, Hankampu (Genealogies of the feudal families), modern edition by Urushiyama Matashirō, ed., 2 vols. (Tokyo, 1926), I, 497-498.

32. Mikami, Edo jidaishi, I, 124.

33. Ibid.

34. Arai Hakuseki, Hankampu, I, 498.

35. Ibid.; Naitō Chisō, ed., Tokugawa jūgodaishi (A history of the fifteen Tokugawa generations), 12 vols. (Tokyo, 1892-1893), I, 9.

36. Mikami, Edo jidaishi, I, 124.

37. Kaga han shiryō (Historical materials of the Kaga domain), comp. Kōshaku Maeda-ke henshūsho (Publication office of the House of Marquis Maeda), 13 vols. (Kanazawa, 1929-1933), I, 846-850.

38. Mikami, Edo jidaishi, I, 124.

39. Date Masamune-Kyō denki shiryō (Historical materials for the biography of Lord Date Masamune), comp. Hanso Date Masamune-Kō Kenshōkai (Han founder Lord Date Masamune Memorial Association; Sendai, 1938), p. 664.

40. Ibid., p. 665.

41. DNS, Series 12, Vol. 1, pp. 66-67, 69.

42. The official annals of the shogunate, the Tokugawa jikki (Vols. 38-47 in KT), under the date Keicho 8th year, 3rd month, states: "This spring the daimyo of the Kansai came up to Edo one after another to have audience with the Dainagon (Hidetada)" (KT,XXXVIII, 80). Cf. also DNS, 12.1:65, and Murdoch, II, 511.

43. DNS, 12.1:61; Tokugawa jikki (Keichō 8th yr., 2nd mo., 21st day), KT, XXXVIII, 80.

44. DNS, 12.1:259; Tokugawa jikki (Keichō 8th yr., 4th mo.), KT, XXXVIII, 81.

45. DNS, 12.1:296-308; Tokugawa jikki (Keichō 8th yr., 5th mo.), KT, XXXVIII, 83.

46. Tokugawa jikki (Keichō 8th yr., 10th mo.), KT, XXXVIII, 95-96.

47. Ibid.

48. DNS, 12.1:465; Date Masamune-Kyō denki shiryō, p. 676.

49. DNS, 12.2:288; Tokugawa jikki (Keichō 9th yr., 6th mo., 2nd day), KT, XXXVIII, 111.

50. DNS, 12.2:62.

51. DNS, 12.2:859.

52. Tokugawa jikki (Keichō 8th yr., 4th mo.), KT, XXXVIII, 81. Cf. also DNS, 12.1:259.

53. In 1602, Kuroda, Katō, and Fukushima stood 7th, 8th and 10th respectively, in the list of feudatories. Each had been raised from around the 200,000-koku level to the ranks of the major daimyo at the 500,000-koku level. See Mikami, Edo jidaishi, I, 106-114 and Murdoch, II, 438-440 for descriptions of the territorial settlement after Sekigahara. Complete lists of daimyo holdings immediately before and after Sekigahara (1600), showing increases, reductions, confiscations and transfers of fiefs, are given in Matsudaira, pp. 517-527 and 528-590.

54. Uesugi and Mōri had, before Sekigahara, ranked next to Ieyasu in wealth and power, with holdings assessed at 1,200,000 koku each and seats on Hideyoshi's Council of Regents. They had been stripped of three-fourths of their possessions and thoroughly humbled. Satake's fief was cut from 500,000 koku to 205,000 koku.

55. For a detailed description of this program and the part the daimyo played, see Tokutomi Iichiro, Kinsei Nihon kokuminshi (A history of the Japanese people in the modern period), 50 vols. (Tokyo, 1935-1936, XII, 4-44; XIII, 41-71.

56. Tokugawa jikki (Keichō 8th yr., 3rd mo.), KT, XXXVIII, 80.

57. In the third month of 1603, Ieyasu ordered seventy-seven of the leading lords to furnish labor for laying out the streets of Edo and for the canal-digging operations, at the rate of one man per 1000 koku of assessed wealth. See

Tokugawa jikki (Keichō 8th yr.), KT, XXXVIII, 76;DNS, 12.1:104.

58. Although the actual presence of the daimyo was not compulsory, the Tokugawa jikki notes early in the year 1606 the arrival in Edo of many daimyo from western Japan coming to oversee the work on Edo castle. See the entry for Keichō 11th yr., 2nd mo., KT, XXXVIII, 405; also Tokutomi, XII, 44.

59. Detailed accounts of Ikeda's visit are found in the Tokugawa jikki (Keichō 8th yr., 4th mo.), KT, XXXVIII, 81; and DNS, 12.1:259.

60. Miura Kikutarō, Nihon hōseishi (A history of Japanese legislation), 3rd ed. (Tokyo, 1910), p. 271.

61. Cf. below, pp. 64-70.

62. See the Tokugawa jikki (Keichō 14th yr., 11th mo., 26th day), KT, XXXVIII, 482; Naitō, I, 104; Miura Kikutarō, p. 261.

63. Cf. below, p. 49.

64. Matsudaira, pp. 266-267. See also Miura Kaneyuki, II, 379.

65. Tokutomi, XII, 55; Murdoch, II, 704.

66. For text see Kinreikō, I, 90ff.; and Hagino, pp. 769ff. For a translation of this code, see Hall, pp. 290ff.

67. The Shoku Nihongi, the second of the six official court histories (Rikkokushi) of the pre-feudal period, covers the years 697-791. It was completed in 797 in 40 kan. One of the modern printed editions appears as Vol. II of the KT (1935 ed.).

68. The reference to "horsemen" did not mean only attendants who were actually on horseback, but included those samurai who were qualified by rank to ride horses in time of war, even though they customarily traveled in the lord's retinue on foot (Hibata, p. 379).

69. Kinreikō, I, 90; Hall, p. 290.

70. Matsudaira, p. 493.

71. The eleventh article was revised; the fifth and ninth articles were dropped. See Kinreikō, I, 93; Hall, pp. 291-292; Matsudaira, p. 493.

72. Tokutomi, XII, 52.

73.  Peter Pratt, History of Japan, Compiled from the Records of
     the English East India Company, 1882, ed. M. Paske-Smith,
     2 vols. (Kobe, 1931), II, 14. The published version of
     Cocks's diary omits this particular entry. Cf. The Diary
     of Richard Cocks, Cape Merchant in the English Factory in
     Japan, 1615-1622, with correspondence, ed. Edward Maunde
     Thompson, 2 vols. (Tokyo, 1899). Additional notes by N.
     Murakami.

74.  Matsuura Takanobu (1591-1637), lord of Hirado since 1614
     when he succeeded his grandfather, Shigenobu.  See Watanabe,
     p. 509.

75.  Pratt, II, 18.

76.  Kinreikō, IV, 516; cf. translation by Hall, pp. 293-294.

77.  Bungen, meaning "social status" or "wealth," refers in this
     context to the magnitude of fiefs held of the shōgun by
     his vassals, according to which the latter were required
     to maintain a definite quota of troops. In the Kan'ei era
     (1624-1643), the quotas ranged from a complement of 21 men
     of all ranks for a 1,000-koku fief-holder to one of 235
     men for a daimyo at the 100,000-koku level (Hibata, p. 380).

78.  Tokugawa jikki (Kan'ei 12th yr., 6th mo., 30th day), KT,
     XXXIX, 684.

79.  Ibid., XXXIX, 684 (Kan'ei 12th yr., 7th mo., 1st day).

80.  Ibid., XL, 271 (Kan'ei 19th yr., 5th mo., 9th day).

81.  Ibid., XL, 272 (Kan'ei 19th yr., 5th mo., 14th day).

82.  Ibid., XL, 286 (Kan'ei 19th yr., 9th mo., 1st day).

83.  Cf. below, p. 49.

84.  Mikami, Edo jidaishi, I, 125.

85.  DNS, 12.2:852-853. Maeda Toshinaga's mother, who had
     been sent as a hostage to Edo in 1600, was given a mansion
     outside of the Ōte gate of Edo castle.  This later became
     the first official residence of the Maeda han in Edo.

86.  DNS, 12.1:61; Tokugawa jikki, KT, XXXVIII, 76.

87.  DNS, 12.1:296-308; Tokugawa jikki, KT, XXXVIII, 83.

88.  DNS, 12.1:416.

89.  DNS, 12.2:853.

90.  Quoted in Murdoch, p. 511.

91. Tōdō in 1599 sent a younger brother to Edo ostensibly as a page to Hidetada, but in reality as a hostage. See Shokafu, V, 717.

92. Daimyo of Takata (Echigo--350,000 koku).

93. Daimyo of Kōfu (Kai-240,000 koku).

94. Tokutomi, XIII, 80.

95. Asano kafu, cited in Tamura Eitarō, Kinsei Nihon kōtsūshi (History of transportation in modern Japan; Tokyo, 1935), p. 265.

96. Tokugawa jikki, KT, XXXVIII, 66. According to the official bakufu genealogical compilation, this marks the beginning of the hostage system under the Tokugawa; see Shokafu, VI, 893. Cf. Murdoch, II, 398-399.

97. Tokutomi, XIII, 80; Mikami, Edo jidaishi, I, 131-132.

98. Date Masamune-Kyō denki shiryō, p. 665.

99. DNS, 12.2:315-316; Tokugawa jikki (Keichō 9th yr., 6th mo., 20th day), KT, XXXVIII, 112; Shokafu, V, 707.

100. Mikami, Edo jidaishi, I, 129-130.

101. Tokugawa jikki, KT, XXXVIII, 404; Shokafu, V, 717.

102. Mikami, Edo jidaishi, I, 129; Tokugawa jikki, KT, XXXVIII, 458. Tōdō, who had risen from a small daimyo of 80,000 koku under Hideyoshi to a 200,000-koku magnate after Sekigahara, was further rewarded at this time by another 20,000-koku increase in his assessment.

103. DNS, 12.6:199; Ihara Gi, Tokugawa jidai tsūshi (Common history of the Tokugawa period; Tokyo, 1928), p. 247.

104. Shokafu, VI, 893.

105. Tokutomi, XII, 54.

106. Mikami, Edo jidaishi, I, 131.

107. Ibid., I, 130; cf. Murdoch, II, 704, n. 5.

108. Mikami, Edo jidaishi, I, 131.

109. Ibid., p. 133.

III.  Structure and Operation of the System

1.  Miura Kikutarō, p. 261.

2.  For details on sekisho administration, see Tamura Eitarō, pp. 242-261; Ono Kiyoshi (section entitled "Sekisho sōran," paginated separately),pp. 1-24; Hibata Sekko, pp. 216-230; Curtis A. Manchester, pp. 86ff.

3.  Kokushi daijiten, III, 1768.

4.  The occupants of the gan-no-ma or the "chamber of the wild geese," one of the halls in the shogun's palace occupied by specified fudai daimyo when attending court.  For a list of gan-no-ma daimyo as of 1835, see Kokushi daijiten, II, 670.

5.  Koji ruien, Vol. 16, p. 168; Katsu Kaishū, Suijinroku, KZ, III, 262.

6.  See Kokushi daijiten, II, 529-530.

7.  Yuasa Jōzan (1708-1781) states in his miscellany, Bunkai zakki, that when the months of travel for the sankin kōtai were determined, weather conditions were the primary consideration.  The sanke and the tozama were assigned the third and fourth months respectively, because these were the best for travel, the days being long and the weather neither too hot or cold.  See the Nihon zuihitsu taisei (Collection of Japanese miscellanies; Tokyo, 1931), series 3, VII, 587.

8.  Sankin dates for the various daimyo are usually given in the bukan (books of heraldry or directories of the military nobility, which were published during the Tokugawa period by several private publishing houses).  A large number of bukan have been reproduced in Hashimoto Hiroshi, ed., Daibukan (Great military mirror), 12 vols. (Tokyo, 1935-1936). Reference has been made to this work and an original edition of the Taisei bukan.  For the sankin dates of 266 daimyo ca. 1830, see Matsudaira, pp. 685-692.

9.  Miura Kikutarō, p. 263.

10.  Matsudaira, p. 675.  According to the Taisei bukan, II, 209B, Matsumae reported on alternate years between the tenth month and the second month of the following year.

11.  Miura Kikutarō, p. 263; Matsudaira, p. 675.

12.  Kokushi daijiten, II, 529.

13. Miura Kikutarō, p. 264. For details see the Tokugawa jikki, KT, XLI, 211-213; and Naitō Chisō, IV, 201.

14. Tokugawa jikki, KT, LXVII, 385; Naitō, IX, 145.

15. Naitō, XII, 148; Miura Kikutarō, p. 264.

16. Tsuchiya Takao, p. 106.

17. This is recorded in the genealogy of the Shimazu family in the Shokafu, I, 164.

18. Mikami Sanji, Edo jidaishi, I, 126.

19. Tokugawa jikki, KT, XLI, 213-214.

20. Miura Kikutarō, p. 264.

21. Hōreki reiten eikan, cited by Honjō Eijirō, "Sankin kōtai seido no keizai kan" (Economic aspects of the sankin kōtai system), Keizai ronsō (Economic review), 3.6:835 (1916).

22. Tokugawa jikki, KT, XL, 217.

23. For a detailed account of the expulsion of the Portuguese and its immediate repercussions, see Murdoch, Vol. II, Chap. 23.

24. Miura Kikutarō, p. 264.

25. Tokugawa jikki, KT, XL, 271; Naitō, IV, 10.

26. Tokugawa jikki, KT, XLIV, 374; Naitō, VII, 161.

27. Honjō, "Sankin kōtai seido...," pp. 835-836; Miura Kikutarō, p. 263.

28. Cf. above, p. 45.

29. Miura Kikutarō, p. 274.

30. Tokugawa jikki, KT, XL, 523. The proportion of foot troops to mounted warriors in this period was roughly 15-20 to 1.

31. Ibid., KT, XLI, 69. For the text of the order quoted see Kinreikō, IV, 522. This order is also reproduced in Tamura, p. 273.

32. Englebert Kaempfer (1651-1716) was a German doctor attached to the Dutch East India Company, who visited in Japan from 1690 to 1692. For Kaempfer's description of the processions he witnessed on his return from Edo in 1692, see below, pp. 77-79.

33. Tamura, p. 266.

34. Ibid., p. 274.

35. See Kinreikō, IV, 523ff., for several examples.

36. Reference is to the ninth article of the first buke shohatto.

37. Tokugawa jikki, KT, XLIV, 225; Miura Kikutarō, p. 275.

38. Guards for the remaining gates were furnished by hatamoto. See Matsudaira, p. 390.

39. The names of the gates, the class of daimyo assigned to each, and the maximum number of men to be stationed at each location were as follows:

| Gate | Class of daimyo | | | Total guard detail |
|------|-----------------|--|--|-------------------|
| Ōte | fudai | 100-150,000 | koku | 175 men |
| Uchi-Sakurada | fudai | 50- 90,000 | " | 95 " |
| Nishimaru-Otē | fudai | 40- 90,000 | " | 95 " |
| Soto-Sakurada | fudai | 40- 60,000 | " | 70 " |
| Kandabashi | tozama | 40- 60,000 | " | 70 " |
| Wadagura | fudai | 20- 30,000 | " | 57 " |
| Hanzō | fudai | 20- 30,000 | " | 57 " |
| Tokiwabashi | tozama | 20- 30,000 | " | 57 " |
| Babasaki | fudai | 20- 30,000 | " | 51 " |
| Takebashi | fudai | 20- 30,000 | " | 51 " |
| Tayasu | fudai | 20- 30,000 | " | 51 " |
| Hitotsubashi | fudai | 20- 30,000 | " | 51 " |
| Gofukubashi | tozama | 10- 20,000 | " | 51 " |
| Kajibashi | tozama | 10- 20,000 | " | 51 " |
| Sukiyabashi | tozama | 10- 20,000 | " | 51 " |
| Hibiya | tozama | 10- 20,000 | " | 51 " |
| Saiwaibashi | tozama | 10- 20,000 | " | 51 " |

40. Tōeizan at Ueno and Zōjōji at Shiba (both in Edo) were Buddhist temples enjoying the special patronage of the Tokugawa.

41. Kinreikō, IV, 524-527. See also Miura Kikutarō, pp. 275-278.

42. Kinreikō, IV, 528-529.

43. Ashigaru (lit., "foot-light") were warriors on foot of humble rank below a samurai but above all other grades of common soldiery.

44. Chūgen (lit., "middlings") derived their name from their intermediate position in rank between samurai and the komono pages. Ninsoku were more laborers and weapon-bearers than soldiers.

45. Bajō (lit., "on horse") referred to a mounted samurai, hence a knight.

46. Date Kenji, "Edo ni okeru shokō no shōhiteki seikatsu ni tsuite" (On the life of the feudal lords in Edo as consumers), Rekishigaku kenkyū (Journal of the historical science society), 4.4:389 (1935).

47. Miura Kikutarō, p. 271.

48. See "jōshi" in Kokushi daijiten, III, 1382. Information on the type of envoy, if any, to which a daimyo was entitled was usually given in the bukan.

49. Ikeda Kōen, Edo jidaishi jō (History of the early Edo period), Vol. IX of the Nihon jidaishi (History of Japan by periods), 14 vols. (Tokyo, 1926-1927), p. 370.

50. The sōshaban were masters of ceremony and etiquette at the shogun's court.

51. The tsukaiban were originally military orderlies and scouts who in peacetime became more or less low-level administrative aides to the shogun. For details on their varied function, see Kokushi daijiten, III, 1785.

52. Miura Kikutarō, p. 272, lists as his fifth category, "tsukaiban as envoy only before departure."

53. Taisei bukan (1853 ed.), I, 58, 101, 134, 194.

54. Ikeda, p. 369.

55. Ono Kiyoshi, Pt. 1, p. 132.

56. Miura Kikutarō, p. 272.

57. Ono Kiyoshi, Pt. 1, p.132.

58. Miura Kikutarō, p. 273.

59. See Honjō Eijirō, ed., Nihon keizaishi jiten, I, 673-674, 1167; Kokushi jiten, III, 669.

60. This information on gifts presented and received is taken from data given in the Taisei bukan (1853 ed.), passim. Cf. Honjō, Nihon keizaishi jiten, p. 673.

61. Kokushi jiten, III, 669.

62. For interesting details on the specifications and manner of presenting these gifts, see Ono Kiyoshi, Pt. 1, pp. 197-201 and Pt. 2, pp. 17ff. See also Hibata, p. 402.

63. For a list of the monthly offerings of the Tokugawa daimyo of Wakayama (Kii) and the Maeda house of Kanazawa (Kaga), see Hibata, p. 403.

64. Ono Kiyoshi, Pt. 1, p. 205.

65. Miura Kikutarō, p. 274.

66. Kokushi jiten, III, 669.

67. Tokugawa jikki, KT, XLI, 215.

68. Nonaka Jun et al., eds., Dai Nihon sozeishi (History of Japanese taxation), 3 vols. (Tokyo, 1926-1927), III, 224-225; Kokushi jiten, III, 669-670.

69. Tamura, pp. 285-287.

70. Twenty-five others were jōfu or "retained at the capital," and were thus exempt at this time.

71. See Neil Skene Smith, ed., "Materials on Japanese Social and Economic History: Tokugawa Japan," TASJ, second series, 14:61 (1937). For further details and a list of the daimyo tabulated, see Tamura, pp. 287-307; and Aoe Shū, Dai Nihon Teikoku ekitei shikō (Draft history of the post stations of Japan), Vol. X in Nihon sangyō shiryō taikei (Compendium of materials on Japanese industry), 13 vols. (Tokyo, 1928), p. 461.

72. For names of the eight daimyo so privileged, see Tamura, p. 300.

73. Orders to this effect were issued as early as 1714 and were repeated in 1799 (Aoe, pp. 471, 511).

74. Tamura, p. 308.

75. For the text of the road or travel orders of the Zeze han and of the Matsudaira han of Himeji (Harima), see ibid., pp. 308-312.

76. Ibid., pp. 338ff.

77. Ibid., pp. 313-320; Hibata, pp. 209-212; see also Smith, pp. 63f.

78. For a good detailed description of the system of rules governing the processions and their equipment, see Matsudaira, pp. 289-313. Lists of daimyo who were privileged to use or display certain types of equipment are given in Tamura, pp. 355-361.

79. Saitō Ryūzō, Kinsei Nihon sesōshi (History of modern Japanese life; Tokyo, 1925), p. 267.

80. Tamura, p. 351. Sketches of these spear sheaths, halberds, and umbrella were printed in the various bukan.

81. Only twenty of the leading daimyo had the privilege of displaying gold-crested hasami-bako. For further details, see Saitō, p. 268.

82. Tamura, p. 350.

83. For a detailed description and a sketch of this device, see Hibata, pp. 397-398.

84. Ibid., pp. 391-393; Saitō, pp. 269-270.

85. Saitō, p. 269.

86. Ibid., p. 271.

87. Murdoch, II, 704, n. 5.

88. Englebert Kaempfer, History of Japan, Together with the Description of the Kingdom of Siam, 1690-1692, 3 vols. (Glasgow, 1906), II, 331.

89. Kaga Shōun Kō den, cited in Date, p. 387.

90. Kaempfer, II, 332-335. Cf. Hibata's analysis of an illustration of a daimyo train made by the famous wood-cut artist Andō Hiroshige (1797-1858); see Hibata, pp. 384-391.

91. Tamura, pp. 370-375.

92. Tsuchiya, pp. 98-99.

93. Tamura, p. 376.


IV. The Economic Effects of the Sankin Kōtai

1. The following list of official and actual assessments at the end of the Tokugawa period (1867) is given in Toba Masao, "Edo jidai no rinsei" (Forestry administration in the Edo period), in case 9 of the Iwanami koza: Nihon rekishi (Iwanami series on Japanese history), 18 cases (Tokyo, 1933-1935), pp. 24-25:

| Daimyo | Han | Official taka (in koku) | Actual taka (in koku) |
|---|---|---|---|
| Maeda | Kanazawa (Kaga) | 1,022,700 | 1,353,300 |
| Shimazu | Kagoshima (Satsuma) | 770,800 | 869,500 |
| Date | Sendai (Mutsu) | 622,000 | 958,400 |
| Tokugawa | Wakayama (Kii) | 555,000 | 539,400 |
| Hosokawa | Kumamoto (Higo) | 540,000 | 721,000 |
| Asano | Hiroshima (Aki) | 426,000 | 488,000 |
| Mōri | Yamaguchi (Suō) | 369,000 | 713,600 |
| Ikeda | Tottori (Inaba) | 325,000 | 428,100 |
| Ikeda | Okayama (Bizen) | 315,200 | 469,100 |
| Hachisuka | Tokushima (Awa) | 257,900 | 442,700 |
| Yamanouchi | Kōchi (Tosa) | 242,000 | 494,500 |
| Satake | Akita (Dewa) | 205,800 | 312,000 |
| Nambu | Morioka (Mutsu) | 200,000 | 308,600 |
| Uesugi | Yonezawa (Dewa) | 147,200 | 284,700 |
| Tsugaru | Hirosaki (Mutsu) | 100,000 | 331,200 |
| Maeda | Toyama (Etchū) | 100,000 | 159,200 |
| Maeda | Daishōji (Kaga) | 100,000 | 83,700 |
| Sagara | Hitoyoshi (Higo) | 22,000 | 64,700 |
| Nambu | Hachinohe (Mutsu) | 20,000 | 40,000 |

2. Cf. George C. Allen, A Short Economic History of Modern Japan, 1867-1937 (London, 1946), pp. 20-21.

3. Tax rice was often measured by the hyō ("bales") containing .4 of a koku.

4. Quoted in Date Kenji, Pt. 1, 4.4:391 (1935).

5. The financial history of the Kaga han has been given detailed treatment by Tsuchiya, pp. 53-346.

6. The rate at which new ricelands increased may be seen from the following tabulation of figures given by Tsuchiya (ibid., p. 54), showing the total amount of reclaimed land at various times between 1646 and 1868:

| Year | Total Reclaimed Land (in koku) | Increment (in koku) |
|---|---|---|
| 1646 | 59,272 | 59,272 |
| 1664 | 159,115 | 99,843 |
| 1684 | 204,355 | 45,240 |
| 1711 | 261,371 | 57,016 |
| 1717 | 261,371 | none |
| 1746 | 261,371 | none |
| 1755 | 261,371 | none |
| 1760 | 261,371 | none |
| 1787 | 261,510 | 139 |
| 1789 | 261,510 | none |
| 1868 | 333,512 | 72,002 |

7.  Ibid., p. 60.

8.  Ibid., p. 61.

9.  The figures for the rice tax income and the amount of rice
    surplus shipped to Edo and Osaka at various times during the
    eighteenth and nineteenth centuries by the Kagan han are
    as follows:

| Year | Rice Tax Receipts (in koku) | Osaka shipments (in koku) |
|------|-----------------------------|---------------------------|
| 1701-1715 | 247,553* | 88,530* |
| 1767 | 250,000 | 88,000 |
| 1788 | 235,967 | 80,000 |
| 1804-1805 | 234,648* | 96,500* |
| 1824-1833 | 233,819* | 51,000* |
| 1845 | 251,304 | 70,000 |
| 1851 | 247,638 | 80,000 |
| 1868 | 250,094 | 60,400 |

(Note:  Figures marked with asterisk represent averages for
        the years indicated.)

These statistics show how little change there was in the
basic rice revenue of the han and in the amount sent to
Osaka, which provided the han with most of its money income.
(Ibid., pp. 88-89, 103, 105, 140, 142-148, 154-155.)

10. Ibid., pp. 103-104.

11. These figures are taken from budget estimates for the years
    given reproduced in Tsuchiya on the following pages:  pp.
    124-126 (1791), pp. 127-138 (1803), pp. 142-149 (1835), and
    pp. 150-153 (1848).

12. Tamura, pp. 388-390.

13. Tsuchiya, p. 133.

14. Ibid., p. 385.

15. The figures of 9,000 kamme is arrived at by adding together
    the total income from sales of rice and other produce in 1801
    (7,000 kamme), receipts from money taxes (1,500 kamme), and
    assessments on vassals' holdings (500 kamme).  Above data
    are taken from Tsuchiya's discussion of the sources of income
    of the Satsuma han (ibid., pp. 354-358).

16. Ono Takeo, Kyū Saga han no kinden seido (The equal field
    system of the old Saga domain; Tokyo, 1928), p. 44, n. 16.

17. Tamura, p. 390.

18. Ibid., pp. 390-391.

19. Takimoto Seiichi, Nihon hōken keizaishi (History of feudal economy in Japan; Tokyo, 1930), p. 138.

20. According to a survey made in 1869 by the new Meiji government, the distribution of land in the city of Edo was as follows: 11,962,000 tsubo (roughly 9,530 acres) or 68.6 per cent held by the military class, 2,661,000 tsubo or 15.6 per cent held by temples and shrines, and 2,696,000 tsubo or 15.8 per cent held by the townspeople. The greater part of the 68.6 per cent designated as military land was occupied by the yashiki or estates of the daimyo and the hatamoto. See Kōda Shigetomo, Edo to Ōsaka (Edo and Ōsaka; Tokyo, 1934), p. 17.

21. Date, 4.4:382.

22. Kōda, p. 17.

23. Date, 4.4:382.

24. Ibid.

25. Kaga han shiryō, III, 527.

26. Date, 4.4:383.

27. After the Restoration in 1868, this estate was taken over by the imperial family and became the site of the Akasaka Detached Palace.

28. Date, 4.4:383.

29. Ibid., p. 384.

30. According to Toba (p. 11), there occurred in Edo between 1601 and 1866 about 90 major fires destroying areas in excess of 10 chō (about 25 acres).

31. These figures are given in Date, 4.4:386.

32. Ibid., p. 385.

33. Date-ke monjo, in Dai Nihon komonjo, iewake monjo (Ancient documents of Japan, documents arranged according to ownership), comp. Tokyo Teikoku Daigaku Shiryō Hensansho (Tokyo Imperial University Historiographical Institute), 54 vols. (Tokyo, 1904- ), Pt. 3, VII, 354.

34. Tsuchiya, p. 106.

35. Date, 4.4:385-386.

36. Ibid., p. 388; Aomori kenshi, published by Aomori-ken (Aomori prefecture), 8 vols. (Aomori, 1926), IV, 401.

37. Shokkaben, in NKS, XXVI, 572.

38. Temmei roku, by Shōji Kōki in NKS, XXIV, 90.

39. Date, 4.4:386.

40. Ibid., p. 387.

41. Tsuchiya, pp. 98-99.

42. See above, p. 62.

43. Date, 4.4:387.

44. Ibid.

45. Tsuchiya, pp. 98-99. The 3,000 kamme was for stipends and allowances to retainers. An additional 450 kamme was alloted to salaries for hired personnel.

46. Date, 4.4:388.

47. Keizaidan, by Kaiho Seiryō in NKS, XVIII, 575.

48. Fujutsui, by Gamō Kumpei in Mishima Kichitarō, ed., Gamō Kumpei zenshū (Complete works of Gamō Kumpei; Tokyo, 1911), p. 357. Cf. translation of this passage in Honjō Eijirō, The Social and Economic History of Japan, pp. 215-216.

49. See Date, 4.4:389-395 (1935), and 6.6:555-565 (1936).

50. Ibid., 4.4:390.

51. Ibid., p. 391.

52. Ibid., p. 392.

53. Ibid., p. 393.

54. Ibid., pp. 393-394.

55. Ibid., p. 394.

56. Ibid., p. 395.

57. This table is based on figures cited by Date, 6.6:555-559.

58. This was particularly true of the Arima han which in 1814 allotted 1,303,972 kamme (21,733 ryō) or 32 per cent of its budget for Kyoto-Osaka needs. About half of this allotment was for freight charges, stipends for kuramoto or warehouse agents, and other costs of marketing the rice surplus--the main source of the han's cash revenue.

Interest payments on debts took almost all of the remainder.  For a detailed breakdown see ibid., 6.6:588.

59.  About a third of the home budget for the Maeda han in
     1747 was for expenses directly connected with the
     lord's trip to Edo.  See ibid., 6.6:556; Tsuchiya, pp. 91ff.

60.  The Satsuma han did not depend primarily on the sale of
     the surplus from its rice tax for its cash income.  Rice
     sales supplied only about a tenth of its commodity sales.
     Satsuma also enjoyed a highly profitable trade with the
     Ryukyus and China.  For details see Tsuchiya, pp. 347-543.


## V.  Contemporary Critiques of the System

1.  For Kumazawa Banzan's biography, see Inoue Tetsujirō,
    Nihon Yōmeigakuha no tetsugaku (The philosophy of the
    Yōmei school in Japan), new ed. (Tokyo, 1928), pp. 173-231;
    Robert Cornell Armstrong, Light from the East:  Studies in
    Japanese Confucianism (Toronto, 1914), pp. 142-149; Galen
    M. Fisher, "Kumazawa Banzan, His Life and Ideas," TASJ,
    second series, 16:221-258 (1938).

2.  Daigaku wakumon by Kumazawa Banzan appears in NKS, I,
    119-175.  For an English translation of this work see
    Galen M. Fisher, tr., "Dai Gaku Wakumon, A Discussion
    of Public Questions in the Light of the Great Learning,
    by Kumazawa Banzan," TASJ, second series, 16:259-356
    (1938).  Unfortunately Fisher's translation is full of
    errors and should be used with care.

3.  The trenchant criticism of the bakufu administration
    contained in this work is said to have been the cause
    of his final exile and retirement from public life in
    1687.

4.  Daigaku wakumon, NKS, I, 151; Fisher, p. 311.

5.  Daigaku wakumon, NKS, I, 142; Fisher, pp. 297-298.

6.  Daigaku wakumon, NKS, I, 150-151; Fisher, p. 311.

7.  Daigaku wakumon, NKS, I, 151; Fisher, p. 314.

8.  Daigaku wakumon, NKS, I, 151-152; Fisher, p. 314.

9.  Kumazawa arrives at this figure by pointing out that
    the average lord of a 100,000-koku domain has a total
    actual revenue of 50,000 koku, since 50 per cent of
    the crop is kept by his peasants.  After paying out
    four-fifths of this 50,000 koku in stipends and allowances

to his samurai, the lord actually nets only 10,000 koku
for his own upkeep (NKS, 1, 152). Fisher misses this point
entirely. His translation (pp. 314-315) reads: "A lord
of a castle of 100,000 koku, a medium sized fief, would
pay a tax of 50,000 koku at a rate of 50 percent, or
10,000 koku at the rate of 10 percent....The tax of 50,000
koku really becomes a 40 percent tax, when the 10,000 koku
stored for food and reserve has been deducted."

10. Daigaku wakumon, NKS, I, 152; Fisher, p. 315.

11. Daigaku wakumon, NKS, I, 153; Fisher, p. 315.

12. Daigaku wakumon, NKS, I, 153; Fisher, pp. 316-317.

13. For this judgment and a brief discussion of Ogyū Sorai's
    achievements see John Joseph Spae, Itō Jinsai, A Philosopher,
    Educator and Sinologist of the Tokugawa Period, Monumenta
    Serica, Monograph XII (Peiping, 1948), pp. 76-80.

14. The kogakuha, its origin and its social outlook, is discussed
    in ibid., pp. 72-74.

15. Seidan, by Ogyū Sorai, preface written in 1727, appears
    in NKS, III, 339-530.

16. For a description of Ogyū's position at the Edo court
    and his relations with Yoshimune, see Murdoch, III, 340-344.

17. Seidan, NKS, III, 406.

18. Ibid., p. 385.

19. Ibid., p. 386. Cf. translation in Honjō, The Social and
    Economic History of Japan, p. 123.

20. See the Taiheisaku, in NKS, III, 554-555. Cf. Honjō,
    Social and Economic History of Japan, p. 123.

21. Seidan, NKS, III, 403.

22. Ibid., p. 376.

23. Ibid., p. 404.

24. Ibid., p. 406.

25. Ibid., p. 407.

26. Ibid., p. 380.

27. Muro Kyūsō was a pupil of Kinoshita Jun'an (1621-1698),
    a Confucianist of the Chu Hsi or Sung school and teacher
    of the statesman Arai Hakuseki (1657-1725). Muro became
    a functionary of the shogunate in 1711 upon Hakuseki's

recommendation. See Papinot, p. 413. For evaluations
of Muro Kyūsō as a philosopher, see Armstrong, pp. 65-77;
and George William Knox, "A Japanese Philosopher," TASJ,
20.1:1-133 (1892).

28. Murdoch, III, 341.

29. The Kenkaroku by Muro Kyūsō appears in NKS, III, 133-226.

30. Muro reported what had taken place at his interviews with
    the shogun to one of his pupils, Aochi Tōdaifu, who re-
    corded the information in letters to his brother, Kurando.
    These letters and others received by the two brothers
    from Muro himself were later compiled in a work known as
    Kenzan hissaku, which appears in NKS, II, 167-661.

31. Kenzan hissaku, NKS, II, 515; Murdoch, III, 360.

32. Kenkaroku, NKS, III, 155.

33. Ibid., NKS, III, 155-156; Kenzan hissaku, NKS, II, 517-518.

34. Honjo Eijirō, "Sankin kōtai seido no keizai kan," 4.4:530.
    Cf. also Shibusawa Eiichi, ed., Tokugawa Keiki-Ko den
    (Biography of Prince Tokugawa Keiki), 8 vols. (Tokyo, 1918),
    II, 92-93.

35. Yoshimune was familiar at first hand with the hardships
    imposed upon the daimyo. He had performed the sankin kōtai
    for almost twenty years as a daimyo before he became
    shogun, from 1697 to 1705, as the lord of Nibu (Echizen--
    30,000 koku), and from 1705 to 1716 as the daimyo of
    Wakayama, the seat of the Kii branch of the Tokugawa house.

36. Kenzan hissaku, NKS, II, 519.

37. For text of this order see the Kinreikō, IV, 517-518;
    and Miura Kikutarō, pp. 266-267.

38. Yoshida Tōgo, Tokugawa seikyōko (Survey of Tokugawa politics
    and education; Tokyo, 1918), p. 175.

39. For a table published in 1722 showing the revised sankin
    dates of the 267 daimyo of that date, see Hibata, p. 381.

40. Kinreikō, IV, 518.

41. Mikami Sanji, Edo jidaishi, II, 155.

42. For the order restoring the old schedule and abolishing
    the rice tax, see Kinreikō, IV, 518-519.

43. For biographical details on Nakai Chikuzan, see Honjō
    Eijirō, ed., Nihon keizaishi jiten, II, 1214-15. The
    Sōbō kigen, written by Nakai Chikuzan in 1789, appears

in NKS, XVI, 261-450. This work has been ranked by
Profesor Honjō with Ogyū Sorai's Seidan as one of the
outstanding works on Tokugawa institutions (Nihon keizaishi
jiten, II, 1214).

44. Matsudaira Sadanobu (1758-1829) was the seventh son of
    Tayasu Munetake (d. 1769), one of the sons of the eighth
    shogun, Yoshimune. In 1774, he was adopted by Matsudaira
    (Hisamatsu) Sadakuni (1728-1790) and, in 1783, succeeded
    him as daimyo of Shirakawa (Mutsu--110,000 koku). In 1787,
    he was appointed a senior councillor (rōjū) and three years
    later became regent (hōsa) to the eleventh shogun, Ienari.
    Until his retirement in 1812, he took a leading part in the
    bakufu administration.

45. Sōbō kigen, NKS, XVI, 301-302.

46. Ibid., p. 303.

47. Ibid.

48. Ibid., pp. 305-306.

49. Ibid., p. 307.

50. Ibid., pp. 306-307.

51. Yoshida, pp. 288-289. Matsudaira Sadanobu's proposals
    are found in a work entitled Kankodori (dates unknown)
    in Ema Seihatsu, ed., Rakuō-Kō isho (The literary remains
    of Lord Rakuō), 3 vols. (Tokyo, 1893), Vol. I. The pro-
    posal on the sankin kōtai is also quoted in Honjō,
    "Sankin kōtai seido no keizai kan," 4.4:531.

52. Sōbō kigen tekigi by Jin Ikō, NKS, XXIV, 536-537. For
    details on Jin Ikō's background, see the bibliographical
    notes by Takimoto Siichi, the editor of the NKS, Vol.
    XXIV, p. xii.

53. The Sōbō kigen tekigi appears in NKS, XXIV, 521-561.

54. Ibid., p. 536.

55. Ibid., pp. 538-539.

## VI. The End of the System

1. This type of violation was apparently common since early in the eighteenth century. In a memorial presented to the shogun Yoshimune shortly after 1716, Sakai Tadataka (1648-1720), ex-lord of Umayabashi (Kozuke--150,000 koku), pointed out that the sankin kōtai schedules were being ignored by many of the lords. He asserted that the daimyo with domains along the Tōkaidō were without exception remaining in Edo and thus neglecting their responsibilities as territorial rulers. See Mikami Sanji, Edo jidaishi, II, 135-136.

2. Matsuura Kiyoshi (style: Seizan), Kasshi yawa (Night tales of Kasshi), completed between 1821 and 1841 in 200 kan. The modern edition is in 6 volumes, constituting Vols. 8 to 13 in the third series of the Kokusho kankō kai sōsho (Series of the Society for the Publication of Japanese Texts), 260 vols. (Tokyo, 1906-1922).

3. Ibid., 3rd series, IX, 292-293.

4. The text of this edict may be found in the Zoku Tokugawa jikki (Vols. 48-52 in KT), Vol. 49, p. 438. It is cited also in Miura Kikutarō, p. 269; and in Honjō Eijirō, "Sankin kōtai seido no keizai kan," 4.4:538.

5. Rin Shihei (1738-1793), a samurai scholar of the Date han of Sendai, was the author of two famous works, the Sangoku tsūran (1786) and Kaikoku heidan (1792), in which he tried to warn of the peril to Japan of Russian expansionism and argued the necessity for strengthening Japan's coastal defenses against foreign attack. For expressing these ideas too forcefully and for exalting the authority of the emperor to the prejudice of the shogunate, Rin was imprisoned in 1793 and died that year while in confinement. See Papinot, p. 148; Murdoch, III, 426; Sansom, The Western World and Japan, pp. 213-214. Rin also expressed himself on the subject of the sankin kōtai, declaring in a memorial to his lord that it was the principal cause of the bankruptcy of the daimyo. For text of this memorial, see Tamura, pp. 403-405.

6. For an excellent discussion of the role of these men and their ideas in the Restoration movement, see Sansom, The Western World and Japan, pp. 248-274.

7. Matsudaira Shungaku (also known as Yoshinaga) was born into the Tayasu branch of the Tokugawa family, and was adopted into the Echizen house, the ranking kamon daimyo.

8. Abe Masahiro (1819-1857), lord of Fukuyama (Bingo--110,000 koku) was senior councilor from 1843 to 1857.

9. For a discussion of Abe's request for advice and the response from the daimyo, see Murdoch, III, 589-593; Sansom, The Western World and Japan, p. 282.

10. Shibusawa, ed., Tokugawa Keiki-Kō den, II, 93.

11. The full text of this memorial is reproduced in Hamano Shōkichi, ed., Kaikyū kiji (Record of the past; Tokyo, 1899), appendix, pp. 122-128. It is quoted in Honjō, "Sankin kōtai seido no keizai kan," p. 535.

12. Honjō, p. 535. Abe is reported to have remarked that such proposals were not only uncalled for but unhealthy for the person making them (Shibusawa, II, 93-94).

13. Keiki (also read Yoshinobu) was a son of the lord of Mito, Tokugawa Nariaki (1800-1860), the leader of the anti-foreign and loyalist party which opposed the opening of the country to foreign intercourse and advocated the restoration of imperial power. Keiki figured in the succession dispute in 1858 at the death of the thirteenth shogun, Iesada, when he was presented by his father as the candidate for the shogunacy against the rival claim of Iemochi of the Kii branch. The latter was championed successfully by the faction headed by the tairō, Lord Ii Naosuke (1815-1860), the signer of the Harris treaty of 1858. Keiki and Matsudaira Shungaku were among the leaders of the movement supported by many of the leading feudatories and adherents of the Tokugawa house to save the bakufu by making concessions to the Kyoto court, which was then becoming the rallying point of a growing number of anti-bakufu samurai.

14. The office of seiji sōsai was newly created in the seventh month of 1862 by command of the emperor and lasted until 1864. Its function was to reform the bakufu administration and take over the direction of affairs, temporarily replacing in this capacity the shogun, who was proving unable to cope with the pressing problems of the times. See Kokushi daijiten, II, 1517; cf. also Papinot, p. 550.

15. Yokoi Shōnan's writings have been compiled in Yokoi Tokio, ed., Shōnan ikō (The literary remains of Shōnan; Tokyo, 1889). For a brief discussion of Yokoi Shōnan's career and ideas, see Sansom, The Western World and Japan, pp. 266-269.

16. Yokoi, p. 146. Also quoted in Honjō, "Sankin kōtai seido no keizai kan," p.535.

17. Tokutomi, XLVII, 293.

18. The reforms of 1862 included, in addition to the revision of the sankin kōtai, the purge of almost all the officials connected with the negotiation of foreign treaties, the punishment by reduction of income and by confinement of the supporters of Lord Ii Naosuke (Ii had dealt similarly with opponents of his policy four years earlier), the reorganization of the bakufu military and coastal defense system to strengthen the country against foreign attack, and such minor changes as revision of official dress regulations.

19. Okabe Nagatsune was also a Commissioner for Foreign Affairs (gaikoku bugyō) since 1861.

20. Yokoi, p. 374. Cited in Honjō, "Sankin kōtai seido no keizai kan," p. 536; Tokutomi, XLVIII, 21.

21. Ōkubo Ichiō (also known as Tadahiro) was a junior councilor (wakadoshiyori) in 1857 and was now a secretary to the shogun (sobayō toritsugi).

22. Sansom, The Western World and Japan, p. 268. Cf. Shibusawa, II, 98.

23. For the text of these regulations see Kinreikō, I, 399-401. See also Honjō, "Sankin kōtai seido no keizai kan," p. 536; Tokutomi, XLVIII, 159-162; Shibusawa, II, 94-98; Ihara Gi, pp. 808-809.

24. Quoted in Murdoch, III, 723. This work, which is supposed to be a contemporary record of events by a Kyoto resident, has been translated by Sir Ernest M. Satow (Japan 1853-1864 Genji Yume Monogatari, by Baba Bunyei [Tokyo, 1905]).

25. For a full discussion of the bakufu's abortive attempt to restore the sankin kōtai system, see Hara Denzō, "Genji gannen sankin kōtai oyobi saishi zaifu sei no fukkyū jijō" (The circumstances of the revival of the sankin kōtai and family hostage system in 1864), Rekishi chiri (Historical geography), 33.2:130-135 (1919). For a brief account, see also Ihara, pp. 926-929.

# BIBLIOGRAPHY

## Bibliographical Note

The principal sources for this study have been the published collections of official and private documents of the Tokugawa era available in the United States as of 1951. It was unfortunately not possible for the author to conduct any of his research in Japan, where he could have had access to the documentary materials in public and private archives or special collections which might have been pertinent to this study. Some of these materials have, however, since been incorporated into the printed collections being published by the Historiographical Institute of Tokyo University and other organizations engaged in compiling historical materials. The author regrets that he has not been able to examine these later accretions or to take into account studies of Tokugawa feudal society published in the last fifteen years. It may be said, however, that postwar Japanese scholars have devoted relatively little attention to the subject of Tokugawa institutional development and that no recent studies of the sankin kōtai have been made.

The most useful documentary sources for this study were the Tokugawa kinreikō, the chief source for the statutes which defined the sankin kōtai; the Tokugawa jikki and the Zoku Tokugawa jikki (Vols. 38-47 and 48-52, respectively, of the Shintei zōho kokushi taikei), the official annals of the Tokugawa shogunate; Section 12 of the Dai Nihon shiryō, a rich collection of public and private documents pertinent to the history of the early years of the shogunate; the Nihon keizai sōsho, which provided the texts of the treatises by Tokugawa writers on the sankin kōtai system; and the Kaga han shiryō, which are the published documents of the Maeda family. The Koji ruien furnished many helpful details concerning the establishment and regulation of the system. Indispensable for a picture of the actual structure of the system at any given time were the bukan or books of heraldry and directories of the military peerage published regularly for popular reference during the Tokugawa period. A large number of bukan have been published in the Daibukan, edited by Hashimoto Hiroshi.

Secondary materials on the sankin kōtai system are relatively scanty. Kurita Motoji gives the best concise summary in his article "Sankin kōdai" in the historical

encyclopedia Kokushi jiten (Vol. IV, pp. 483-485). A brief
outline of the institutional structure of the system is found
in Miura Kikutarō, Nihon hōseishi (pp. 260-279). Mikami
Sanji evaluates the system as an instrument of political
control in his essay "Edo bakufu no jūyō naru seisaku," in
Edo jidai shiron. Honjō Eijirō discusses the economic aspects
of the system as seen by contemporary Tokugawa writers in
"Sankin kōtai seido no keizai kan," in Keizai ronsō. Date
Kenji's article, "Edo ni okeru shokō no shōhiteki seikatsu
ni tsuite" (in Rekishigaku kenkyū), and Tsuchiya Takao's
Hōken shakai hōkai katei no kenkyū provided much statistical
data on the economic impact of the system on daimyo finances.

Allen, George C., A Short Economic History of Modern Japan,
    1867-1937 (London, 1946).

Aoe Shū 青江秀 , Dai Nihon Teikoku ekitei shikō 大日
    本帝國驛遞志稿 (Draft history of the post
    stations of Japan), Vol. X in Nihon sangyō shiryō taikei
    日本産業史料大系 (Compendium of materials
    on Japanese industry), 13 vols. (Tokyo, 1928).

Aoki Busuke 青木武助 , Shintei Dai Nihon rekishi shūsei
    新訂大日本歴史集成 (New revised composite
    history of Japan), 5 vols. (Tokyo, 1933).

Aomori kenshi 青森縣史 (History of Aomori prefecture),
    published by Aomori-ken 青森縣 (Aomori prefecture),
    8 vols. (Aomori, 1926).

Arai Hakuseki 新井白石 , Hankampu 藩翰譜 (Genealogies
    of the feudal families), modern edition by Urushiyama
    Matashirō 漆山又四郎 , ed., 2 vols. (Tokyo, 1926).

Armstrong, Robert Cornell, Light From the East: Studies in
    Japanese Confucianism (Toronto, 1914).

Asakawa Kanichi, The Early Institutional Life of Japan:  A
    Study in the Reform of 645 A.D. (Tokyo, 1903).

----"Some Aspects of Japanese Feudal Institutions," TASJ,
    46.1:76-102 (1918).

----The Documents of Iriki (New Haven, 1929).

Biot, Eduard, Le Tcheou Li ou Rites des Tcheou (Paris, 1851).

Cocks, Richard, The Diary of Richard Cocks, Cape Merchant in the English Factory in Japan, 1615-1622, with correspondence, ed. Edward Maunde Thompson, 2 vols. (Tokyo, 1899).  Additional notes by N. Murakami.

Courant, Maurice, "Les clans japonais sous les Tokugawas," Annales du Musée Guimet, Bibliothèque de Vulgarisation, 15:1-82 (1904).

Couvreur, S., Dictionnaire classique de la langue Chinoise (Ho Kien Fou, 1911).

Dai Nihon komonjo, iewake monjo 大日本古文書, 家わけ 文書 (Ancient documents of Japan, documents arranged according to ownership), comp. Tokyo Teikoku Daigaku Shiryō Hensansho 東京帝國大學史料編纂所 (Tokyo Imperial University Historiographical Institute), 54 vols. (Tokyo, 1904- ).

Dai Nihon shiryō (see under DNS).

Date Kenji 伊達研次, "Edo ni okeru shokō no shōhiteki seikatsu ni tsuite" 江戸に於ける諸侯の消費的 生活に就いて (On the life of the feudal lords in Edo as consumers), Rekishigaku kenkyū 歴史學研究 (Journal of the Historical Science Society), 4.4:389-395 (1935), 6.6:555-565 (1936).

Date Masamune-Kyō denki shiryō 伊達正宗卿傳記史料 (Historical materials for the biography of Lord Date Masamune), comp. Hanso Date Masamune-Kō Kenshōkai 藩祖伊達正宗公顯彰会 (Han founder Lord Date Masamune Memorial Association; Sendai, 1938).

DNS: Dai Nihon shiryō 大日本史料 (Japanese historical materials), comp. Tokyo Teikoku Daigaku Shiryō Hensansho, 176 vols. (Tokyo, 1901- ).

Droppers, Garret, "The Population of Japan in the Tokugawa Period," TASJ, 22.2:269-331 (1894).

Ema Seihatsu 江間政發, ed., Rakuō-Kō isho 樂翁 公遺書 (The literary remains of Lord Rakuō), 3 vols. (Tokyo, 1893).

Fisher, Galen M., tr., "Dai Gaku Wakumon, A Discussion of Public Questions in the Light of the Great Learning, by Kumazawa Banzan," TASJ, second series, 16:259-356 (1938).

208

----"Kumazawa Banzan, His Life and Ideas," TASJ, second series, 16:221-258 (1938).

Gubbins, J.H., "The Feudal System in Japan under the Tokugawa Shoguns," TASJ, 15.2:133-141 (1887).

Hagino Yoshiyuki 萩野由之 et al., eds., Nihon kodai hōten 日本古代法典 (Ancient Japanese laws; Tokyo, 1903).

Hall, John Carey, "Japanese Feudal Laws III--The Tokugawa Legislation," TASJ, 38.4:269-331 (1911).

Hamano Shōkichi 濱野章吉 , ed., Kaikyū kiji 懷舊紀事 (Record of the past; Tokyo, 1899).

Hara Denzō 原傳藏, "Genji gannen sankin kōtai oyobi saishi zaifu sei no fukkyū jijō" 元治元年參覲交代及び妻子在府制の復舊事情 (The circumstances of the revival of the sankin kōtai and family hostage system in 1864), Rekishi chiri 歴史地理 (Historical geography), 33.2:130-135 (1919).

Hashimoto Hiroshi 橋本博, ed., Daibukan 大武鑑 (Great military mirror), 12 vols. (Tokyo, 1935-1936).

Hibata Sekko 樋畑雪湖 , Edo jidai no kōtsū bunka 江戸時代の交通文化 (Transportation culture of the Edo period; Tokyo, 1931).

Honjō Eijirō 本庄榮次郎 , "Sankin kōtai seido no keizai kan" 參覲交代制度の經濟觀 (Economic aspects of the sankin kōtai system), Keizai ronsō 經濟論叢 (Economic review), 3.6:828-841 (1916),4.4:521-540 (1917).

----The Social and Economic History of Japan (Kyoto, 1935).

----, ed., Nihon keizaishi jiten 日本經濟史辞典 (Dictionary of Japanese economic history), 2 vols. (2nd ed., Kyoto, 1942).

Hotta Masaatsu, ed., Kansei chōshū shokafu (see under Shokafu).

Ihara Gi 井原儀 , Tokugawa jidai tsūshi 德川時代通史 (Common history of the Tokugawa period; Tokyo, 1928).

Ikeda Kōen 池田晃淵 , Edo jidaishi jō 江戸時代史上 (History of the early Edo period), Vol. IX of the Nihon jidaishi 日本時代史 (History of Japan by periods), 14 vols. (Tokyo, 1926-1927).

Inoue Tetsujirō 井上哲次郎, Nihon Yōmeigakuha no tetsugaku 日本陽明學派の哲學 (The philosophy of the Yōmei school in Japan), new ed. (Tokyo, 1928).

Izomodera Manjirō, Taisei bukan (see under Taisei bukan).

Kaempfer, Englebert, History of Japan, Together with a Description of the Kingdom of Siam, 1690-1692, 3 vols. (Glasgow, 1906).

Kaga han shiryō 加賀藩史料 (Historical materials of the Kaga domain), comp. Kōshaku Maeda-ke henshusho 侯爵前田家編輯所 (Publication Office of the House of Marquis Maeda), 13 vols. (Kanazawa, 1929-1933).

Katsu Kaishū 勝海舟, Suijinroku 吹塵錄 (Records), Vols. III and IV of Kaishū zenshū 海舟全集 (Complete works of Kaishū), 10 vols. (Tokyo, 1928).

Kawakami Tasuke 川上多助, "Toshi to shite no Kamakura" 都市としての鎌倉 (Kamakura as a city), Rekishi chiri 歷史地理 (Historical geography), Vol. 3, No. 4 (1918).

Kinreiko: Shihōshō 司法省 (Ministry of Justice), Tokugawa kinreikō 德川禁令考 (Survey of Tokugawa laws), 6 vols. (Tokyo, 1931-1932).

Knox, George William, "A Japanese Philosopher," TASJ, 20.1:1-133 (1892).

Kōda Shigetomo 幸田成友, Edo to Ōsaka 江戸と大阪 (Edo and Osaka; Tokyo, 1934).

Koji ruien 古事類苑 (Encyclopedia of ancient matters), revised popular ed., 60 vols. (Tokyo: Jingū Shichō 神宮司廳 [Office of Shrine Affairs], 1933-1936).

Kokushi daijiten: Yashiro Kuniharu 八代國治 et al., eds., Daizōtei kokushi daijiten 大增訂國史大辞典 (Further revised and supplemented dictionary of Japanese history), 7th ed., 6 vols. (Tokyo, 1930).

Kokushi jiten 國史辞典 (Dictionary of Japanese history), 4 vols. (Tokyo, 1940-1943).

KT: Kuroita Katsumi 黑板勝美, ed., Shintei zōho kokushi taikei 新訂增補國史大系 (Revised and supplemented compendium of Japanese history), 58 vols. (Tokyo, 1929- ).

Kurita Motoji 栗田元次, Edo jidai jō 江戸時代上 (The early Edo period), Vol. IX of Sōgō Nihonshi taikei 綜合日本史大系 (Synthetic survey of Japanese history; Tokyo, 1926).

Kuroita Katsumi (see under KT).

KZ: Kaishu zenshū (see under Katsu Kaishū).

Legge, James, The Lî Kî, A Collection of Treatises on the Rules of Propriety or Ceremonial Usages, Vol. XXVIII in F. Max Müller, ed., The Sacred Books of the East (Oxford, 1885).

----The Chinese Classics, 2nd ed., 7 vols. (Oxford, 1895).

Manchester, Curtis A., "The Development and Distribution of Sekisho in Japan," Ph.D. thesis (University of Michigan, 1946).

Matsudaira Tarō 松平太郎, Edo jidai seido no kenkyū 江戸時代制度の研究 (A study of the Edo period administrative system; Tokyo, 1919).

Matsuura Kiyoshi 松浦清, Kasshi yawa 甲子夜話 (Night tales of Kasshi), 6 vols. (Vols. 8-13 in the third series of the Kokusho kanko-kai sosho 國書刊行会叢書 [Series of the Society for the Publication of Japanese Texts], 260 vols. [Tokyo, 1906-1922]).

Mikami Sanji 三上参次, "Edo bakufu no jūyō naru seisaku" 江戸幕府の重要なる政策 (Important policies of the Edo Shogunate), Edo jidai shiron 江戸時代史論 (Essays on Edo period history; Tokyo, 1915), pp. 31-65.

----Edo jidaishi 江戸時代史 (A history of the Edo period), 2 vols. (Tokyo, 1944).

Mishima Kichitarō 三島吉太郎, ed., Gamō Kumpei zenshū 蒲生君平全集 (Complete works of Gamō Kumpei; Tokyo, 1911).

Miura Kaneyuki 三浦周行, Hōseishi no kenkyū 法制史の研究 (Studies in legal history), new ed., 2 vols. (Tokyo, 1943-1944).

Miura Kikutarō 三浦菊太郎, Nihon hōseishi 日本法制史 (A history of Japanese legislation), 3rd ed. (Tokyo, 1910).

Murdoch, James, History of Japan, 3 vols. (London, 1925-1926).

Naitō Chisō 内藤耻叟 , ed., Tokugawa jūgodaishi
德川十五代史 (A history of the fifteen Tokugawa
generations), 12 vols. (Tokyo, 1892-1893).

Nakamura Kōya 中村孝也 , "Daimyo no kenkyū" 大
名の研究 (A study of the daimyo) in Miyake Hakase
koki shukuga kinen rombunshū 三宅博士古稀
祝賀記念論文集 (Collection of mono-
graphs commemorating the 70th birthday of Dr. Miyake;
Tokyo, 1929), pp. 329-385.

Nihon zuihitsu taisei 日本隨筆大成 (Collection of
Japanese miscellanies), 3 series, 37 vols. (Tokyo,
1927-1931).

NKS: Takimoto Seiichi 瀧本誠一 , ed., Nihon
keizai sōsho 日本經済叢書 (Documentary
series on Japanese economics), 36 vols. (Tokyo, 1914-1917).

Nonaka Jun 野中準 et al., eds., Dai Nihon sozeishi
大日本租税史 (History of Japanese taxation),
3 vols. (Tokyo, 1926-1927).

Ono Kiyoshi 小野清 , Tokugawa seido shiryō 德川制
度史料 (Historical materials on the Tokugawa administrative system; Tokyo, 1927).

Ono Takeo 小野武夫 , Kyū Saga han no kinden seido
舊佐賀藩の均田制度 (The equal field
system of the old Saga domain; Tokyo, 1928).

Papinot, E., Historical and Geographical Dictionary of Japan
(Yokohama, 1910).

Pratt, Peter, History of Japan, Compiled from the Records of
the English East India Company, 1882, ed. M. Paske-Smith,
2 vols. (Kobe, 1931).

Ryō Susumu 龍肅 , Kamakura jidai no kenkyū 鎌倉時
代の研究 (A study of the Kamakura period; Tokyo, 1945).

Saitō Ryūzō 斎藤隆三 , Kinsei Nihon sesōshi 近世
日本世想史 (History of modern Japanese life;
Tokyo, 1925).

Sansom, George B., Japan: A Short Cultural History, rev. ed.
(New York, 1943).

----The Western World and Japan (New York, 1950).

212

Shibusawa Eiichi 澁澤榮一, ed., Tokugawa Keiki-Kō den 德川慶喜公傳 (Biography of Prince Tokugawa Keiki), 8 vols. (Tokyo, 1918).

Shihōshō (see under Kinreikō).

Shimmi Kichiji 新見吉治, Nihon ni okeru buke seiji no rekishi 日本に於ける武家政治の歴史 (The history of feudal military rule in Japan; Osaka, 1941).

Shimonaka Yasaburō 下中彌三郎, ed., Daijiten 大辞典 (Encyclopedia), 26 vols. (Tokyo, 1933).

Shokafu: Hotta Masaatsu 堀田政敦 (1758-1832), ed., Kansei chōshū shokafu 寛政重修諸家譜 (Kansei collated genealogies), modern printed ed., 9 vols. (Tokyo, 1918). First ed. completed in 1812 in 1530 kan.

Smith, Neil Skene, ed., "Materials on Japanese Social and Economic History: Tokugawa Japan," TASJ, second series, 14:1-176 (1937).

Spae, John Joseph, Itō Jinsai, A Philosopher, Educator and Sinologist of the Tokugawa Period, Monumenta Serica, Monograph XII (Peiping, 1948).

Taisei bukan: Izumodera Manjirō 出雲寺萬次郎, Taisei bukan 大成武鑑 (Taisei military mirror), 3 vols. ([Edo], 1853).

Takekoshi Yosaburō, The Economic Aspects of the History of the Civilization of Japan, 3 vols. (New York, 1930).

Takimoto Seiichi 瀧本誠一, Nihon hōken keizaishi 日本封建經済史 (History of feudal economy in Japan; Tokyo, 1930).

----, ed., Nihon keizai sōsho (see under NKS).

Tamura Eitarō 田村榮太郎, Kinsei Nihon kōtsūshi 近世日本交通史 (History of transportation in modern Japan; Tokyo, 1935).

TASJ: Transactions of the Asiatic Society of Japan.

Toba Masao 鳥羽正雄, "Edo jidai no rinsei" 江戸時代の林政 (Forestry administration in the Edo period), in case 9 of the Iwanami koza: Nihon rekishi 岩波講座：日本歴史 (Iwanami series on Japanese history), 18 cases (Tokyo, 1933-1935).

Tokugawa kinreikō (see under Kinreikō).

Tokushi biyō 讀 史 備 要 (Handbook of Japanese history),
comp. Tokyo Teikoku Daigaku Shiryō Hensansho (Tokyo, 1933).

Tokutomi Iichirō 德 富 猪 一 郎 , Kinsei Nihon kokuminshi
近 世 日 本 國 民 史 (A history of the Japanese people in
the modern period), 50 vols. (Tokyo, 1935-1936).

Tsuchiya Takao 土 屋 喬 雄 , Hōken shakai hōkai katei
no kenkyū 封 建 社 會 崩 壞 過 程 の 研 究
(A study of the process of decay of feudal society), 2nd
ed. (Tokyo, 1930).

Watanabe Yosuke 渡 邊 世 祐 , Daimyō hen 大 名 編
(Volume on the daimyo), Vol. III of the Ruishū denki Dai
Nihonshi 類 聚 傳 記 大 日 本 史 (A biographical
history of Japan), 15 vols. (Tokyo, 1934).

Yamaga Sokō 山 鹿 素 行 , Buke jiki 武 家 事 紀
(Chronicle of the feudal military families), modern ed.,
3 vols. (Tokyo, 1915-1918). Compiled in 1673.

Yashiro Kuniharu (see under Kokushi daijiten).

Yokoi Tokio 橫 井 時 雄 , ed., Shōnan ikō 小 南 遺 稿
(The literary remains of Shōnan; Tokyo, 1889).

Yoshida Tōgo 吉 田 東 伍 , Tokugawa seikyōko 德 川 政
教 考 (Survey of Tokugawa politics and education;
Tokyo, 1918).

# GLOSSARY

Abe Masahiro 阿部正弘
agemai 上米
Akizuki Tanenaga 秋月種長
Andō Hiroshige 安藤廣重
Aochi Kurando 青地藏人
Aochi Tōdaifu 青地藤太夫
Arima Toyouji 有馬豊氏
Asano kafu 淺野家譜
Asano Nagamasa 淺野長政
Asano Nagashige 淺野長重
Asano Yoshinaga 淺野幸長
ashigaru 足輕
Azuma kagami 吾妻鏡
Babasaki 馬場先
bajō 馬上
budōjō 武道場
bukan 武鑑
buke shohatto 武家諸法度
bungen 分限
Bunkai zakki 文會雜記
chabentōki 茶便當器
chō 町
chōnin 町人
Chu-hou pei-mien erh chien
  t'ien-tzu yüeh chin 諸侯
北面而見天子曰覲

chūgen 中間
Chü li 曲禮
dai-gasa 臺笠
Daigaku wakumon 大學或問
daikan 代官
daimyō 大名
date dōgu 伊達道具
Date Hidemune 伊達秀宗
Date-ke monjo 伊達家文書
Date Masamune 伊達正宗
de-onna ni iri-deppō 出女に
入り鐵砲
Endō Yoshitaka 遠藤慶隆
fuchi 扶持
fudai 譜代
Fujutsui 不恤緯
Fukushima Masanori 福島正則
gaikoku bugyō 外國奉行
gakumonjo 學問所
Gamō Kumpei 蒲生君平
gan-no-ma 雁間
go-tairō 五大老
Gofukubashi 吳服橋
gokenin 御家人

Hachisuka Yoshishige 蜂須賀至鎮

haidai 盃臺

hairyō mono 拜領物

hanchi 半知

Hanzō 半藏

hasami-bako 挾箱

Hassaku 入朔

hatamoto 旗下

Hibiya 日比谷

Hidetada [Tokugawa] 秀忠

hitojichi 人質

Hitotsubashi 一橋

Hitotsubashi Keiki 一橋慶喜

Hitotsuyanagi Naomori 一柳直盛

honjin 本陣

Horeki reiten eikan 寶曆令典永鑑

Hori Hideharu 堀秀治

hosa 輔佐

Hosokawa Tadaoki 細川忠興

Hosokawa Tadatoshi 細川忠利

hyō 俵

hyōjōsho 評定所

Iemitsu [Tokugawa] 家光

Iemochi [Tokugawa] 家茂

Ienari [Tokugawa] 家齊

Ienobu [Tokugawa] 家宣

Iesada [Tokugawa] 家定

Ietsuna [Tokugawa] 家綱

Ieyasu [Tokugawa] 家康

Ii Naosuke 井伊直弼

Ikeda Mitsumasa 池田光政

Ikeda Tadatsugu 池田忠繼

Ikeda Terumasa 池田輝政

Ikoma Kazumasa 生駒一正

jifuku 時服

Jin Ikō 神惟考

jinsei 仁政

jinya-mochi 陣屋持

jisha bugyō 寺社奉行

jitō 地頭

jitsudaka 實高

jōdai 城代

jōfu 定府

jōshi 上使

jōshu 城主

jōshu-kaku 城主格

jōshu-nami 城主並

jun-kokushu 準國主

jusshoku 述識

Kaga Shōun Kō den 加賀松雲公傳

kago 駕籠

Kaiho Seiryō 海保青陵

Kaikoku beidan 海國兵談

Kajibashi 鍛治橋

kaku 格

kami yashiki 上屋敷

Kamigata 上方

kamme 貫目

kamon 家門

Kandabashi 神田橋

Kan'ei 寛永
kan'i bu 官位部
kanjō bugyō 勘定奉行
Kankodori 諫皷鳥
kariage 借上
karō 家老
katabira 帷子
Katō Kiyomasa 加藤清正
Katō Tadahiro 加藤忠廣
Katō Yoshiaki 加藤嘉明
Keichō 慶長
Keiki [Tokugawa] 慶喜
Keizaidan 經濟談
Kemmu shikimoku tsuika 建武
　　式目追加
Kenchō 建長
kenjō mono 獻上物
Kenkaroku 獻可錄
Kenzan hissoku 兼山秘策
kiku-no-ma 菊間
kimbanshi 勤番士
Kinoshita Jun'an 木下順庵
kirimai 切米
kogakuha 古學派
koku 石
koku daka 石高
kokushu 國主
komono 小者
kosode 小袖
kōtai yoriai 交代寄合
Kumazawa Banzan 熊澤番山

kunimochi 國持
kunimochi-nami 國持並
kura-iri 藏入
kuramoto 藏元
Kuroda Nagamasa 黑田長政

Li chi 禮記

machi bugyō 町奉行
madai 馬代
Maeda Toshiie 前田利家
Maeda Toshinaga 前田利長
Maeda Toshitsune 前田利常
Maeda Tsunatoshi 前田綱紀
mangoku ijō 萬石以上
Masuda Nagamori 増田長盛
Matsudaira Hideyasu 松平秀康
Matsudaira Nobutsuna 松平信綱
Matsudaira Sadakuni 松平定邦
Matsudaira Sadanobu 松平定信
Matsudaira Shungaku (Yoshinaga)
　　松平春嶽（慶永）
Matsudaira Tadamasa 松平忠昌
Matsudaira Tadateru 松平忠輝
Matsuura Atsunobu 松浦篤信
Matsuura Hisanobu 松浦久信
Matsuura Shigenobu 松浦鎮信
Matsuura Takanobu 松浦隆信
metsuke 目付
Minamoto no Yoritomo 源賴朝
Mizuno Tadayuki 水野忠之
Mōri Terumoto 毛利輝元

Moriyama 守山
mujō 無城
Muro Kyūsō 室鳩巣
myōden 名田

Nabeshima Katsushige 鍋島勝茂
Nabeshima Naoshige 鍋島直茂
Nabeshima Narinao 鍋島齊直
Nabeshima Tadashige 鍋島忠茂
nagamochi 長持
nai jih chin ssu-yüen ch'un-
    mu 乃日觀四岳羣牧
naidaka 内高
naka yashiki 中屋敷
Nakae Tōju 中江藤樹
Nakai Chikuzan 中井竹山
Nakasendō 中仙道
Nambu Shigenao 南部重直
nengu 年貢
ninsoku 人足
Nishimaru-Ōte 西丸大手
nōhei 農兵
norimono 乘物

ōban'yaku 大番役
ōbiroma 大廣間
Oda Nobunaga 織田信長
Ogyū Sorai 荻生徂徠
Okabe Nagatsune 岡部長常
Ōkubo Ichiō (Tadahiro) 大久保
    一翁（忠寬）
ōmetsuke 大目付

omotedaka 表高
ōrōka 大廊下
Ōte 大手
ōyuka 大床

ri 里
Rikkokushi 六國史
Rin Shihei 林子平
rōjū 老中
rōnin 浪人or牢人
rusui 留守居
ryō 兩
ryōshu 領主
ryoshuku seikatsu 旅宿生活

Sagara Nagatsune 相良長毎
Saiwaibashi 幸橋
Sakai Tadataka 酒井忠擧
sampu kenjō 參府獻上
Sangoku tsuran 三國通覽
sanke 三家
sankin kōtai 參覲（勤）交
    代（替）
Satake Yoshinobu 佐竹義宣
sei-i tai shōgun 征夷大將軍
Seidan 政談
seiji sōsai 政事總裁
Seizan 靜山
sekisho 關所
"Sekisho sōran" 關所總覽
shimadai 島臺
Shimazu Iehisa 島津家久

Shimazu Tadahisa 島津忠久
shimo yashiki 下屋敷
shimpan 親藩
shita yado 下宿
Shōchō 正長
shōen 莊園
Shōji Kōki 正司考祺
Shokkaben 食貨辨
Shoku Nihongi 續日本紀
shōmyō 小名
shōnin 證人
shoshidai 所司代
Shu ching 書經
shugo 守護
Shun tien 舜典
sobashū 側衆
sobayō toritsugi 側用取次
sobayōnin 側用人
Sōbō kigen 草茅危言
Sōbō kigen tekigi 草茅危言
　摘議
sōshaban 奏者番
Soto-Sakurada 外櫻田
Sukiyabashi 數寄屋橋

Taiheisaku 太平策
tairō 大老
taka 高
Takebashi 竹橋
tamari-no-ma 溜間
tate-gasa 立傘
Tayasu 田安

Tayasu Munetake 田安宗武
teikan-no-ma 帝鑑間
Temmei roku 天命錄
tenryō 天領
tetsudai 手傳
Tōdō Takatora 藤堂高虎
Tōeizan 東叡山
Tōkaidō 東海道
toki kenjō 時獻上
Tokiwabashi 常盤橋
Tokugawa jikki 德川實紀
Tokugawa Mitsusada 德川光貞
Tokugawa Nariaki 德川齊昭
Tokugawa Yorinobu 德川賴宣
Toyotomi Hideyori 豐臣秀賴
Toyotomi Hideyoshi 豐臣秀吉
tozama 外樣
tsubo 坪
Tsugaru Nobumasa 津輕信政
tsukaiban 使番
tsuma-ori gasa 爪折傘
Tsunayoshi [Tokugawa] 綱吉

Uchi-Sakurada 內櫻田
uchimono 打物
Uesugi Kagekatsu 上杉景勝

Wadagura 和田倉
waka-doshiyori 若年寄
waki honjin 脇本陣

Yamanouchi Kazutoyo 山內一豐
yanagi-no-ma 柳間

yashiki 屋敷
Yokoi Shōnan 横井小楠
yōmei gakuha 陽明學派
Yoshimune [Tokugawa] 吉宗

Yuasa Jōzan 湯淺常山
Zōjōji 増上寺
Zoku Tokugawa jikki 續德川
實紀

INDEX

226

# HARVARD EAST ASIAN MONOGRAPHS

1. Liang Fang-chung, The Single-Whip Method of Taxation in China

2. Harold C. Hinton, The Grain Tribute System of China, 1845-1911

3. Ellsworth C. Carlson, The Kaiping Mines, 1877-1912

4. Chao Kuo-chün, Agrarian Policies of Mainland China: A Documentary Study, 1949-1956

5. Edgar Snow, Random Notes on Red China, 1936-1945

6. Edwin George Beal,Jr., The Origin of Likin, 1853-1864

7. Chao Kuo-chün, Economic Planning and Organization in Mainland China, A Documentary Study, 1949-1957

8. John K. Fairbank, Ch'ing Documents: An Introductory Syllabus

9. Helen Yin and Yi-chang Yin, Economic Statistics of Mainland China, 1949-1957

10. Wolfgang Franke, The Reform and Abolition of the Traditional Chinese Examination System

11. Albert Feuerwerker and S. Cheng, Chinese Communist Studies of Modern Chinese History

12. C. John Stanley, Late Ch'ing Finance: Hu Kuang-yung as an Innovator

13. S.M. Meng, The Tsungli Yamen: Its Organization and Functions

14. Ssu-yu Teng, Historiography of the Taiping Rebellion

15. Chun-Jo Liu, Controversies in Modern Chinese Intellectual History: An Analytic Bibliography of Periodical Articles, Mainly of the May Fourth and Post-May Fourth Era

16. Edward J.M. Rhoads, The Chinese Red Army, 1927- 1963:
    An Annotated Bibliography

17. Andrew J. Nathan, A History of the China International
    Famine Relief Commission

18. Frank H.H. King (ed.) and Prescott Clarke, A Research
    Guide to China-Coast Newspapers, 1822-1911

19. Ellis Joffe, Party and Army: Professionalism and
    Political Control in the Chinese Officer Corps,
    1949-1964

20. Toshio C. Tsukahira, Feudal Control in Tokugawa Japan:
    The Sankin Kōtai System

21. Kwang-Ching Liu, ed., American Missionaries in China:
    Papers from Harvard Seminars

22. George Moseley, A Sino-Soviet Cultural Frontier: The
    Ili Kazakh Autonomous Chou

23. Carl F. Nathan, Plague Prevention and Politics in
    Manchuria, 1910-1931

24. Adrian Arthur Bennett, John Fryer: The Introduction
    of Western Science and Technology into
    Nineteenth-Century China

25. Donald J. Friedman, The Road from Isolation: The
    Campaign of the American Committee for Non-
    Participation in Japanese Aggression, 1938-1941

26. Edward Le Fevour, Western Enterprise in Late Ch'ing
    China: A Selective Survey of Jardine, Matheson
    and Company's Operations, 1842-1895

27. Charles Neuhauser, Third World Politics: China and the
    Afro-Asian People's Solidarity Organization,
    1957-1967

28. Kungtu C. Sun, assisted by Ralph W. Huenemann, The
     Economic Development of Manchuria in the First
     Half of the Twentieth Century

29. Shahid Javed Burki, A Study of Chinese Communes, 1965

30. John Carter Vincent, The Extraterritorial System in
     China: Final Phase

31. Madeleine Chi, China Diplomacy, 1914-1918

32. Clifton Jackson Phillips, Protestant America and the
     Pagan World: The First Half Century of the
     American Board of Commissioners for Foreign
     Missions, 1810-1860

33. James Pusey, Wu Han: Attacking the Present through
     the Past

34. Ying-wan Cheng, Postal Communication in China and its
     Modernization, 1860-1896

35. Tuvia Blumenthal, Saving in Postwar Japan

## DATE DUE

| MAY 2 5 1996 | | | |
|---|---|---|---|
| | | | |
| | | | |
| | | | |
| | | | |
| | | | |
| | | | |
| | | | |
| | | | |
| | | | |
| | | | |
| | | | |
| | | | |
| | | | |
| | | | |